The Complete Bread Machine Bakery Book

The Complete Bread Machine Bakery Book

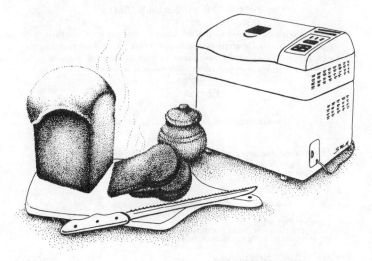

Richard W. Langer

Illustrations by Susan McNeill

LITTLE, BROWN AND COMPANY ❖ BOSTON ❖ NEW YORK ❖ TORONTO ❖ LONDON

First Edition

Illustrations copyright © 1996 by Susan McNeill

Portions of the text were previously published in The Bread Machine Bakery Book, More Recipes for Your Bread Machine Bakery, *and* Bread Machine Sweets and Treats.

Library of Congress Cataloging-in-Publication Data

Langer, Richard W.
    The complete bread machine bakery book / Richard W. Langer ;
illustrations by Susan McNeill. — 1st ed.
        p.   cm.
    Includes index.
    ISBN 0-316-51303-2
    1. Bread.   2. Automatic bread machines.   I. Title.
TX769.L2735   1996
641.8'15 — dc20   96-1783

10   9   8   7   6   5   4

QHAW

Published simultaneously in Canada by Little, Brown & Company (Canada) Limited

PRINTED IN THE UNITED STATES OF AMERICA

To Uncle Robert —
and his *"handgemachte"*

Contents

The
Complete
Bread Machine
Bakery Book

1 · Hey, I Bake Real Bread; Why Would I Use One of Those Machines?

FOR YEARS I'VE ENJOYED the pleasure of baking bread in our country kitchen, kneading and fussing with the dough while watching the horses outside mowing down the lawn that I never get around to mowing myself. So one would think I'd be one of the last people in the world to use a bread machine. But I do. They make sense, I've found, for even ardent bakers.

Bread making is not a daily activity for most people, and never has been. In eastern Finland, for instance, from ancient times to the present, the tasty, dark *hapanleipä* with its distinctive hole in the center has traditionally been baked but twice a year. Hundreds of the flat loaves would be suspended from a pole threaded through the holes and stored in the granary or larder. Needless to say, by the time another baking marathon was due, the bread had acquired some hardiness — and so had the Finnish teeth, renowned for their pearly whiteness and durability.

In the Currier and Ives New England of the era before the turn of the century, bread was baked once or twice a week. At least that was the norm for most rural families. Urban families had given up baking, electing to buy fresh loaves as needed from the baker.

Then came preservatives and supermarkets. Bread gave way to baked foam only a little less enduring and flavorful than plastic.

So, nostalgic for that special treat unmatched by newer substitutes — a loaf of bread fresh and fragrant from the oven — people began baking again. But baking done every day can turn from a pleasant task to tedium. Besides, it's only on weekends that most of us have the hours required to enjoy guiding the yeast through its stages of leavening, and by Wednesday or Thursday, staleness has overcome the result of our efforts. Let's face it, in an era in which *Time* magazine has made stress a cover story, finding enough hours on a daily basis to bake bread is not something the average individual can indulge in even thinking about. Enter the bread machines.

I still bake braids and rings the traditional way most Saturdays, because there are many things that a bread machine cannot do. It's not a substitute for home baking. But it's a great addition to it. On weekday evenings I often fill the machine before going to bed, set the timer so the bread will be finished just as we're getting up, and for breakfast we have a fresh, hot loaf.

Much to the chagrin of my wife, Susan, I then proceed to make toast of this wonderful loaf. I can see her point of view, but fresh bread like this makes *real* toast. Most people have never tasted *real* toast, crisp and desert-dry on the outside, moist and soft on the inside. It beckons the taste buds to smile, even when the day is gray and dreary outside.

Apart from toast for breakfast, the freshly baked loaves in all their possible variety can turn a simple meal of soup and bread into a quick, economical repast of epicurean proportions. And coming home from work to the aroma of fresh herb bread may not be exactly like coming home from school when one was nine or ten or thereabouts to Mom's freshly baked cookies set out with a glass of milk, but it's spirit-warmingly close. It's also surely far more homey and comforting for today's latchkey children, who must let themselves in after school because both parents are away at work, to return to a kitchen redolent of cinnamon or chocolate from a loaf of raisin pumpernickel or two-chocolates bread cheerfully doing its thing in a bread machine than to return to a cold empty house.

Come to think of it, I wouldn't be surprised to see the more enterprising of real estate agents soon buying up bread machines so they could arrange to have the aroma of baking bread wafting from the kitchens of houses they are showing. Our sense of smell is one of our most primal faculties, awakening all kinds of nostalgic memories and emotions. We are really quite vulnerable to scents.

On a less subjective plane, a bread machine makes a great deal of practical economic sense. The ingredients for even the richest loaf of homemade bread cost but a fraction of what the store-bought finished product brings. So within a year the machine should have paid for itself. Meanwhile there will have been a steady supply of nutritious, flavorsome bread from its obliging, compact oven — all as free as it can be of additives and questionable ingredients. With a bread machine, you know what's cooking. And you can key its output to your mood and inclination.

2 · Sugar and Spice and Flour and Rice

ONE OF THE ADVANTAGES of home baking with a bread machine is that you know what goes into every loaf. You can accommodate family whims and dietary needs or restrictions, use nothing but the finest and freshest ingredients, and rest assured that you are truly producing the staff of life.

As bread machines have proliferated, so have specialized flours and mixes catering to their use. The recipes in this book, however, are designed primarily around standard flours commonly available in the supermarket. Where the occasional rarer ingredient is called for, it will be found either in health-food stores or from the mail-order suppliers listed at the back of the book.

The special bread flour found increasingly on grocery shelves as bread machines multiply is a high-gluten flour, containing more of this protein than ordinary flour can boast. Gluten is what adds elasticity and stretch to a batch of dough, trapping the gas released by the fermenting yeast and enabling the bread to rise. All wheat flour contains some gluten, however, and in working with any of the recipes presented here, I've found no need for the special bread flour on the market. In some cases, in fact, the extra gluten in bread flour causes a dough to overflow its pan unpredictably. The one place where I do suggest using bread flour is in a recipe with a high proportion of oatmeal, which seems to benefit from a dose of the higher-gluten flour.

By all means use bread flour if that's what you have around. For that matter, you can use bleached flour instead of the unbleached, if you prefer. I just like the latter because the bleaching process involves chlorinating the flour; unbleached flour is whitened naturally, through aging.

There's a raft of other flours, among them whole-wheat, rye, barley, buckwheat, millet, semolina, and brown rice, used for the recipes in this book. Many of these flours contain perishable oils from the germ, or heart, of the grain and are best kept refrigerated if you're going to have them around for more than a month or so, as otherwise they can spoil and lend a bitter taste to your bread. This isn't much of a problem in our corner of New England except in the summertime. However, if you live in a warmer region, refrigeration year-round is a good idea.

Speaking of refrigeration, most books on baking will tell you that the ingredients for a loaf of bread should be at room temperature before being used. I've always abided by this axiom myself. But given the premise that the principal attraction of a bread machine is its convenience, the idea of waiting half an hour or so for the eggs and milk and flour and what have you to warm up before starting one's baking seems contradictory to the mission of the machine. So, modifying my habitual routine, I've baked all the breads in this book with any refrigerated ingredients taken straight from their storage spot as needed. It's worked out just fine. By the time the machine's kneading blade has performed its initial mixing ritual, the ingredients have become quite warm and cozy. The one exception, a large cold block of butter, I've dealt with simply by cutting the bar into small pieces before adding it to my batter.

However, if you store rarely used specialty flours in the freezer, a practice well worth adopting, let them warm up half an hour or so before using them. One thing that's helpful is to freeze the flour in small, more or less recipe-sized bags rather than in large containers.

Speaking of recipe portions, you may wonder why I do not specify sifting the flour or particularly the confectioners' sugar used for any of the loaves described in this book. Well, it seemed to me that since the whole principle of using a bread machine is supposed to be its convenience, it would be more useful to the reader and baker for me to adjust the amount of any given ingredient so the flour sifter would not have to be hauled out. Certainly any clumping of such ingredients as sugar is taken care of by either the kneading blade of the bread machine, if it's responsible for the mixing, or the beaters of the electric mixer, if that's what's doing the blending.

Convenience does need to give way to a little advance planning occasionally. For example, like flour, chunky ingredients frozen to retain their freshness, such as nuts and dried fruits, need half an hour's defrosting as well. The exception that proves the rule is chocolate chips, which I suggest keeping in the freezer for certain sweets precisely so they will keep their separate identity when added to a dough.

Starters frozen in premeasured batches need more time, as much as three to four hours, to thaw, for in order to do their job properly they need to be bubbly when incorporated into the dough they are expected to leaven. This natural thawing produces more flavorsome bread, to my mind. However, it is possible to save time by zapping a batch of starter in your microwave, using the method recommended in your machine's instructions for thawing bread dough. Stir in a tablespoon of flour as soon as you take the starter from the microwave, and make sure it's revived enough to be bubbly before using it to bake your bread.

Each of the specialty flours adds its own characteristic taste and texture to the bread in which it's used. Whole wheat, as the name implies, includes the entire wheat kernel. It also contains a lot of bran, which contributes healthful dietary fiber. The germ and the bran are what give this flour its distinctive light brown color. But these heavier components also slow the rise of the whole-wheat, as opposed to white-flour, dough. That's why some of the newer bread machines have a whole-wheat mode among their settings.

The whole-wheat setting extends the dough's rising time so that the heavier mixes can catch up with their airier counterparts. However, a lot of machines do not provide this option, and even those that do retain the shorter rising period for their rapid-bake cycle. So, to make life simpler, most of the breads in this book have been baked on the short cycle, spanning roughly three hours. The regular cycle takes around four hours, the whole-wheat setting five, and the crisp mode available on a few machines seven hours from start to finish. Generally the only noticeable difference in the loaf these settings yield is that it's a bit taller and more open in texture.

Bran, the protective coating surrounding the kernels of grains, for years announced its presence in breads mostly in the coffee-counter muffins carrying its name. Bran as a cereal sold listlessly from the grocer's shelves. Then, in the late eighties, the American Medical Association released a study indicating that a high-fiber diet including oat bran might help reduce blood cholesterol. Suddenly there wasn't enough oat bran procurable at any price.

The craze is over now, but bran is still a good ingredient for bread, adding texture and flavor as well as nutrition and roughage. I prefer unprocessed wheat bran to oat bran. The wheat variety has more fiber and better flavor than the oat does.

Use rye flour in your bread, and your loaf will maintain a low profile, dense and compact, regardless of the setting you use in baking it, for this flour contains little gluten. The higher the proportion of rye in a recipe, then, the smaller the loaf will be. But that's the way rye breads have always been, fine textured — and tasty indeed.

Rye comes in a number of grades, the two most common ones being medium and the darker pumpernickel. Pumpernickel is the coarser of the two and contains a lot of bran. It's a nice flour for dense breads. Unfortunately, it's not readily available in this country. So for all the recipes in this volume calling for rye flour, including the pumpernickel recipes, I've used the medium variety, usually labeled simply as rye and available at most supermarkets. Some health-food stores do carry real pumpernickel flour, and it can be substituted for the medium rye in the recipes with good results.

Mention barley, and I think of beef and barley soup, a dish I toss into the same category as I do okra, both being somewhat slimy and not favorites of mine. But barley does make a good bread, nutty and very fine in texture.

Millet, as I keep insisting to the kids, really isn't birdseed. True, your standard modern cage-bird mix is full of its tiny yellow spheres, but millet has been a staple of the human race for millenniums. At one time it was more popular than rice in China, and it is still a major food crop in Africa. Whole millet adds a lovely crunch to bread.

Rice is the "daily bread" of more than half the population of the earth. It is central particularly to the diet of peoples in the tropics. Rice and bread are rarely found in each other's company, as we tend to eat but one starchy food at a time. But rice flour gives bread a silky quality. It's also a valuable ingredient in gluten-free loaves for those who can't eat regular bread because of gluten intolerance. Even baking whole rice into a loaf results in a surprisingly good bread, as our family discovered quite by accident.

Corn is normally regarded as a vegetable, and corn on the cob is probably America's favorite in that category of foods. But in fact corn is a grain. As cornmeal, it lends an agreeably gritty texture to bread.

The color of cornmeal is traditionally divided by the Mason-Dixon line. North of that boundary, the meal is yellow; south of it, white. For baking purposes the two are interchangeable — but don't try to tell that to anyone with set ideas about the rightful color of the meal.

Whole-grain cornmeal, stone- or water-ground, contains the germ, and so profits from storage in the refrigerator. Degermed cornmeal, because it has had the spoilable oily part of the seed removed, doesn't need to be kept refrigerated. Then again, it's less nutritious than whole-grain cornmeal. For baking purposes, it doesn't matter which you use.

Cornmeal adds flavor as well as texture to breads, not to mention extra nutrition. Try experimenting with some in your favorite recipe. But stay away from an all-cornmeal formula. Without some wheat-based flour as a binder in the mix, your bread machine is likely to dispense hot crumbs — tasty hot crumbs, I'll grant you, but crumbs nonetheless.

Another flavorsome and nutritious addition to bread is oats. Oats are, or at least were for a very long time, the mainstay of Scottish sustenance. Despite Samuel Johnson's definition of them as "a grain which in England is generally given to horses, but in Scotland supports the people" and my own childhood memories of the sticky porridge that appeared in my bowl at breakfast time at my aunt's and if not finished off reappeared at dinnertime fried, oats really are a tasty grain. There were simply times when folks had too many of them. Again harking back to Scotland, in olden days in that country there was a holiday called Oatmeal Monday, a midterm celebration at Scottish universities when fathers of the poorer students would traditionally bring them a sack of oats to nourish them for the remainder of the term.

Steel-cut oats, the ones common to Scottish and Irish oatmeal, are the least processed form of this cereal outside of whole oat groats. The oats have been chopped by sharp steel blades to reduce the cereal's normal cooking time from a couple of hours to somewhere in the neighborhood of forty minutes. Because no heat is generated by the blades, steel-cut oats are supposed to retain more flavor and nourishment than rolled oats. They add a lot of texture to a bread and are worth experimenting with.

Rolled oats, the ones most common in this country, have been softened slightly by steam and then flattened between steel rollers.

Quick oats are rolled a little thinner, and instant oatmeal is squashed paper-thin and then dehydrated. All can be used in breads, but the instant oatmeal adds the least texture and nutrition. I don't recommend it in the recipes in this book, simply because a bread machine can handle any of the other, more nutritious forms in which this cereal is found.

Semolina, milled from protein-rich durum wheat with only the bran layer removed, will be found listed in some of the recipes in this book, along with amaranth, cousin of the colorful cockscomb planted in many an annual flower garden. These are both nutritious additions to bread. The more familiar wheat germ can enrich a blander flour as well.

The grains have always dominated European and American bread baking. But flours made from potatoes, beans, and other legumes have often been used to supplement the more traditional flours. In earlier times, these admixtures were for the most part instances of manifest adulteration, the grain flours up until a century ago being reasonably expensive, while flour from other sources could often be had at a cheaper price.

Sometimes, however, the blending of different flours produced a genuinely more wholesome commodity. An outstanding example of such a loaf is Ezekiel bread, a recipe for which will be found among the multigrains. Another is the rich, baking-powder-leavened teff nut bread.

Potatoes make for a heavenly light loaf, as a good Hungarian potato bread will testify. Buckwheat, a relative of rhubarb, better known to some in its hulled and cooked form, kasha, lends a loaf distinctive robustness. Seeds like sunflower and flaxseed contribute a piquancy both visually attractive and very nutritious.

Eggs add extra protein to a bread, and their yolks add color. Eggs also help the dough to rise. Their leavening is a physical effect, based on the swelling of the whites, where other leavening agents work their magic by means of a chemical reaction, releasing carbon dioxide.

Egg-based breads usually need more oil or butter than might otherwise be called for, to keep from drying out. Loaves rich in egg tend to go stale rather quickly. But in the unlikely event that you have leftovers of such loaves, they make great bread puddings.

Besides the extra shortening, extra salt is needed in egg breads, to counteract their natural blandness. On the whole, I don't use much salt in my loaves, which is why a taste range is given for that seasoning in the recipes. Susan was put on a low-salt diet when carrying our first child some twenty years ago, and between that and numerous years of pureeing items from the day's menu for baby food, we've never gone back to a heavy hand with the salt shaker. Nevertheless, salt affects bread in more ways than taste. It enhances the effectiveness of the gluten in the flour, helping to loft the dough. It also keeps the dough from rising too fast and then collapsing.

However, if you come across an old recipe for salt-rising bread, don't assume from the name that such bread used no yeast. The dough for salt-rising bread was kept warm and expanding in a container of heated rock salt; in those cozy environs the wild yeasts did their thing.

Yeast is the most common leavening agent used in bread making. It is available in fresh form as cake yeast, dried under the name active dry yeast, and in a new so-called rapid-rise version. The recipes in this book all call for active dry yeast. Cake yeast is not readily proofed and dispersed throughout a dough mixed and rested in a baking machine, while rapid-rise yeast will often cause the dough to overflow the pan before the end of the machine's allotted resting cycle and ooze into a real mess around the heating coils.

Yeasts are one-celled, naturally occurring wild plants that multiply incredibly rapidly, given the right conditions. Those conditions include warmth, moisture, and carbohydrates. The first of these is supplied by the bread machine's diminutive oven, the last by the flour and, often, sugar. The trick is to balance the proportions of flour, sweeteners, and liquids to achieve a blend the yeast can work with.

Provided with these necessities, the yeast initiates a fermentation process the by-product of which is carbon dioxide gas. The gas becomes ensnared in the fabric of the dough, and the gluten in the dough acts like spandex, stretching into miniballoons full of carbon dioxide. Once the bread has begun to bake, the fermentation stops, arrested by the penetrating heat. But the bubbles remain. They are what give bread its familiar porous texture.

While domesticated yeast is the primary leavener in homemade breads today, it wasn't always so. Sourdough was the mainstay of bread making in pioneer days, and some of the starters passed on from generation to generation came to this country from the Old World, hoarded carefully on the long transatlantic voyages by settlers from Europe. Sourdough remains alive and well today, and is regaining favor among bread aficionados. But it is, remember, a wild thing. A bit different from the other leaveners, sourdough and its care have a chapter to themselves.

Baking soda and baking powder were also much-used leaveners in earlier days, especially when the warmth, time, and tending that yeast breads required were scarce. Baking soda is the oldest chemical leavening agent around. It is traditionally combined with acidic liquids like buttermilk in a recipe. Being alkaline, the baking soda reacts with the acid in these liquids to produce carbon dioxide. The reaction is a very quick one, which is why these breads have traditionally been rushed from the batter bowl to a preheated oven.

But there's no way to rush the current generation of bread machines, so pure baking-soda breads do not fare well in these devices. Adding extra baking soda to a recipe in an attempt to boost the gas output doesn't work.

Traditional baking powder is a combination of baking soda and cream of tartar, an acid. Double-acting baking powder, the only kind available commercially today, uses calcium phosphate and sodium aluminum sulfate as its acids. The term "double-acting" refers to the fact that this powder releases gas twice, once when it comes in contact with moisture, a second time when heated. It is the fact that it produces carbon dioxide on heating, which baking soda by itself does not do, that makes baking powder utilizable in a bread machine.

Like sourdough, baking powder has a way with a loaf distinctively its own, as you will see — and taste — whenever working with it. The chapter devoted to baking-powder, or quick, breads contains a number of exceptionally tasty loaves raised with the help of this riser. But cultivated yeast remains the monarch of the leavening world.

Which brand of yeast to use is a question I'm often asked, and the answer to that question is bound to be subjective. Yeasts do vary, and people tend to use what has served them well in the past. Some bakers swear that imported European yeasts work best in bread machines. Others find that whatever is available on the supermarket shelf, which usually turns out to be Fleischmann's or Red Star, suits them fine. As it so happens, I use Red Star, simply because it's the one yeast I can purchase in bulk, and I go through pounds and pounds of yeast when I'm developing and refining the recipes for a book.

The fermentable sugar that boosts the growth of baker's yeast in many bread recipes can come from a variety of sources. White sugar, brown sugar, molasses, corn syrup, maple syrup, honey, even barley malt — all have their place in bread making. Each adds a slightly different taste to a loaf, all add tenderness to it as well, and all can normally be substituted one for the other, although not necessarily on a one-to-one basis. In substituting a granular sugar for a syrupy one, for instance, you may need to increase the amount of liquid called for in the recipe. Don't be afraid to experiment.

Almost anything can go into a loaf of bread, and nowhere is this more true than when it comes to the liquids that can be pressed into service. Cider's been used; so has tea, notably in Irish currant bread. The broth left from cooking vegetables substitutes nicely for the water or other liquid called for in a recipe, adding both extra nourishment and extra flavor. Such broths have a natural affinity with herb, vegetable, and savory breads.

Where you substitute a broth for milk in a recipe, you do need to know that the resulting loaf will not be quite as soft and tightly grained as the milk loaf would be. Milk breads are exceptionally tender.

Whole milk and skim milk can be used interchangeably in almost all of the recipes in this book. I happen to prefer the whole; it gives a richer, softer crumb. But skim milk can usually be substituted for it with no real loss in flavor and very little loss in texture.

In general, water makes a crust crisper and the loaf inside chewier than milk does. Milk browns the crust and adds tenderness and keeping quality. Buttermilk does the same, only better. You'll find it a common ingredient in quick-bread recipes, because its acidity sets off the requisite reaction in baking soda and baking powder.

Cream, sour cream, cottage cheese, and yogurt are other dairy products prized for their tenderizing role in bread making. I often use a dollop of nonfat dry milk for added flavor and nourishment in a loaf calling for water as its liquid. Noninstant powdered dry milk is even more nourishing, because it has not been heated as much as the instant variety during the drying process. However, it has a tendency to form lumps unless whipped into the water before being mixed with flour. It is also not as readily available as the common nonfat instant variety.

Butter is by today's fitness standards a naughty little richness sometimes occurring in bread. But it does serve a function, helping the dough to stretch and making the yeast's leavening task easier. It also makes for a moister, richer-tasting loaf. I use unsalted butter; it's reputed to blend more smoothly with other ingredients than salted butter does. Of course, with a bread machine everything gets thrown around in the mixing and agitating cycle, so I'm not sure if that point carries the value it once did. In any case, if what you have around your house is salted butter, don't put off your baking on that account. Simply adjust the amount of plain salt you use in a given recipe accordingly.

Oil has greater cachet than butter in many circles these days. If you are on a restricted cholesterol intake, you can substitute canola oil for butter. It will work in the recipes in this book with only a minor loss in taste. Also you'll find a number of the recipes calling for olive oil, which imparts its own bit of flavor while at the same time being right for the cholesterol-conscious. Incidentally, a small but nifty tip comes to mind in connection with using oil in bread making: where a recipe calls for both oil and a gooey sweetener such as molasses, if you measure out the oil first, the syrup will slide out of the same spoon or cup cleanly.

Lecithin, which you'll note in a few of the recipes included in this book, is a natural phosphatide, or phospholipid, derived from soybeans, corn, egg yolk, and other sources. It acts as an emulsifier and wetting agent, facilitating the mixing of ingredients and, in the case of bread, interacting with the gluten found in flour to add elasticity and leavening power to the dough. It particularly helps solid whole-grain breads to rise. Most health-food stores carry it.

The health-food stores and alternative-lifestyle purveyors are also good sources for the occasional odd ingredient like flaxseed or a specialty flour not available at the supermarket. Other sources for ingredients you might not have on hand are listed at the back of the book.

The proportions of herbs and spices to the other ingredients in the recipes in this book are pretty much middle of the road, and you can add to or subtract from the quantities listed to the point of doubling or halving them without affecting the loaves as a whole. Fresh herbs can also be substituted for dried ones, and dried for fresh. However, if you substitute fresh chopped onions for the dehydrated minced variety or for onion flakes, you'll have to add a lot more to achieve the same degree of oniony flavor. You'll also have to reduce the amount of liquid called for in the recipe by one to two tablespoons. Onions are 99 percent water.

3 · Tips and Tricks for Electronic Baking

NONE OF MY REGULAR BREAD PANS have bucket-hoop handles like the ones on bread machine pans. This would be no big deal were it not for the fact that the unaccustomed hoop provides such an inviting handhold. Even when grasping the pan with potholders, one is prone to grab the hoop with a bare hand absentmindedly on occasion — at least I am, as my mildly burned fingertips will attest. Apart from that all too repeatable learning experience, one soon adjusts to the differences between traditional baking and its bread machine counterpart.

Differences there are, though. Consider, for instance, the order in which the ingredients are mixed. The sequence varies even from machine to machine.

The instructions for some bread machines specify that the liquids are to be measured into the pan first, then the solids, then the yeast. This particular sequence is presumably designed to keep the yeast from percolating down into the liquids at the bottom of the pan and being activated by the moisture too soon. But that becomes a real peril only when you are setting the timer to mobilize the machine at some future point. If your bread is to be baked in the ordinary course of events, such restraining measures aren't needed.

The directions supplied with other machines state that you are to put the yeast in the pan first, a little bit in each corner, then cover it with the solid ingredients, pouring the liquids in last. What reasoning lies behind this order, I'm not sure.

The problem of where and when to add the yeast is solved very neatly where a machine has a separate yeast dispenser. The leavening is simply added there after all the other ingredients have been placed in the baking pan. This dispenser can also be used for baking powder. But in that case you have to be supercareful not to pack the powder down in the slightest. Baking powder is very fine; it does not flow as readily as the granular yeast for which the dispenser was designed. On the whole, I find it safer to put the baking powder right in with the other ingredients when making quick breads, even in a machine with a yeast dispenser.

This might be the place to mention two things to be remembered about bread machines. First, they are Japanese in origin, and Japan's traditional cuisine is not bread-based. Although the Japanese like bread, it is a relatively new and foreign commodity. Part of its popularity probably stems from this very fact. However, because bread does not have a long cultural heritage in those islands, the breads assimilated do not have the broad range of ingredients, textures, and flavor taken for granted in European-based cultures. The second thing to remember is that while bread machines may be turning Japan into the land of the rising yeast, they were designed by engineers, not bakers. The combination of these two factors perhaps explains why the manufacturers' recipe booklets tucked in with the machines seem so mundane and repetitive.

Bread machines are capable of far more than the monotonous examples of culinary art presented in the makers' brochures. But you do have to experiment, sometimes modifying both the ingredients and the mixing sequence given in traditional recipes to the logistics of the machine. For instance, you can't simply toss a little more flour into the dough during kneading when it just doesn't feel right.

Sometimes what's needed is a simple alteration in the manufacturer's instructions on placing ingredients in your machine. For example, when baking a heavy loaf such as a pumpernickel or a rye or one using buttermilk, sour cream, and other dense liquids, you may end up with a half-baked mess the consistency of custard topped by caked flour. What has happened in this case is that, because the engineering considerations involved in designing a mixing blade that will pull easily out of a finished loaf conflict with the scientific principles of mixing and agitation, the machine has failed to blend and knead the ingredients properly. It's been doing what's known in the propeller industry as cavitating, the blade carving out an air-filled void in the material surrounding it and then spinning rapidly with reduced efficiency.

You can achieve approximately the same sorry results by failing to put the mixing blade back in the pan after washing those two components. That's something I did more than once at the beginning of my adventure with bread machines, if only because putting something in the bottom of a pan is so counterintuitive to someone accustomed to regular baking pans.

At any rate, if you end up with unincorporated flour lining the top or outer edges of your loaves, try reversing the order of the ingredients, adding the liquids last. Don't attempt this in a recipe you are planning to use with the overnight timer unless your machine has a separate yeast dispenser; the yeast would certainly be activated too soon. Then again, the culprit in a cavitating bread machine is usually a dough heavy in eggs or milk products, and because of possible spoilage, you wouldn't be letting such a dough sit overnight anyhow.

Another remedy for cavitation may be to alter the consistency of the dough you're working with to suit your machine better. The design of a bread machine's baking pan is such that most doughs should, after some mixing and machine kneading, form a ball around the blending blade. This ball will then run around the edges of the pan picking up extra bits of flour and other ingredients that may have temporarily clung to the nonstick walls. When you've heard the dough being agitated for quite a while during the first kneading, take a peek and see if the ball of dough is forming. It's perfectly all right to lift the lid of a bread machine and sneak a look at what's happening inside during the preliminary kneading cycle, even though the manual will warn you against it. I peek all the time. Just don't open the lid on a machine that has a separate container for leavening built into it at about the time when the yeast is scheduled to be released into the dough, for obvious reasons. You also want to refrain from disturbing the environment of the miniature bakery later in the bread-making process, when the bread is rising. And I burned my nose once peeking during the baking cycle.

A dough that is too soft to form a ball will sometimes fail to pick up all the flour from the edges of the pan. Typically, a loaf that emerges from your electronic oven with a swirly pattern on top is telling you that your particular machine had a problem mixing that particular batter. This is not an uncommon occurrence when one is first trying out a recipe for a soft, moist, milk-based bread or working with a sticky dough like that for teff or rice bread. A little extra flour will often firm up the dough and improve the final results.

If, conversely, you find when you slice open a finished loaf that the ingredients are not evenly dispersed, the next time you try the recipe, add a bit more liquid than it calls for. Some variations in loaf density are due to the composition of the flour used, which differs from brand to brand and even from harvest to harvest within the same brand.

Bread machines do have their idiosyncrasies, just as conventional ovens do, and even identical ingredients used with the very same recipe may result in different loaves. As a general rule, however, you can count on white breads and doughs rich in eggs to rise the most, heavy ryes and corn or bran breads the least.

This doesn't mean that you should double a recipe to get a full-sized loaf. I've tried that, mostly to my sorrow. Some breads simply don't rise to the top of the pan in a bread machine. Early on in my exploration of bread machines, I tried to make a full-sized corn bread — and laid an egg. What I achieved was a large golden loaf with a raw oval blob in the middle. The baking cycle of the machines is such that the heat of their ovens cannot penetrate the center of so large and solid a loaf long enough to bake it properly.

While my trial-and-error adventures with doubling recipes ended in disaster, other innovations in bread making with a machine proved quite workable. I've tried any number of concoctions, including simply dumping a chocolate and a date-nut box-cake mix along with the requisite egg and water into the baking pan to see what the machine would do with them. The results were certainly on par with conventionally baked box cakes. Once I even dumped some leftover spaghetti into the pan with some oregano, basil, and garlic powder, thinking to make an Italian loaf; that particular endeavor was voted out of this book by my family.

At one point Revell, our ten-year-old son, proposed adding M&Ms or Skittles to a batch of bread I was making. I objected that the hard candy might scratch the pan's nonstick finish.

"Then why not Froot-Loops bread," teased our daughter Genevieve, nine years his senior. I was saved only by Revell's "Oh, disgusting!"

Then there was the time, during a singularly frenetic baking session, when I ascended from the basement with a couple of half gallons of ice cream retrieved from the big freezer downstairs to replenish the smaller one in the kitchen refrigerator. Revell, not too busy building his nth balsa-wood sailboat for the pond to notice my passage, looked up and said, "You're not."

"Not what?"

"Going to make ice-cream bread."

"Oh, come on..."

"Well," Tanya chimed in from behind the easel in her room to which she was tacking filaments of lace in an intricate pattern for her graduation dress, "why not? How about baked Alaska, Dad?"

I left hanging the reference to that namesake of the forty-ninth state and helped myself to some ice cream in the hot kitchen, where three machines were at the moment busy churning the dough for refried bean, Bulgarian cheese, and beer bread, respectively. Ice-cream bread, indeed!

All the same, experimenting is part of the fun of owning a bread machine, and for each failure there's a spectacular success. Use the recipes in this book to familiarize yourself with the range of nutritious and flavorsome breads you can bake in your electronic oven. But don't stop there. By all means do go on to create your own personalized loaves.

Conventional or experimental, most breads bake well in a bread machine set to its quick, or short, cycle. Baking-powder breads, in fact, will usually work only if baked quickly. On the other hand, some solid loaves like rye and blue-cheese breads profit from the long full cycle, to give the leavening time to raise the dough as much as possible.

Light, medium, or dark settings for loaf color are pretty much up to the individual baker. With rare exceptions, I use whatever setting the machine itself selects automatically when it's turned on. Known in computerese as the default setting, this is what the manufacturer has deemed the most-often-used selection.

As to which of all the bread machines works the best, the answer to that depends largely on the features you're looking for. Someday a machine somewhere will incorporate them all. Meanwhile, you'll need to decide which ones are most important to you.

Right now, some of the baking machines have a window that lets you see how a loaf is progressing; others do not. Some beep at you; some beep and flash at you. Some have a separate yeast dispenser, which assures that the yeast will not come in contact with any liquids until the proper time for it to do so.

Eventually, I hope, the machines will have a similar separate compartment for additions like raisins, dates, nuts, and so on. As things stand now, these ingredients tend to become a bit mashed during the prolonged kneading cycle. Certain machines do have a special beeper that can be set to signal the end of the mixing cycle, when such ingredients can more safely be added in the expectation that they will remain whole and unbroken. But a beeper doesn't usually work for me. Invariably I've stepped out of the kitchen for just a minute when those three little beeps have sounded the "add now" signal, and my raisin bread has remained raisinless and my nut bread has baked without the nuts. Besides, what if I hadn't been home? With a release compartment for the raisins and the nuts like that for yeast, the breads could make themselves all by themselves while I was gone.

Different makes and models of bread machines produce somewhat different breads from a single recipe. For instance, the instant-mashed-potato bread recipe in this book results in a loaf with a more open texture, a chewier consistency, and a smaller size when baked in a National or Panasonic machine than it has when made in a Hitachi. A Hitachi-made loaf of the same bread is larger, but a little drier and crustier. Each loaf, however, has a worthy texture and taste of its own.

Speaking of things larger, the first bread machines all produced 1-pound loaves of bread. Now some of the machines, such as the National and Panasonic large-loaf models, make an oblong 1½-pound loaf. The Hitachi can also bake a large-size loaf, although it will be a tall bread rather than an oblong one. I have included recipes for big loaves as well as for small in this book, but on the whole I find that most machines make a bread more even in texture and consistent in quality in the original 1-pound size. So some of the recipes remain listed in a single, small size. This doesn't mean they can't be baked in a larger-model bread machine. They'll just be 1-, not 1½-, pounders.

Certain recipes, however, do not lend themselves to either large-quantity measurements or to large pans. The ingredients called for are too viscous or too unwieldy to be collected by the willing but small kneading blade from all the corners of an oblong pan like that of the Panasonic or the National 1½-pound-loaf model, for example. Or they may be too weighty to be kneaded by the blade of a machine like the Hitachi, whose pan, because it is so tall, can physically contain the ingredients for either a small or a large loaf but may not be able to mix the greater batch. Here again the recipes will be designed only for the small, or 1-pound, loaf.

The major functional difference between the various machines lies in the power of their kneading blades. DAK and Welbilt models do not deal well with a heavy dough, for instance. If these machines seem to be struggling with the task of kneading a bread, barely turning the dough around in the baking pan, you may need to add a bit of extra liquid, a tablespoonful at a time.

Two extended baking cycles have been added to the National and Panasonic machines now on the market. The aforementioned one for whole-wheat breads allows more time for nonwhite bread doughs to rise. Since this setting is not an option on many of the other bread machines, however, most of the recipes for whole-wheat and multi-grain breads in this book have been created to work with either the rapid or the regular baking mode of your bread machine.

The second new setting was designed to facilitate a crisp crust on a bread. Essentially all this setting does is to extend the time allowed for rising even further. Yet most of the snappiness of a crust still depends on the ingredients used and the oven environment during baking. No bread machine yet devised will yield the brittle shell of a true French baguette that sends shards flying across the room when a piece of the loaf is broken off. That bread can be baked properly only in an oven misted with cold water.

The microelectronics underlying today's bread machines could make possible the baking of a true baguette in tomorrow's electronic oven, however. The only modification needed would be the addition of a water reservoir and a misting mechanism. The water reservoir would add but fractionally to the cost of the machine. The mister, being a mechanical mechanism, might add as much as 20 percent to the price. Still, those two refinements are improvements one can hope the electronic ovens of the future will incorporate.

Meanwhile, all the breads in this book can be baked in any of the machines currently on the market — with two caveats. First, the heavier doughs, as mentioned, will probably need some extra liquid if they're to be kneaded in a DAK or a Welbilt. Quite simply, these machines are somewhat underpowered. Second, machines like the large Panasonic model featuring the oblong, more traditional loaf-shaped pans need a bit of initial supervision before they are left to their job. Thick or sticky doughs are sometimes not picked up from the corners of the rectangular pan by the kneading blade. Keep handy a rubber spatula with which to scrape down the sides of the pan about five or ten minutes into the preliminary mixing cycle. However, remember that the lid on a machine featuring a separate container for leavening should be opened either before or after the yeast has been dispensed, not during that operation, in order to avoid a shower of yeast granules.

One improvement I seriously hope future bread machines incorporate is some better means of access for cleaning. This would allow me to be even bolder than I am in my baking experiments, no longer daunted by the prospect of scraping out the burned remains of some failed dough from heating coils deep within the machine. I particularly remember an experiment of mine with a blue-corn bread, the failed results of which, a steaming, oozing blue blob whose closeup on videotape could have been used in a remake of *It Came from Outer Space,* still rested on a cooling rack in the center of our kitchen table when in walked Tanya, our mature high-school senior, with her date. I don't recall his name, perhaps because he never came back. . . .

Speaking of cleaning, it is possible to glaze and garnish a loaf of bread without removing it from the machine, and I've done it that way, but some of the glaze usually dribbles down between the bread and the sides of the pan to sizzle into a sticky mess, and some of the seeds or other embellishments always bounce off and fall into the machine. Adding glazes and toppings in situ is, as things now stand, asking for trouble; and so I dutifully remove the loaves, add the finishing touches I envision as appropriate, and return them to the bread baker to bake on.

In the way of components, some bread machines come with a thicker baking pan than others do. The thicker pan seems to me to make better bread. Loaves appear to bake less evenly in the thinner pans, and often they have a disproportionately thick bottom crust.

Day-to-day fluctuations in temperature, the vicissitudes of altitude and atmosphere, variations in flour quality — such things can all affect the loft and lightness and uniformity of a loaf. Yet, overall, bread machines turn out consistently good, tasty loaves.

Whatever the bread you bake, when it comes from the oven hot and fragrant, your final task is to get the loaf out of its pan. Rapping the pan on the side of the counter helps, although the loaf still will not slide out quite as easily as one from a regular bread pan, as the beater in the bottom of a bread machine pan is loath to let its loaf

go. Twiddling the screw at the bottom of the pan a few times —
wearing an oven mitt — helps here.

Once the loaf is free, let it rest on a rack to cool for ten to twenty
minutes before slicing it. Otherwise the retained steam will make
your slices sticky. That wait, as the aroma of fresh-baked bread fills
the room so irresistibly, may be the hardest part of baking with a
bread machine.

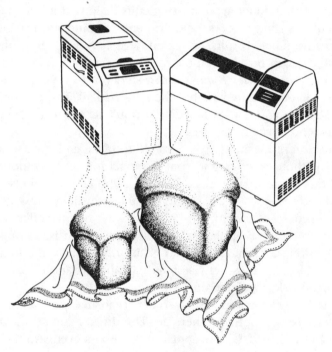

4 · My Bread Machine Has a Sweet Tooth!

BREAD MACHINES REWARD THEIR owners with all the pleasure and nourishment of homemade loaves in return for only minutes of preparation time and a minimum of bother.

"If only they could bake pastries as well!" is the echoing cry of today's busy gourmet. Well, they can.

Now, I'll be the first to admit that bread machines have their limitations when it comes to traditional cakes and quick breads. Their pans restrict the shape of the loaves they eject to a monotonous sameness, and the crusts they produce are thicker than those of cakes and quick breads baked in conventional ovens in conventional cake or loaf pans.

Someday, probably soon, in fact, bread machines will become true home bakeries. It would take next to nothing for their manufacturers to reprogram the microchip controller directing all their actions to include a short baking-powder-bread cycle, for instance, or an initial egg-beating cycle for true cake batters.

It would also cost the manufacturers very little, if anything, to offer an assortment of pan shapes for the machines. At present, the round pans of DAK and Welbilt bread machines lend the sweets baked in them a more traditional cake shape than do the square pans of, say, the Hitachi or the Panasonic, while the oblong pan of the larger Panasonic yields a loaf looking more like the traditional loaf of bread. Why not simply offer buyers a selection of pan shapes as optional extras? After all, what cook has only one pie tin or cake pan?

Meanwhile, until the bread machine with all these accoutrements of the well-stocked bakery arrives on the market, I'll keep exploring ways around the limitations of the ones available. Being an inveterate experimenter, and liking cakes as much as I do bread, I've come up with a number of recipes adapted for bread machines that yield really delightful treats capable of satisfying just about anyone's sweet tooth. With little more effort than tossing the ingredients into the pan and pressing a button, you can coax from any of the bread machines currently on the market a wide range of sweets, from a fragrant, spicy kumquat tea loaf to a devilishly dense chocolate cake, and from the simplest *biscotti* to a spectacular *panettone farcito*.

While a loaf is cooling, you'll have time to make a sauce for it, shave some chocolate to sprinkle over it, or whip up a quick icing. None of the treats included in this volume should take more than 10 or 15 minutes to assemble, and many are quickies that take only a minute or two. "Oh, how sweet it is," as Jackie Gleason used to say.

When I came to this country as an immigrant in the late forties, bread was still central to my life. Even in Sweden, neutral during the war and undamaged physically, the economic consequences of that worldwide confrontation were great, and so we ate a lot of bread. Very good bread.

Most of the bread I found in this country was a puffy white tasteless disaster compared with the solid peasant loaves to which I was accustomed. The ice cream, however, was fantastic, a boy's dream come true. It could make up for just about anything.

One day about six months after we had reached these shores, I was in a local candy store learning English, of which I had known not a word before arriving in the States, by reading *Fox and the Crow* and other comic books. A boy about my age entered, swaggered up to the soda fountain, and asked for an ice cream sandwich.

An ice cream sandwich! I had never heard of such a marvelous thing. Here were my two favorite foods combined. I too swaggered up to the counter and, in my best English, requested "one ice cream sandwich, please, on rye."

Besides expectations, appearance has much to do with what is considered a cake and what is not. The classic European tortes, such as the Sacher torte of Vienna, are not really sweet at all by modern cake-mix standards. It is their opulent fillings and frostings that make them so.

The fluffy cake as we know it relies on eggs, and often baking powder, to give it loft and lightness. It also happens to incorporate a fair amount of sugar. A bread machine, however, does not easily handle quantities of any of those ingredients. Eggs it cannot beat; baking soda it renders helpless by long sitting; large amounts of sugar kill the yeast it must rely on for leavening power. In short, to use contemporary jargon, bread machines don't do cakes, at least as we usually think of them.

On the other hand, they do turn out very rich loaves when called upon to do so. And a very rich loaf with a rich filling or frosting is fit for display in any *pâtisserie* window. Certainly it is fit to be served on your prettiest cake plate. One doesn't even miss the reduced calories in the layers themselves. Maybe, in fact, for some that's an added advantage of bread machine cakery.

Of course, a bread machine loaf fresh from the electronic oven is also delicious unadorned, simply sliced and served with perhaps a fruit spread or sweet butter. The choice is yours, then — plain or fancy, designer dessert or down-home fare. In either case, the loaf whose finished look you're contemplating is apt to be a pretty nutritional one as pastries go.

Many of the sweet loaves whose recipes are found in this book are very healthy fare indeed. A number of them incorporate dried fruits and nuts, full of vitamins and minerals, and ingredients such as the millet and semolina flours used in many of them offer much more nourishment than cake flour does.

A white whole-wheat flour newly developed at Kansas State University of Agriculture and Applied Science that has all the vitamins, minerals, and fiber of the whole-wheat kernel without the faint bitter aftertaste of whole wheat promises to become an excellent substitute for white flour. While it appeared on the market too late for me to test it with a variety of loaves, you'll find it in the Zwieback and Cherry Milk Loaf recipes in this book, where I put it to use with great success. This flour will likely replace all-purpose flour in a good many of my future recipes.

You may be surprised to find cake flour only rarely in any of the recipes in this volume. Cake flour would seem the flour best suited of all to delicate, sweet loaves, because it's lighter than ordinary flour. And indeed it is suited to true cakes, which rely on eggs or baking powder rather than yeast for their leavening power. But, as it happens, cake flour also contains less gluten than all-purpose flour, and gluten is what allows bread dough to expand as it is leavened by the yeast. So cake flour, contributing less of that elastic, airy quality, results in a smaller, denser yeast bread.

Yeast converts the carbohydrates in a bread dough to carbon dioxide gas, which is what expands the dough, giving the finished loaf its light, airy texture. These carbohydrates — from white sugar to brown and from corn syrup to molasses — also contribute much of a loaf's flavor. In a bread dough, however, they cannot be used in overly large quantities, because the yeast is easily smothered by sugars. This is why the recipes in this book will produce lovely loaves, and often very rich-tasting ones, but never the ultrasweet ones associated in many people's minds with true cakes. You'll find the chocolate loaves, particularly, sumptuous but unsweet, so don't expect brownies from a bread machine. Do expect a surprising richness and intense flavor.

In case you're wondering about sugar substitutes, they don't work in the bread machine bakery. Most of them lose their sweetness in the prolonged high temperatures of the oven, leaving a bitter after-taste in the baked loaf.

The liquid used in a cake recipe is almost always a dairy one. Water makes for a crisp crust, often desirable on a bread, seldom on a cake. Generally speaking, the richer the liquid, the more tender the loaf and softer the crust will be. Thus many of the cake recipes in this book call for cream, either sweet or sour, or buttermilk or yogurt.

Butter, for which canola and other light oils often can be substituted, also adds tenderness to a loaf. The butter I use is the unsalted variety, simply because that's what's at hand in our household, but salted butter is fine so long as you adjust the amount of salt you use accordingly. As for substituting an oil for the butter in a recipe, where either is fine, I have listed both — for example, "1 table-spoon unsalted butter or canola oil." Where I have felt that butter is strongly preferred, I have indicated the substitute in parentheses. Where only butter will do, no alternative is presented.

One normally doesn't think of salt in connection with sweets. Many cake recipes don't call for it. However, what we're working with here is yeast-based loaves, and the fact is that a little salt in the dough regulates and stabilizes the activity of the yeast.

Eggs are a supplementary leavening agent. They help to make a loaf wonderfully light. But the dozen eggs called for in a conven-tionally made torte, say, won't be found in the recipes for bread machine sweets — which, I might add, is all to the good for those watching their cholesterol consumption. The eggs for a cake, whole or separated, are whipped to a froth, something a bread machine can't do. The purpose served by all that whipping, which is to incorporate air into the batter, is here served primarily by the yeast and kneading.

Browsing for ingredients, both in different stores and among the pages of mail-order bakery catalogs, often affords inspiration for new treats to coax from the bread machine. That's how I discovered the dried bananas that suggested the fabulous Banana Chocolate Loaf. It's also how macadamia nuts precipitated the Luau Loaf.

All manner of nuts and dried fruits make their appearance in these recipes. I've become quite partial to the dried fruits, from the familiar dates and prunes to blueberries and cherries — yuppie raisins, our daughter Tanya calls them. They are preferable to fresh ones in bread machine baking for a number of reasons.

For one thing, dried fruits tend to hold together more during the machine's heavy kneading process, resulting in chunks of contrast in the finished loaf rather than a homogeneous texture. For another thing, the intense, concentrated essence of the dried fruits adds much more flavor than their fresh or canned counterparts do. The moisture in undried fruit limits the amount of it that you can use.

Because the dried fruits are so concentrated — it takes anywhere from six to ten pounds of fresh fruit to produce a pound of dried — these wonderful tidbits are expensive. But they are well worth the price for their flavor and ease of use, not to mention nutrition. Stored in an airtight container, they keep almost indefinitely, which is another advantage they have over fresh fruit. They're available at a moment's notice.

From a tea loaf flecked with festive bits of dried cranberries or blueberries to a loaf adorned with a Satin Chocolate Glaze or a luscious caramel cream sauce is a very short step. And once that step is taken, what you'll find is that a cake has happened. Frostings, glazes, ice cream, toppings, nuts, and fruits all make opulent desserts out of simple loaves.

Commercial icings and syrups can be used to embellish most of the treats in this volume. However, I've also included recipes for homemade versions of the buttercreams, sauces, and other accompaniments that have seemed to go best with the different loaves I've baked. All of these additions are quickly made and applied, to match the quick-and-easy focus of bread machine baking.

Take that simple standby of the traditional kitchen, confectioners'- sugar icing. It's a no-fail crown for a cake that can be varied in a myriad of ways, for example, by substituting a liquid such as fruit juice, maple syrup, or hot fudge sauce for the plain water usually called for. If you add too much liquid by mistake, you can remedy it by simply adding more sugar. If it becomes too stiff, you can just dilute it with more liquid. It's almost impossible to botch.

A confectioners'-sugar icing lends itself to many different applications. Swirl it over a high-domed loaf or cut the entire loaf, except for the crusts, into squares an inch or two across and make petits fours of them. Trimming away the crusts, which leaves the remainder of a loaf much more cakelike, might at first seem rather wasteful. But there are great dessert uses for them, from homey bread puddings to wickedly rich fondues.

Petits fours look difficult to create, but they're really not, although it's true that they used to be. The classic fondant icing for petits fours is classically time-consuming to make, necessitating long cooking of the sugar syrup, cooling on a marble slab, and much folding and kneading — not exactly bread machine convenience.

Then too, the traditional method of frosting petits fours is something of a bother. First they are placed on a rack set in turn on waxed paper or a marble countertop and then coated with dribbled icing. Any fondant dripping off the pastries is then scraped up and reused. We're talking a glorious mess here.

But the cubes can be iced by simple dipping. Have a rack set on waxed paper or a cookie sheet ready to receive them once they're iced. Spear a cube with a fork and dip it into the saucepan holding the icing until all the sides except the bottom are coated, then lift it out and hold it above the saucepan for a moment to let most of the excess coating drip back into the pan. Now point it as right side up as you can over the rack and, using a second fork to help it along, slide the iced petit four off the first fork onto the rack. A little extra icing will still drip through onto the waxed paper or cookie sheet, but not a great deal.

Petits fours are prettily garnished with a strawberry — perhaps partly quartered, as one might cut a radish to reveal its white interior, and opened enough to hold a dollop of whipped cream or hard sauce — or with kiwifruit circles or a kumquat sliced almost but not quite all the way through from top to stem and spread out to form a fan.

A single chocolate curl makes a striking statement on a white iced petit four. Curls are easily scraped from a square of semisweet chocolate with a vegetable parer if the chocolate is first warmed for a minute or two in the palm of your hand. For a nice accent on a colored icing, a chunk of fresh coconut can be pared in a similar fashion to form lacy white curls. Handle gently, for they will not only look, but be, very delicate. That's the beauty of them.

Another attractive white decoration is rosettes made from hard sauce piped through a pastry bag or a cookie press fitted with a star tip. If you pipe the rosettes out onto a foil-lined cookie sheet or tray and place them uncovered in the freezer, once hardened they can be transferred to a rigid container and kept frozen for up to six months, ready for use whenever a festive accent is needed.

Besides being cut into petit four squares, a dessert loaf can be served simply in slices spread with a soft buttercream icing. Like the rosettes, any extra buttercream left over can be frozen for later use. When it's needed, merely defrost it and whip it up again with an electric mixer for a couple of minutes until it is fluffy once more.

A soft icing can be scooped onto slices of a dessert loaf and swirled into a pretty pattern, or it can be spread over the slices and smoothed to a sheen with a spatula. A serrated knife run over it will create waves or ripples, depending on whether you draw the knife straight across the icing or zigzag it as you go.

For a contrasting motif on a buttercream icing, lay a paper doily over it, dip a small, soft brush like those used in watercolor (but not one that's been so used) into some cocoa, and tap it lightly over the doily with your forefinger. Remove the doily and you'll have an attractive stenciled pattern decorating the slice. If the buttercream is a chocolate or a mocha one, stencil it with confectioners' sugar instead of cocoa.

Another decorative touch for a frosted loaf is a piped design. Piping icings now come in handy toothpastelike tubes complete with a variety of screw-on pattern tips. A striking design can be created by piping circles or lines of a trimming frosting onto the cake and then modifying its outlines by drawing a toothpick through the bands or stripes.

A square of semisweet chocolate microwaved in a plastic bag adaptable to that use makes a simple homemade decorating icing.

Cut off a tiny corner of the bag, press the chocolate into that corner, and squeeze the bag gently. The chocolate will flow in a slender ribbon wherever you direct it.

Fruit is an age-old adornment for sweets. Sliced strawberries or grapes can be patterned to form a rose or a rosette covering the entire top of a cake. Peach or pear slices, fresh or canned, lend themselves to spiral and herringbone motifs. Pineapples make sunny daisies, especially if centered with a chocolate-dipped cherry. And, of course, orange and lemon slices can be slit and coiled into shapely curves, while their zest can be julienned and scattered in curls wherever you'd like a bright accent.

For added sparkle, canned fruits can be glazed with the syrup in which they were packed, reduced by about two thirds by boiling. Fresh fruits can be similarly glazed with apricot preserves or apple jelly brought to the simmering point. Dip the fruit in the glazing mixture, or drop it in and then remove it with a slotted spoon, and allow it to set for a few minutes before transferring it to your cake.

Nuts, chopped or whole, are another wonderful garnish for your bread machine bakery sweets. Almonds, particularly, lend themselves to being arranged in attractive patterns, from a pineapple of overlaid sliced blanched ones anchored in whipped cream to richly hued toasted ones garnishing some fabulous chocolate confection in a carefree scatter pattern. To brown almonds, bake them on a cookie sheet in a 350-degree F. oven or, for quicker results, crisp them in a dry skillet over medium heat, stirring to toast them evenly.

For whipped cream toppings, if the only cream you can find is the ultrapasteurized variety, that bane of the culinary arts, make sure it is very cold before trying to beat it. I've been known to put it in the freezer compartment of the refrigerator for a few minutes before attempting that endeavor, along with the bowl and beaters.

In the process of turning your bread machine loaves from plain to fancy treats, you'll acquire some leftovers. Not to worry. From simple brown Betty to elegant fondue, the crusts and crumbs from your baking, frozen for safekeeping till needed, will be put to excellent use.

Both a bread pudding and a fondue want a crusty, slightly stale bread. So it's an advantage to have on hand the trimmings from loaves used for other treats. Then too, the variety of loaves the different recipes in this book yield makes a basic fondue or bread pudding capable of almost infinite variety as well.

Even the crumbs from your loaves won't go to waste. They can be used to make delicious piecrusts of every flavor to fill with mousses and creams and summer fruit — quick, delightful desserts that the original designers of bread machines probably never dreamed of, and all of them tantalizingly different.

5 · Basic Breads and Toast

IT WAS TOAST that first sold me on the idea of a bread machine. Oh, I'll grant, I'm enough of a baking enthusiast that I'll try almost anything, from a wild South Pacific yeast to a new long-handled Danish spring whisk, at least once. But to my mind there was something not quite proper about a bread machine. Even the combination of words making up the name clashed, both with each other and with the image of a cozy, sunny kitchen with a wood stove and a calico cat dozing on the warming shelf that the making of home-baked bread conjures up. All the same, the temptation of fresh toast every morning was real and undeniable.

All of the basic breads presented here make great toast. Some of the recipes in this section call for more than one type of flour, and readers may wonder why they have been put here rather than with the other multigrain breads. Certain flours are very solid, and some quite strong in taste; rye is an outstanding example. Breads using these flours often need the balance of a less dense constituent, hence the mix. But those associated with a particular grain are still thought of as the basic bread of that type in that they are staples, which is why they are included here. These are the breads one bakes over and over again, adding the occasional unusual loaf for accent.

Fluffy White Bread

W hite bread is everywhere, so why bother to bake it at home? Well, I can think of half a dozen reasons. For one thing, nothing can match the taste of a truly fresh-from-the-oven loaf of bread. And unless you live next to a bakery, nothing can match the aroma, either. Besides, the electronic oven makes it all so easy, there's no real reason not to.

Then there's the matter of ingredients. You know what's in a loaf of bread you've made yourself — and what's not in it. You can limit or eliminate entirely unwanted elements like sugars, sodium, cholesterol, gluten, and certainly such additives as preservatives and "flavor enhancers." But probably the most compelling reason for baking a homemade loaf of old-fashioned fluffy white bread is that it's the kind of bread many of us grew up with — comfort food, they call it.

Here, then, is a homemade bread as simple and light as it is good. For a pleasant surprise, once in a while add a couple of drops of almond, vanilla, or other extract to the dough mix. That barest hint of modification may not be part of the memory, but the unexpected variation may well stir up new dreams.

SMALL	LARGE
½ cup water	¾ cup water
½ cup milk, whole or skim	¾ cup milk, whole or skim
1 tablespoon canola oil	4 teaspoons canola oil
a few drops almond, vanilla, or other extract (optional)	a few drops almond, vanilla, or other extract (optional)
2 cups unbleached all-purpose flour	3 cups unbleached all-purpose flour
2 tablespoons sugar	3 tablespoons sugar
¼ to 1 teaspoon salt to taste	½ to 1½ teaspoons salt to taste
1½ teaspoons active dry yeast	2 teaspoons active dry yeast

If the directions for your bread machine instruct you to place the yeast in the very bottom of the pan, you will need to reverse the order in which you incorporate the liquids and dry ingredients. Otherwise pour the water and milk into your baking pan and add the canola oil, flavoring extract as desired, flour, sugar, salt, and yeast, reserving the leavening for its own separate dispenser if your machine has one.

Bake the loaf on your machine's quick cycle.

Basic White Bread

Here's a lofty, light loaf of bread that those guarding against cholesterol can enjoy guilt-free. It's superior to store-bought diet bread, yet it contains none of the shortening usually associated with a tasty bread.

A quarter of a cup of toasted sesame seeds or a couple of teaspoonfuls of caraway seeds will add a delicious extra burst of flavor to the loaf. But don't attempt to use the Japanese black sesame seeds. Sprinkled over the top of the bread as it comes hot from the oven, they can add striking color contrast. Mix them into the dough, however, as I once did, and you'll have blue-black bread. It might taste fine, but somehow or other blue-black bread is aesthetically unacceptable.

> 1 cup water
> 1/4 cup toasted sesame or 2 teaspoons
>   caraway seeds (optional)
> 2 cups unbleached all-purpose flour
> 1 tablespoon nonfat dry milk
> 2 tablespoons sugar
> 1/4 to 1 teaspoon salt to taste
> 1 1/2 teaspoons active dry yeast

Pour the water into the baking pan of your bread machine, unless the instructions for your machine specify that the leavening is to be placed in the pan first and the liquid last, and add the sesame or caraway seeds if desired. Then add the flour, dry milk, sugar, salt, and yeast. In machines equipped with a separate dispenser for the leavening, the yeast should be added to the dispenser after all the other ingredients have been placed in the pan.

A quick bake cycle can be used with this bread.

Milk Bread

One of my most memorable meals ever was an early-morning one in Braunau am Inn served on a balcony overlooking the Austrian Alps. The day was postcard-picture perfect, sunny and sufficiently warm for comfort but still cool enough to make the steam rising from my generously sized cup of hot chocolate clearly visible. The hot chocolate came with a basket of small, fresh rolls, among which were some deliciously tender milk breads.

The larger milk loaf, similar to challah, resulting from the recipe given here achieves its sunny yellow appearance through the addition of eggs. The dough is so soft and sticky that it could never be kneaded by hand, so in effect what you have here is a soft, golden loaf that only a bread machine can make. The three eggs, incidentally, raise the volume of ingredients to very nearly the maximum that most bread machines can handle, which is one reason why the recipe calls for less yeast than usual.

½ cup milk, whole or skim
1 tablespoon dark corn syrup
3 eggs
3 tablespoons unsalted butter
2 cups unbleached all-purpose flour
¼ to ½ teaspoon salt to taste
1 teaspoon active dry yeast

GLAZE

1 egg
1 tablespoon cold water
poppy seeds for garnish

Measure the milk and corn syrup into your baking pan, break the eggs into the liquids, and add the butter, cutting it into small chunks if it's not soft, as otherwise, since you're using a relatively large amount, it may not blend altogether evenly into the dough. Next measure in the flour and salt. Distribute the yeast according to the instructions given for the particular bread machine you have.

Use a quick bake cycle and, if available, a light loaf setting for this loaf. As soon as it has finished baking, take it from the machine and remove it gently from its pan. Beat the egg and cold water together for the glaze, brush this mixture over the dome of the loaf with a pastry brush, and sprinkle it with poppy seeds. Then ease the bread gently back into the pan, pop it back into the machine, and close the lid. The residual heat will bake the glaze on within a minute or two. Pull the pan out once more and remove the loaf, carefully so as not to dislodge the poppy seeds, to a rack to cool.

Golden Milk Bread

There's a small bakery down the street from my uncle's house in Vienna. I remember on visits to that city going each morning to pick up fresh rolls, always *handgemacht,* "handmade," for breakfast. The long arm of the industrial age has reached even into the ancient order of bakers, and now most of the little kaiser rolls are shaped by machine. For bread connoisseurs like my uncle, however, nothing will do but the original version, and so some establishments still sell the hand-shaped rolls — for twice the price of the others. To be honest, I can't taste the difference.

The same Viennese bakery carried a golden yellow milk bread that I always found superlative. The owner of the establishment attributed its special flavor to the extra egg yolks and the cream used in place of milk in the recipe. Here it is, adapted for the bread machine.

Should you be wondering what to do with the egg whites left from the baking of this bread, the Viennese answer would be to make meringues, those wisps of sugar and air served with chestnut puree, chocolate, and other wickedly rich dessert delights. But that's a confection for another book. . . .

SMALL	LARGE
¾ cup heavy cream	1 cup heavy cream
3 tablespoons unsalted butter	¼ cup unsalted butter
1 tablespoon honey	2 tablespoons honey
1 egg	1 egg
2 egg yolks	3 egg yolks
2 cups unbleached all-purpose flour	2¾ cups unbleached all-purpose flour
½ to 1½ teaspoons salt to taste	1 to 2 teaspoons salt to taste
1 teaspoon active dry yeast	1½ teaspoons active dry yeast

Pour the cream into your bread machine baking pan and measure in the butter. If you are using butter still cold from the refrigerator, cut it into chunks before placing it in the pan to ensure its blending evenly with the other ingredients. Spoon in the honey and add the egg and egg yolks, the flour, salt, and, last, the yeast, reserving the leavening for its own container where a separate dispenser is provided for it. If the instructions for the machine you have specify placing the leavening in the bottom of the pan first thing, you'll need to remember to add the flour and salt next, the cream, butter, honey, and eggs last.

Bake the loaf on your machine's quick cycle.

Sour Cream Bread

Here's a loaf that uses no liquids in the traditional sense, just sour cream for moisture. My original recipe for this bread called for water as well. But that version, when attempted in my machine, demonstrated quite graphically why bread machines should be designed for easier cleaning. It was smoke-alarm time.

This is not to discourage experimentation. I simply dropped the water from the recipe altogether and ended up with a soft, moist, white bread with a lovely puffed crown.

The loaf is perfect for French toast, its open texture holding the butter and pools of syrup delectably.

1 cup sour cream
2½ cups unbleached all-purpose flour
1 tablespoon dark brown sugar
¼ to 1 teaspoon salt to taste
1½ teaspoons active dry yeast

Scoop the sour cream into your baking pan and add the flour, brown sugar, and salt. Position the yeast according to the directions given for your machine, unless you have a machine with its own dispenser for leavening, in which case the yeast should be measured into the dispenser the very last thing.

A quick bake cycle gives the best results with this recipe.

French Sandwich Bread

French bread brings to mind those long, thin baguettes of cinematographic and novelistic allure a couple of which I would tuck under my arm each morning to transport from the *boulangerie* in Restinclières, one of those tiny villages that dot the south of France, to the small stone farm cottage at the outskirts of town that was our home for one memorable spring. Like most patrons of the *boulangerie,* I would break off a piece of the bread to nibble on my stroll. Rarely did more than a loaf and a half make it home. Often there remained but one loaf, which occasioned another walk before lunch.

Then on Tuesday and Thursday afternoons, a large white van proclaiming itself to be a mobile *charcuterie* and featuring a wide array of cheeses along with its many pâtés and sausages would ring its bell outside the cottage, and at least once a week we would treat ourselves to a substantial slab of Roquefort, which made of a buttered baguette a delectable feast. And so I would take yet another stroll to the bakery to pick up yet more baguettes.

But there's a whole other side to French bread. Among the loaves not so well known abroad is *pain de mie,* a popular sandwich loaf, square as befits its purpose, baked in a special pan with a sliding cover. As the dough rises, the cover keeps it from expanding freely.

The result is the traditionally shaped fine-textured sandwich loaf equally brown on all sides.

I tried to achieve this effect in the Hitachi bread machine that doubles as a rice cooker, not to mention a jam maker, and thus has a lid for its pan. But the results were unpredictable and not really worth the number of times the dough forced the cover off and spilled over onto the heating coil. It's better simply to accept that this bread as baked in the electronic oven is going to emerge with a slightly rounded top. The squarish shape of the machine's pan will give you a close approximation of the real thing on the other five sides, and the flavor and texture will be right on target.

Make sure the butter called for in the recipe is either soft or sliced very thin before being added to the other ingredients, as otherwise it is apt not to be incorporated evenly in the batter. You may notice at the beginning of the mixing cycle that the dough seems far too dry and the machine seems to be simply stirring flour. Give it time, and it will churn together the well-kneaded dough for a good, rich sandwich loaf.

SMALL
½ cup water
¼ cup unsalted butter
2 cups unbleached all-purpose
    flour
1 teaspoon sugar
½ to 1½ teaspoons salt to taste
1 teaspoon active dry yeast

LARGE
1¼ cups water
½ cup unsalted butter
4 cups unbleached all-purpose
    flour
2 teaspoons sugar
1 to 2 teaspoons salt to taste
1½ teaspoons active dry yeast

Pour the water into your bread machine baking pan and add the butter, remembering to slice it fairly thin if taking it cold from the refrigerator, as such a quantity dumped unceremoniously into the pan will fail to blend smoothly with the other ingredients. Measure in the flour, sugar, salt, and yeast, reserving the leavening to place in its separate dispenser if this feature is provided on your machine. If the directions that came with the model you have specify spooning the leavening into the pan at the start of operations, however, add the flour, sugar, and salt before the water and butter.

Bake the loaf on your machine's quick, or rapid-bake, cycle.

Faux French White Bread

European flour is softer than the bread flour found in the United States. In some ways it's more like our cake flour. I once tried to duplicate the texture by mixing some cake flour in with the bread flour I was using, hoping, among other things, to achieve in some miraculous random way the crisp crust crowning so many of the loaves and rolls I remembered from the Continent.

My experiment didn't work out as I'd hoped. The bread that emerged from my electronic oven was soft and tender inside and out. But it was a very nice, homely sort of bread, "a welcome change," as my wife, Susan, put it, "from a rich diet of the more colorful and heavily flavored breads." She likes slices of this loaf toasted for breakfast with butter and apricot jam. It's marvelous with a bitter orange marmalade as well.

You'll note that a bit of barley malt syrup is used in the recipe given here. Malt, available at health-food stores and by mail order, is extracted from sprouted barley. An enzyme in it called diastase produces the natural sugar maltose, which is what imparts the familiar malt flavoring to real, old-fashioned malted milk. Barley malt syrup is a viscous semiliquid that adds a warm flavor to what otherwise might be bland fare. Make sure you use plain barley malt syrup, not the hop-flavored malt sold for home beer brewing. Hop malt has a bitter taste.

SMALL

1 cup sour cream or yogurt,
    regular or low-fat
¼ cup water
1 tablespoon olive oil
1 tablespoon barley malt syrup
1½ cups unbleached all-purpose
    flour
1 cup cake flour
¼ cup whole-wheat flour
½ to 1½ teaspoons salt to taste
1½ teaspoons active dry yeast

LARGE

1½ cups sour cream or yogurt,
    regular or low-fat
⅓ cup water
4 teaspoons olive oil
1 tablespoon barley malt syrup
2½ cups unbleached all-purpose
    flour
1½ cups cake flour
½ cup whole-wheat flour
1 to 2 teaspoons salt to taste
2 teaspoons active dry yeast

Scoop the sour cream or yogurt into the baking pan of your bread machine and add the water, olive oil, and barley malt syrup, unless the instructions for your machine specify that the yeast is to be placed in the bottom of the pan first thing, in which case these liquid ingredients should be added last, after all the dry ingredients. Measure in the all-purpose, cake, and whole-wheat flours, the salt, and the yeast, placing the leavening in its own separate dispenser if your machine has one.

To bake the loaf, set your machine to its rapid cycle.

Beer Bread

B eer and bread have been intertwined in history ever since the Egyptians discovered zymurgy, whose listing in the dictionary I found as a child, much to my delight, to be the very last entry and a rare and challenging appendage in a game of Scrabble. Zymurgy, the art of fermentation, involves the harnessing of yeast to produce beer, bread, soy sauce, or any of a number of other less-familiar fermented products.

Egyptologists recently unearthed some apparently viable grains of wheat at the ancient Egyptian ruins of Tel el Amarna. They've planted a crop of this wheat and are planning to replicate the beer of the Pharaohs. "Whether there was one sourdough for bread and another for beer, we do not know," they observe. Outside of that comment, I've found no reference to the bread of the Pharaohs, the focus of the research seemingly being on the beer.

Considerable analysis is being devoted to the matter of regulating the temperature of the brew-to-be. "It gets pretty hot in Tel el Amarna, and excessive heat would destroy the enzymes needed to make sugar," the scientists reason. The ancient Egyptian zymologists' solution seems to have been to use special porous pottery for the fermentation process, enabling evaporation to cool the liquid as it rested.

There were no hops in ancient Egypt with which to flavor the Pharaohs' brew. Research seems to indicate that herbs, cinnamon, even dates, were used for this purpose.

Whatever the case, beer, albeit of the hopped variety, has long been used in Europe as the liquid of choice in many breads, to which it adds, besides keeping quality, a pleasantly rough texture and its own distinctive flavor. Dark beers like porter and stout contribute extra tang. It's a good idea to let the beer go flat before using it for bread. Otherwise the beating action of the kneading blade may cause the frothy dough to foam over.

SMALL

1 cup (²/₃ of a 12-ounce can or
   bottle) flat beer
1 tablespoon canola or olive oil
2¹/₄ cups unbleached all-purpose
   flour
2 tablespoons sugar
1¹/₂ teaspoons active dry yeast

LARGE

1¹/₂ cups (1 12-ounce can or
   bottle) flat beer
2 tablespoons canola or olive oil
3¹/₂ cups unbleached all-purpose
   flour
¹/₄ cup sugar
2 teaspoons active dry yeast

If the instructions for the bread machine you have specify that the leavening is to be placed in the bottom of your baking pan first thing, add the flour and sugar before the beer and oil. Otherwise, pour the beer into the pan, followed by the canola or olive oil, then measure in the flour, sugar, and yeast. If your machine features a separate dispenser for leavening, spoon the yeast in there.

Use your machine's quick cycle for baking this bread.

Buttermilk Whole-Wheat Bread

Buttermilk is one of those old-fashioned farmstead ingredients that aren't used all that often in cooking anymore. But it's still readily available in many supermarkets, and it contributes exceptional tenderness and taste to a loaf of bread. It's a particularly fitting choice of liquid in whole-grain breads, where it adds extra loft as well as flavor.

If for some reason you have difficulty finding buttermilk in your area, put two tablespoons of yogurt or sour cream into a measuring cup and stir in enough milk to give you a level cupful of liquid. From a baking point of view, the combination is a reasonable substitute for buttermilk. Some stores also carry dried buttermilk for reconstituting if demand is not sufficient to keep the fresh product on the shelves.

SMALL

1 cup buttermilk
2 tablespoons canola oil
1 tablespoon unsulphured
  molasses
1¾ cups whole-wheat flour
½ cup unbleached all-purpose
  flour
¼ to 1 teaspoon salt to taste
1½ teaspoons active dry yeast

LARGE

1¾ cups buttermilk
3 tablespoons canola oil
2 tablespoons unsulphured
  molasses
3 cups whole-wheat flour
¾ cup unbleached all-purpose
  flour
½ to 1½ teaspoons salt to taste
2 teaspoons active dry yeast

Pour the buttermilk into your bread machine baking pan and add the canola oil and molasses, unless the instructions that came with the model you have specify that the yeast is to be placed in the bottom of the pan first thing, in which case these ingredients should be added after the dry ones. Measure in the whole-wheat and all-purpose flours, the salt, and the yeast, spooning the leavening into its own dispenser if a separate container is provided for it on your machine.

Use the rapid-bake setting on your machine for this loaf.

Basic All-Whole-Wheat Bread

W hen you combine the proteins of grain with those of dairy products, you create more complete food proteins, balanced like those of meat and fish. In a loaf such as this one, the whole-wheat grain and the buttermilk together provide a source of protein and fiber more acceptable than animal protein to many in today's fat-conscious culture. So here's a balanced loaf that should be as healthy as it is tasty.

> *1 cup buttermilk*
> *1 tablespoon unsulphured molasses*
> *1 tablespoon unsalted butter or canola*
>   *oil*
> *2½ cups whole-wheat flour*
> *2 tablespoons nonfat dry milk*
> *¼ to 1 teaspoon salt to taste*
> *1½ teaspoons active dry yeast*

Remember that if the instructions that came with your bread machine call for the yeast to be placed in the baking pan first, the dry ingredients should be added before the liquids. Otherwise put the buttermilk, molasses, and butter or canola oil in the pan, add the flour, dry milk, salt, and, if the instructions for your machine so direct, the yeast. If your machine has a separate dispenser for leavening, spoon the yeast into the dispenser after all the other ingredients have been measured into the baking pan.

Set the machine to its full bake cycle for this bread.

Light Whole-Wheat Bread

A ll the publicity over the healthfulness of whole grains and fiber aside, if you've spent your entire life eating white bread, then, let's face it, the darker varieties are going to take some getting used to. Nowhere is this more true than among children, whose sensitive taste buds and peer-pressure-prone personalities are apt to find Twinkies the ultimate in lunch-box fare. Well, here's a light whole-wheat bread that you might be able to slip them without their noticing.

The recipe produces an attractive tall loaf. It's a good summer bread that, toasted, accommodates the traditional ingredients of a BLT sandwich magnificently.

> *1 1/4 cups water*
> *1 teaspoon honey*
> *2 cups unbleached all-purpose flour*
> *1/2 cup whole-wheat flour*
> *1/2 cup uncooked oatmeal (not instant)*
> *1/4 to 1 teaspoon salt to taste*
> *1 1/2 teaspoons active dry yeast*

Pour the water into the baking pan of your bread machine and add the spoonful of honey, followed by the all-purpose and whole-wheat flours, the oatmeal, salt, and yeast. Remember, however, to follow the directions that came with your particular machine for incorporating the leavening; if the yeast is to be placed in the pan first thing, then the water and honey should be reserved till last.

Use either the regular or the quick cycle on your machine for baking this loaf.

Basic Rye Bread

Rye bread, that tasty European staple from the oven, is one of those tricky loaves that often fail to meet the expectations of the home baker. The first loaf I made, a decade ago, would still be sitting around if Susan hadn't finally disposed of it. My plan had been to drill three holes in it, providing it with a possible use as a bowling ball.

The recipe that follows makes a nice firm loaf. Because of this, the bread will be about half as tall as some of the lighter, more delicate loaves whose recipes are found in this book, so don't be overcome with disappointment when you pull the pan out and have to peer over the edge to see the bread. Once you've sampled it, you'll love its dense, fine-grained, moist texture.

The instant coffee you'll notice among the ingredients is for color. Old-time rye-bread recipes often called for Postum, a toasted grain-based coffee substitute that can still be used instead of the coffee if preferred and if it's handy. My hunch regarding the origin of this ingredient as a coloring agent in the bread is that, somewhere back in history, one baker or another added some accidentally blackened, burned grain to his loaves rather than simply throwing it out, and the sumptuous-looking darkened loaves became objects of preference. Whatever the case, the dark rye bread you see at the local bakery also has one coloring agent or another added to give it a look of richness.

When slicing loaves fresh from a bread machine, one tends to go for substance, both because it can be tricky to cut thin slices from them and because one doesn't ordinarily want wimpy slices of a good bread anyhow. But this particular rye bread really should be cut into slices no thicker than an eighth to three-sixteenths of an inch across, and it stands up well to such delicate carving.

The bread is superb with sliced hard-boiled eggs and anchovies, a flavorful cheese like Brie or Swiss, watercress and mayonnaise, or sliced cucumbers and butter. Make a whole trayful of small open-faced sandwiches from it for a delightful summer meal.

1¼ cups buttermilk
2 tablespoons olive oil
1 tablespoon dehydrated minced onion
1 cup unbleached all-purpose flour
1 cup rye flour
1 cup whole-wheat flour
¼ cup firmly packed dark brown sugar
1 tablespoon instant coffee, regular or
    decaffeinated, or Postum
1 tablespoon caraway seeds
½ to 1 teaspoon salt to taste
1½ teaspoons active dry yeast

Unless the instructions that came with your bread machine call for starting with the yeast, in which case you will need to remember to reverse the order in which you add the liquid and the dry ingredients, pour the buttermilk and olive oil into your baking pan and add the onion. Then add the all-purpose, rye, and whole-wheat flours, the brown sugar, coffee or Postum, caraway seeds, and salt. Last, add the yeast, following the instructions given for your particular machine. If the model you have features a separate dispenser for leavening, add the yeast there.

Set the machine on its regular full cycle to bake this loaf.

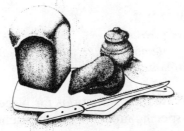

Basic Oatmeal Bread

Oatmeal bread always brings to my mind the Irish. Why that is I'm not exactly sure, since I associate the cereal itself more with the frugal Scots. The Scots make their porridge from the cracked but unflattened grain rather than from the paper-thin rolled oat flakes to which we are accustomed.

Whatever its original nationality, oatmeal bread is undeniably hearty and flavorful. The recipe given here makes a fine-textured, nutty, golden loaf. The use of bread flour instead of plain unbleached flour is helpful in this instance, giving the loaf more loft. But in any case, don't expect a really tall loaf. The bread will be nicely rounded on top, but rather squarish. What it lacks in height it will make up for in taste.

> 1 cup milk, whole or skim
> 2 tablespoons unsalted butter or
>   canola oil
> 2 cups bread flour
> 1 cup uncooked oatmeal (not in-
>   stant)
> 2 tablespoons dark brown sugar
> 1/4 to 1 teaspoon salt to taste
> 1 1/2 teaspoons active dry yeast
>
> G L A Z E
>
> 1 egg white
> 2 tablespoons milk, whole or skim
> oat flakes for garnish

Remember to follow the instructions for placement of the yeast provided with the specific model of bread machine that you have. Put the cupful of milk and the butter or canola oil in the baking pan first, unless directed to reserve the liquids till last, and add the flour, oatmeal, brown sugar, salt, and yeast.

Use either your machine's regular or its quick bake cycle for this bread. When you remove the finished loaf from its pan, while it's still piping hot, quickly whip together the egg white and the two tablespoons of milk and brush this glaze over the top of the hot bread. Either a pastry brush or the more traditional goose feather used in Ireland will do a fine job of this. Sprinkle the dome of the loaf liberally with oat flakes. Some will always fall off. Not to worry. Return the loaf to the pan and the pan to its baking slot in the machine. The oat flakes will cling firmly as the glaze cooks on from the retained heat of the bread and the oven and then cools, imparting the distinctive traditional look that makes oatmeal bread instantly recognizable.

Sesame Oatmeal Bread

The sesame in this loaf comes as a lovely surprise when one bites into it, especially when the seeds are toasted beforehand, although both that step and glazing the finished loaf with more of the decorative grains are optional. The tendency of oatmeal to weigh down a dough, resulting in a fairly compact bread, is compensated for in this recipe by the sour cream, which helps to give a loaf extra height.

SMALL

1 1/4 cups sour cream or yogurt, regular or low-fat

1 tablespoon unsalted butter or canola oil

2 cups unbleached all-purpose flour

3/4 cup uncooked oatmeal (not instant)

1 tablespoon dark brown sugar

3/4 cup sesame seeds, toasted if desired

1/4 to 1 teaspoon salt to taste

1 1/2 teaspoons active dry yeast

LARGE

1 1/2 cups sour cream or yogurt, regular or low-fat

2 tablespoons unsalted butter or canola oil

3 cups unbleached all-purpose flour

1 1/4 cups uncooked oatmeal (not instant)

2 tablespoons dark brown sugar

1 1/4 cups sesame seeds, toasted if desired

1/2 to 1 1/2 teaspoons salt to taste

2 teaspoons active dry yeast

Scoop the sour cream or yogurt into your baking machine bread pan and add the butter or canola oil, unless the instructions that came with your machine specify that the yeast is to be placed in the bottom of the pan first thing, followed by the other dry ingredients and then the liquids. Add the flour, oatmeal, brown sugar, sesame seeds, salt, and yeast, following the directions given for your particular machine in incorporating the yeast.

Bake the loaf on the machine's quick cycle.

Basic All-Semolina Bread

Semolina flour is ordinarily used in the making of pasta. Milled from protein-rich durum wheat with only the bran layer removed, the flour is creamy in color and grainy in texture, rather reminiscent of cornmeal. It makes a rich-looking, great-tasting bread.

Most grocery stores and supermarkets do not carry semolina flour. But just about every health-food store does. The flour is also often available in ethnic markets, particularly Italian and Middle Eastern ones. In the latter it will be found along with the coarser grind used for that region's justly acclaimed couscous.

The recipe given here produces a moist, fine-textured yellow loaf. It's a superlative toasting bread that goes particularly well with coarse-cut English marmalade.

> 1 cup buttermilk
> 1 egg
> 1 tablespoon unsalted butter or canola oil
> 2½ cups semolina flour
> ¼ to 1 teaspoon salt to taste
> 1½ teaspoons active dry yeast

Unless the instructions that came with your bread machine call for starting with the yeast, in which case you will need to reverse the order in which the liquid and the dry ingredients are incorporated into the batter, pour the buttermilk into your baking pan, break in the egg, and add the butter or canola oil. Then measure in the flour, salt, and yeast. If you have a machine with its own dispenser for leavening, add the yeast there.

Use a regular full baking cycle for this loaf.

6 · Multigrain Breads

THE DAILY BREAD that has been part of my life for as long as I can remember has taken a multitude of forms. Like most children growing up in Europe during and after World War II, I didn't have to be reminded to clean my plate, and the pieces of bread with which I did so were broken from many different loaves. Some of the great variety in taste and texture of the breads of the Old World and beyond has been "rediscovered" in this country only during the past decade or so of culinary expansion. For a long time we were a nation of white bread.

I vividly remember being told stories of the great hungers of the 1800s, when in desperation people made bread of anything flour-like in consistency, including the ground bark of trees. Bread has in fact been made of many things besides wheat flours over the years, and in many shapes as well, from the huge free-form loaves of central Europe to the paper-thin *chappatis* of India.

Bread machines will make neither of those. But these electronic ovens can produce a range of delicious multigrain breads far wider than might be imagined from the instruction booklets accompanying the devices. Richly flavorsome, these multigrain breads served merely with butter are close to a meal in themselves.

Even the most basic of breads often contain several different flours. But the recipes in this chapter encompass a broader spectrum of grains. Cornell bread, for instance, formulated by Dr. Clive McCay of the university of that name, was originated to return nourishment to the staff of life for people raised to believe in sliced white fluff as the only socially acceptable bread. The cut-oats and flaxseed bread recipes acknowledge the trend today toward including tasty, uncrushed seeds in bread. Ezekiel bread, well, do try it. It's an unusual delicacy.

Cornell Bread

Today's emphasis on nutrition and flavor in bread suggests that it might be time to take another look at what some readers may remember as "the Cornell formula." Not much has been heard of it lately, but its value is far from spent.

For centuries bread was the staff of life. For centuries it was also an emblem of social stature. Dark, rich bread betokened peasantry; white, bland bread denoted a high social plane.

But increasing wealth in the wake of the industrial revolution and the development of mechanized baking together conspired to put white bread in the baskets of even the poor, and the rank it symbolized within their grasp. The sad corollary was that those who depended on bread for their very subsistence were robbed of its sustenance.

The so-called enriched flours of the twentieth century have all the wheat germ removed from them, because the germ makes the grain hard to mill and the flour hard to keep. True, a few nutrients from the original germ are restored to the flour after milling, but the result is still far less nutritious than even the finest of white flours in the days before modern milling.

In an effort to counter malnutrition among the underprivileged and the institutionalized of America, who earlier in this century lived on bread to a degree inconceivable today, a bread mix designed to deliver more nutrition in white bread was developed at Cornell University. To the processed wheat flour were added nonfat dry milk, soy flour, and wheat germ. Cornell bread had everything going for it: it was inexpensive, it was nourishing, and it was white.

Today's national dietary abundance has given priority to eating less rather than to getting enough to eat, and Cornell bread has fallen into oblivion. However, it is still a nutritious loaf, and one that the undernourished of the present generation, the Fluffernutter school set, take to as if it were, well, white bread.

The Cornell mix can be purchased by mail from some of the suppliers listed in the back of this book. You can also make your own, using the formula below.

BASIC CORNELL FLOUR MIX

1 tablespoon soy flour
1 tablespoon wheat germ
1 tablespoon nonfat dry milk
unbleached all-purpose or bleached
* white flour*

Mix the soy flour, wheat germ, and dry milk in the bottom of a measuring cup. Add enough regular all-purpose or white flour to make one full cup, and stir with a fork to blend.

By multiplying the ingredients proportionately, you can make up a large batch of this mix at one time. It will keep well if stored in an airtight container in your freezer. To make a loaf from it, measure out the amount of flour mix needed and let it reach room temperature before starting your dough.

The Cornell bread recipe given here produces an average-sized, nicely rounded loaf. Unassuming-looking, it nevertheless packs good flavor and nutrition under its modest crown.

1 cup milk, whole or skim
2 tablespoons honey
1 tablespoon unsalted butter or canola
* oil*
2 cups Cornell mix
¼ to 1 teaspoon salt to taste
1½ teaspoons active dry yeast

Pour the milk into the baking pan of your bread machine and add the honey, butter or canola oil, Cornell mix, and salt. Distribute the yeast as directed for your particular machine.

Bake on a quick cycle.

Seven-Grains Bread

Multigrain cereals in a wide variety of mixes are available at health-food stores and some supermarkets. The most popular of these blends is probably one version or another of the seven-grains mixture used here, an Arrowhead Mills mix of coarsely ground wheat, oats, triticale, millet, soybeans, buckwheat, and yellow corn.

A dense, textured bread has no equal as a foil for a good, sharp cheese or a flavorsome pâté, and it was in search of such a bread that I decided to try this combination of grains to vary a whole-wheat loaf I'd been baking for some time. The bread is sweeter than what one might expect from the addition of a mere quarter cup of honey, and, if you prefer, the honey can be omitted and an egg or just the white from a large egg can be used in its place. The loaf is also quite compact and square; for a somewhat lighter texture, 1½ cups of unbleached all-purpose flour can be substituted for 1½ cups of the whole-wheat flour.

> 1 cup seven-grains cereal
> 1½ cups boiling water
> ¼ cup honey or, if preferred,
>   1 egg or the white of 1 large egg
> 3 tablespoons olive oil
> 3 cups whole-wheat flour or 1½ cups
>   unbleached all-purpose flour and 1½
>   cups whole-wheat flour
> ½ to 1 teaspoon salt to taste
> 2 teaspoons active dry yeast

Put the seven-grains cereal mixture in the baking pan of your bread machine and pour the boiling water over it. Let the mush cool to the point where it feels merely warm before incorporating the other ingredients, unless your machine has a separate dispenser for the yeast, in which case no wait is necessary, since the yeast is not added to the dough for the first half hour or so of mixing. Next, add the honey or egg or egg white, the olive oil, the whole-wheat flour or all-purpose and whole-wheat flours combined, and the salt. Top it off with the yeast, unless directed otherwise in the instructions for your machine.

Bake on full cycle, using a medium setting for color if your machine permits this choice.

Sprouted Wheat Bread

This bread is the sixties and seventies revisited with the nineties grafted on. Our children still remember the sprouter in our kitchen and the young shoots we scooped from it into whatever happened to be in the culinary making. Our sprouting has trickled to an occasional event these days, but the diminutive germinated seeds are still nice in a salad, and they add to this bread a grand nutty taste along with extra nutrition.

The celery seed is right on the cutting edge of health-food enhancement, it turns out. Researchers at the University of Chicago Medical Center have discovered that a chemical constituent of celery called 3-n-butyl phthalide lowers blood pressure and cholesterol significantly. Celery is an old Chinese remedy for high blood pressure as well, so maybe it is especially good for us. In any case, the tiny seeds contribute a refreshing piquancy to the loaf.

The measurement for the sprouted wheat in the recipe is for the dry grains to be germinated, because once they've sprouted, it's difficult to pack them, with all their tangled roots, into a measuring cup. Anywhere from one to three days is required for the roots to reach the preferred length of once to twice the length of the seeds themselves. You'll need to take this into account when planning to bake this loaf.

SMALL	LARGE
1 cup water or vegetable broth	*1½ cups water or vegetable broth*
1 tablespoon olive oil	*2 tablespoons olive oil*
1 tablespoon honey	*2 tablespoons honey*
½ cup wheat seeds, sprouted	*¾ cup wheat seeds, sprouted*
1 cup unbleached all-purpose flour	*1½ cups unbleached all-purpose flour*
1 cup whole-wheat flour	*1½ cups whole-wheat flour*
½ cup semolina flour	*¾ cup semolina flour*
1 teaspoon celery seed	*2 teaspoons celery seed*
½ to 1½ teaspoons salt to taste	*1 to 2 teaspoons salt to taste*
1½ teaspoons active dry yeast	*2 teaspoons active dry yeast*

Pour the water or vegetable broth into your bread machine baking pan and add the olive oil and honey, unless the instructions for your machine call for placing the yeast in the bottom of the pan first thing and incorporating the liquids after the other dry ingredients. Measure in the sprouted wheat, the all-purpose, whole-wheat, and semolina flours, the celery seed, and the salt. If your machine has a separate dispenser for leavening, add the yeast there; otherwise, scatter it over the rest of the dry ingredients.

Set your machine to its rapid-bake cycle for this loaf.

Sesame Semolina Bread

Every once in a while, one comes across a loaf of bread that's not simply good, but grand. This loaf qualifies for that accolade. Everyone in the family loves it, and there's never a single slice left over with which to experiment in making a stuffing or dumplings or other entremets.

It's a rather unusual loaf, the semolina flour contributing a soft, silky texture and the sesame seeds a nutty touch. Both those ingredients and the barley malt syrup called for in the recipe are usually available at neighborhood health-food stores. The sesame seeds can generally be bought in bulk there as well, at considerable savings over purchasing them in the small containers found on supermarket spice shelves.

SMALL	LARGE
1 cup water	1¾ cups water
1 tablespoon olive oil	5 teaspoons olive oil
1 tablespoon barley malt syrup	5 teaspoons barley malt syrup
1¾ cups semolina flour	3 cups semolina flour
¾ cup unbleached all-purpose flour	1 cup unbleached all-purpose flour
½ cup sesame seeds	1 cup sesame seeds
½ to 1½ teaspoons salt to taste	1 to 2 teaspoons salt to taste
1½ teaspoons active dry yeast	2 teaspoons active dry yeast

Unless the instructions for your bread machine specify that the yeast is to be placed in the bottom of the baking pan, followed by the other dry ingredients and then the liquids, pour the water into your pan and add the olive oil, barley malt syrup, semolina and all-purpose flours, sesame seeds, and salt. Last, add the yeast, placing it in its own separate dispenser if your machine has that feature. Set your machine to its rapid-bake cycle for this loaf.

Graham Cracker Bread

Snacks in my grade-school days were almost always a pint of milk and a double graham cracker. My own children eat fried graham crackers, which sounds a little weird until one realizes that what they're doing is crushing the crackers and cooking them in butter, thus creating a graham cracker pie crust without the filling.

The reason the school I attended as a youngster served the snacks it did, and the reason we've never really discouraged the fried cracker munchies, is that graham flour ranks high on the nutritional scale, although I should add that the crackers are far sweeter than the flour Dr. Sylvester Graham first promoted as a healthful replacement for white flour back in the 1800s.

The recipe given here utilizes the readily available graham crackers in lieu of graham flour, which is often hard to find. The loaf, slightly sweet but not overpoweringly so, goes splendidly with roast pork or ham. Also, to return the discussion to the halls of learning, slices of this bread sandwiched together with apple butter make great school lunchbox snacks.

SMALL	LARGE
1 cup milk, whole or skim	*1½ cups milk, whole or skim*
2 tablespoons unsalted butter	*3 tablespoons unsalted butter*
2 tablespoons dark corn syrup	*3 tablespoons dark corn syrup*
2 teaspoons vanilla extract	*1 tablespoon vanilla extract*
1¾ cups unbleached all-purpose flour	*3 cups unbleached all-purpose flour*
11 double graham crackers (one package)	*18 double graham crackers*
1 teaspoon cinnamon	*1½ teaspoons cinnamon*
1½ teaspoons active dry yeast	*2 teaspoons active dry yeast*

Pour the milk into your bread machine pan and add the butter. If you are making the large loaf and using butter cold from the refrigerator, cut it into chunks before placing it in the pan, to facilitate its blending with the other ingredients. Measure in the corn syrup, vanilla extract, and flour. Toss in the graham crackers, crushing them in your hand as you go, and the cinnamon, and add the yeast as directed for your machine. Remember to reverse the order of ingredients if so instructed.

Use your machine's quick cycle to bake this loaf.

One Rye Bread

This bread is an adaptation of the Czech Oder River rye. Among my pleasant recollections is one of a memorable evening spent dining on succulent pork sausages served with grand chunks of that bread and accompanied by the original Budweiser, as brewed in the Czech town of Budějovice.

The bread machine version of Oder River rye owes its present name to the fact that in converting the recipe, I had the best results using one measure of everything. Oh, all right, the recipe does happen to call for one 1½ teaspoons of yeast, the standard for almost all the small machine-made loaves I bake, but that's the only exception.

If you don't have any pork sausages handy to go with this bread, try it with herring or a hard cheese or just butter and onions, in the European peasant tradition.

1 cup water or vegetable broth
1 tablespoon canola oil
1 tablespoon unsulphured molasses
1 cup unbleached all-purpose flour
1 cup rye flour
1 cup whole-wheat flour
1 tablespoon cocoa
1 tablespoon dehydrated minced onion
1 tablespoon caraway seeds
1 teaspoon salt
1½ teaspoons active dry yeast

Pour the water or vegetable broth into your baking machine pan and add first the canola oil and molasses, then the all-purpose, rye, and whole-wheat flours, the cocoa, onion, caraway seeds, and salt. Spoon the yeast into its dispenser if your machine has one; if not, scatter the leavening over the other dry ingredients. Should the directions for your machine specify that the yeast is to be placed in the bottom of the pan first thing, however, you'll need to remember to reverse the order in which you add the liquid and the dry ingredients.

Bake the bread on your machine's quick cycle.

Garlic Pumpernickel Bread

Pumpernickel has a longstanding flavor relationship with molasses and onions. Molasses also helps to give a pumpernickel loaf its traditional dark mahogany color. But the onion has no such secondary function, and so substituting garlic for it does little to affect the bread except to enhance its flavor in a way somewhat different from that of the onion.

This fine-textured, compact loaf is elegant sliced thin and served with cold cuts and a horseradish-spiked mustard. There's nothing subtle here, rather a palette of forceful flavors.

Yes, all of those cups of flour do fit into a 1-pound bread machine pan; the loaf is that compact. Lightweight machines such as the DAK and the Welbilt, however, do have problems handling the dough.

SMALL	LARGE
1½ cups water or vegetable broth	2 cups water or vegetable broth
¼ cup unsulphured molasses	⅓ cup unsulphured molasses
¼ cup olive oil	⅓ cup olive oil
2 cups pumpernickel or rye flour	3 cups pumpernickel or rye flour
1 cup unbleached all-purpose flour	1¼ cups unbleached all-purpose flour
1 cup whole-wheat flour	1 cup whole-wheat flour
2 teaspoons garlic powder or 4 cloves fresh garlic, pressed	1 tablespoon garlic powder or 6 cloves fresh garlic, pressed
2 teaspoons instant coffee, regular or decaffeinated, or Postum	1 tablespoon instant coffee, regular or decaffeinated, or Postum
1 teaspoon cocoa	2 teaspoons cocoa
½ to 1½ teaspoons salt to taste	1 to 2 teaspoons salt to taste
1½ teaspoons active dry yeast	2 teaspoons active dry yeast

Unless the instructions for the bread machine you have specify that the leavening is to be placed in the baking pan first, followed by the other dry ingredients and then the liquids, pour the water or vegetable broth, molasses, and olive oil into your pan. Then add the pumpernickel or rye, all-purpose, and whole-wheat flours, the garlic, coffee or Postum, cocoa, and salt. Last, add the yeast, following the instructions given for your particular machine. If the model you have features a separate dispenser for leavening, add the yeast there.

Your bread machine can be set to either its regular or its quick cycle for this loaf.

Raisin Pumpernickel Bread

True pumpernickel is traditionally a sourdough bread, coarse-grained and dark, made from unsifted rye flour. Its Eulenspiegel-esque name derives from the combination of two German words: *pumpern,* to break wind — the idea being that the coarse bread was very difficult to digest — and *Nickel,* a goblin or demon — whose friendlier side is represented by jolly old Saint Nick.

The recipe offered here results in a much milder pumpernickel than that which presumably first earned the name. The loaf is high-domed, with a very soft, silky texture.

The cocoa is included more for the traditional dark color of rye breads than for anything else. The raisins are optional. Revell, raisined out on school-lunch-box-sized cartons of them, prefers the bread without. But if you omit the raisins, you may need to reduce the yeast by half a teaspoon to keep the bread from topping out in your machine.

> *1 ½ cups water*
> *¼ cup unsulphured molasses*
> *¼ cup unsalted butter or canola oil*
> *1 cup raisins (optional)*
> *2 cups unbleached all-purpose flour*
> *1 cup rye flour*
> *1 cup whole-wheat flour*
> *¼ cup cocoa*
> *1 tablespoon cinnamon*
> *¼ to 1 teaspoon salt to taste*
> *2 teaspoons active dry yeast (or 1 ½*
> *teaspoons if the raisins are omitted)*

Pour the water and molasses into your bread machine's baking pan and add the butter, cut into small chunks if it's not soft, to ensure that it blends uniformly into the dough, or substitute canola oil, if you prefer. Next add the raisins, if desired, and the all-purpose, rye, and whole-wheat flours. Measure in the cocoa, cinnamon, and salt. Distribute the yeast according to the directions for your particular machine, remembering to reverse the order in which you add the liquid and the dry ingredients if the instructions for your machine specify that the yeast be placed at the bottom of the pan.

Set your machine on its quick cycle for this loaf.

Molasses Rye Bread

This is a sweet, dense rye bread, redolent of molasses, that goes well with cheeses. It's particularly good with the Scandinavian goat cheese *gjetost,* now frequently available in cheese emporiums on this side of the Atlantic.

The bread is unusual for a rye in that it contains bran in addition to the rye flour. The bran, besides contributing to the long-lasting quality of the loaf, adds a stick-to-the-ribs moistness to it. Because of its denseness, the loaf tends to be brick-shaped, with a flat top instead of a rounded one.

SMALL	LARGE
1¼ cups buttermilk	1¾ cups buttermilk
1 tablespoon unsalted butter or canola oil	4 teaspoons unsalted butter or canola oil
¼ cup unsulphured molasses	½ cup unsulphured molasses
1½ cups unbleached all-purpose flour	3 cups unbleached all-purpose flour
1 cup rye flour	1½ cups rye flour
½ cup unprocessed wheat bran	¾ cup unprocessed wheat bran
½ to 1½ teaspoons salt to taste	1 to 2 teaspoons salt to taste
1½ teaspoons active dry yeast	2 teaspoons active dry yeast

Pour the buttermilk into your bread machine baking pan, unless the instructions for the model you have specify that the yeast is to be placed in the pan first and the liquids last, and add the butter or canola oil and the molasses. Then measure in the all-purpose and rye flours, followed by the bran, salt, and yeast. If your machine is equipped with a separate dispenser for leavening, the yeast should be spooned into the dispenser after all the other ingredients have been placed in the pan.

Use the regular baking cycle on your machine for this loaf.

Russian Black Bread

Here's one of my favorite breads. Still not as black as some of the loaves of European rye my memory conjures up, even with both cocoa and coffee added for color, it's nevertheless very dark and moist and dense.

For all that, it's fairly light in heft. One of the secrets here is the use of bread crumbs in the recipe. Such a reclamation of crumbs may seem the ultimate in modern recycling to bread machine owners with leftover loaves, but it's an age-old custom serving a much more basic function. Bread crumbs add airiness, whether to bread or dumplings or a torte.

You can use either store-bought crumbs, for convenience, or your own homemade variety (see the instructions on making bread crumbs in the chapter "Brown Betty, Crumb Crusts, and Bread Puddings"). Toasting the crumbs is really worth the small effort involved. They can be browned either in the oven or in a skillet over a burner.

For oven toasting, spread the crumbs out on a cookie sheet and pop them into a preheated 400-degree oven for eight to ten minutes or until they are a deep golden brown. For stovetop toasting, which I prefer because it's quicker, put the crumbs in an ungreased steel fry pan over a medium to high flame. Stir continuously until the crumbs are the color of dark oak.

The bread crumbs in this recipe help to lighten the loaf, which would otherwise have the solidness characteristic of so many rye breads. You might note that in the list of ingredients the rye and whole-wheat flours appear first, before the liquids usually heading the roster. This reversal is to improve the mixing, which otherwise is poor because of the large quantity of liquid this recipe calls for.

A good Russian black bread really deserves a befitting glaze. The standard one would be simply egg and water. But a mustard glaze goes very well with this loaf, and sesame seeds on top of that add a superlative burst of flavor.

The bread keeps well, although in our family it's rarely allowed to do so because of its popularity. Great slabs of it with generous slices of meat and a favorite condiment between them make wonderful hearty sandwiches. Try it thinly sliced for canapés as well; it's an excellent foil, both in flavor and in appearance, for savory spreads.

1 cup rye flour
½ cup whole-wheat flour
2 cups warm water
2 tablespoons instant espresso
2 tablespoons unsulphured molasses
2 tablespoons unsalted butter or canola
  oil
1½ cups unbleached all-purpose flour
1 cup toasted bread crumbs
1 tablespoon cocoa
2 teaspoons aniseed
1½ teaspoons caraway seeds
¼ to 1 teaspoon salt to taste
1½ teaspoons active dry yeast

G L A Z E

1 egg
1 tablespoon prepared whole-grain
  mustard
sesame seeds for garnish

Measure the rye and whole-wheat flours into the baking pan of your bread machine. Pour the water into a separate bowl or a large measuring cup and dissolve the instant espresso in it. Then transfer the dilute coffee to the baking pan, add the molasses, butter or canola oil, all-purpose flour, bread crumbs, cocoa, aniseed, caraway seeds, salt, and yeast. If your machine has a separate dispenser for leavening, the yeast should be placed there.

A full bake cycle is needed for this bread, to give the dough time to rise properly. As soon as the bread is baked, remove it from its pan. Whip the egg and mustard together and brush this mixture onto the hot loaf with a pastry brush. Sprinkle with sesame seeds if desired. Slip the loaf back into its pan and return it to the bread machine, where the residual heat will bake the glaze on.

Steel-Cut Oat Bread

The heartiest breads usually contain some whole grain. But many of the cereals when left whole need to be softened before they are used in baking. Even steel-cut oats, which are the chopped version of this grain, are no exception. Accordingly, for this loaf you will need to allow an extra fifteen minutes, say, for the boiling water in which the cut oats are soaked to cool to the point where it will not inadvertently kill the leavening.

The recipe given here yields a loaf in which the steel-cut oats are so scattered that one's teeth and taste buds come upon them with pleasant surprise rather than jaded familiarity. The bread makes a thoroughly satisfying meal in itself sliced into thick slabs slathered with butter and garnished with something crisp like sliced cucumbers or watercress.

> 1 cup steel-cut oats
> 1½ cups boiling water
> 2 tablespoons unsulphured molasses
> 1 egg
> 2 cups unbleached all-purpose flour
> 1 cup rye flour
> ½ cup cornmeal
> 2 tablespoons nonfat dry milk
> ½ to 1 teaspoon salt to taste
> 1½ teaspoons active dry yeast

Measure the oats into the baking pan of your bread machine and pour the boiling water over them. Let them stand until they are no more than warm to the touch before adding the other ingredients unless your machine has a separate dispenser for the yeast, as otherwise the hot liquid will kill the leavening. Spoon the molasses into the mush, break in the egg, and add the all-purpose and rye flours, the cornmeal, dry milk, salt, and, following the instructions given for your particular machine, the yeast.

Bake on full cycle.

Brown Rice Bread

Sometimes the best of breads come about by accident. This is such a loaf. To keep the bread machines humming round the clock when I was experimenting with recipes for this book, I would occasionally leave missives for other family members requesting that they feed the machines' hungry maws in my absence.

Now my notes on bread making, intended primarily for myself, are sometimes not entirely clear to others. "Mrs. K.," my fourth-grade penmanship teacher, who always found my script wanting, would no doubt point out that she'd been right all along about the importance of precision in presentation. For when I left the instructions for a rice loaf by one of the bread machines, I neglected to add the word *flour* after *brown rice*.

Susan, aware of the eccentric nature of some of my experiments, dutifully followed the instructions verbatim. Talk about bombs!

However, the failed attempt also made me think. Although the rice had remained embedded in that particular loaf of bread thoroughly uncooked, resembling so many grains of gravel, instant rice should steam itself nicely in the cooking time allowed by the bread machine's baking cycle. And so it does, producing a truly tasty loaf with plenty of nubbly flavor and a nice texture.

No salt is needed in the recipe, as this ingredient is plentifully provided by the soy sauce.

SMALL
1¼ cups water or vegetable broth
1 tablespoon canola or olive oil
2 tablespoons unsulphured
  molasses
1 tablespoon soy sauce
1 cup unbleached all-purpose
  flour
1 cup whole-wheat flour
1 cup instant brown rice
½ teaspoon pepper
1½ teaspoons active dry yeast

LARGE
1¾ cups water or vegetable broth
5 teaspoons canola or olive oil
3 tablespoons unsulphured
  molasses
2 tablespoons soy sauce
1¾ cups unbleached all-purpose
  flour
1¾ cups whole-wheat flour
1½ cups instant brown rice
1 teaspoon pepper
2 teaspoons active dry yeast

Pour the water or vegetable broth into your bread machine pan and add the canola or olive oil, molasses, and soy sauce. If the instructions for your machine specify that the yeast is to be placed in the pan first, however, remember to reverse the order in which you add the liquid and the dry ingredients. Measure in the all-purpose and whole-wheat flours, then the brown rice and pepper. Scatter the yeast over the other ingredients in the pan or measure it into its own container if your machine has a separate dispenser for the leavening.

Use your machine's rapid-bake cycle for the loaf.

Brown Rice Amaranth Bread

Did the Aztecs, consumers of amaranth in the ancient days, mill it and use the flour to make bread? Failing a definitive answer to that question, I surmise the tiny grains were too small to mill satisfactorily with the technology of the times.

Today amaranth is used primarily in the form of a hot cereal or sprinkled uncooked over salads to add a pleasant textural contrast. I use it to the same purpose in this loaf, where its high protein and fiber nutritionally complement the brown rice, yielding a loaf that is very nearly a balanced low-fat meal in itself. The bread is full-bodied, nutty, sweet, and superb with smooth flavorsome cheeses like Swiss. It's also delightful simply with butter.

SMALL	LARGE
1 cup milk, whole or skim	*1½ cups milk, whole or skim*
2 tablespoons honey	*3 tablespoons honey*
½ cup pecan halves	*¾ cup pecan halves*
1 cup semolina flour	*2 cups semolina flour*
1 cup brown rice flour	*1½ cups brown rice flour*
¼ cup whole-wheat flour	*½ cup whole-wheat flour*
½ cup amaranth seed	*1 cup amaranth seed*
¼ to 1 teaspoon salt to taste	*½ to 2 teaspoons salt to taste*
1½ teaspoons active dry yeast	*2 teaspoons active dry yeast*

Pour the milk into your baking machine bread pan, unless the directions for the model you have specify placing the yeast in the bottom of the pan, followed first by the other dry ingredients and then by the liquids, and measure in the honey, pecans, and semolina, brown rice, and whole-wheat flours. Add the amaranth seed and the salt, then spoon the yeast into the leavening dispenser or, failing that device, scatter it over the other dry ingredients.

Bake the loaf on your machine's quick cycle.

Anadama Bread

Most corn breads contain molasses, honey, buttermilk, or a combination of these ingredients, all of which are acidic and react with baking soda to activate its leavening power. Thus baking soda or baking powder, containing soda, is the leavener traditionally used in making these breads. Anadama is an exception.

There are many versions of Anadama bread — almost as many as there are stories purporting to explain how the loaves' curious name came about. But what sets them all apart from the corn breads is the yeast used instead of baking soda to leaven them. The recipe given here makes a dense, nicely corn-flavored loaf best eaten warm with butter and honey.

¾ cup milk, whole or skim
¼ cup unsulphured molasses
1 egg
2 tablespoons unsalted butter or canola oil
2 cups unbleached all-purpose flour
1 cup cornmeal
½ to 1 teaspoon salt to taste
1½ teaspoons active dry yeast

Pour the milk and the molasses into your bread pan, break in the egg, and add the butter or canola oil, the flour, cornmeal, salt, and yeast. The leavening should be added according to the specific instructions given for your bread machine.

Bake this loaf on either a long or a short cycle, using a light color setting if your machine permits that choice.

Portuguese Corn Bread

Somehow, corn bread has acquired the image of being as American as apple pie. And indeed the quick-bread version, made with baking powder, may well be. But corn bread is also popular in Europe, particularly in the southern countries.

The recipe given here is for a Portuguese corn bread called *bro*, which, like Anadama bread and the Tex-Mex corn bread featured later in this book, uses yeast for its leavening. It usually accompanies dishes like stews that are heavy on the gravy or sauce.

SMALL	LARGE
1 cup water or vegetable broth	*2 cups water or vegetable broth*
2 tablespoons olive oil	*3 tablespoons olive oil*
1½ cups unbleached all-purpose flour	*3 cups unbleached all-purpose flour*
1½ cups cornmeal	*2½ cups cornmeal*
2 tablespoons sugar	*3 tablespoons sugar*
¼ teaspoon ground nutmeg	*½ teaspoon ground nutmeg*
½ to 1½ teaspoons salt to taste	*1 to 2 teaspoons salt to taste*
1½ teaspoons active dry yeast	*2 teaspoons active dry yeast*

Pour the water or vegetable broth and olive oil into the baking pan of your bread machine, unless the instructions for the model you have specify that the leavening is to be placed in the pan first and the liquids last, and add the flour, cornmeal, sugar, nutmeg, salt, and yeast. In machines equipped with a separate dispenser for the leavening, the yeast should be spooned into its container after all the other ingredients have been placed in the pan.

This is a bread for your machine's rapid-bake cycle.

Millet Cornmeal Bread

Millet is an ancient grain much used by the Romans, a fact my high-school Latin studies made memorable. The Romans mixed millet and wheat flours for their bread. But millet is an even more congenial complement of corn; added to a corn bread, the seeds, left whole, add crunchy bursts of extra flavor.

Revell, who keeps a bird feeder stocked with seed for the English sparrows, jays, cardinals, and other feathered friends that winter over on our farm, has suspected me of raiding his supplies on occasion for this loaf, but it's not true. I buy the millet from a local health-food store, where you will find it as well.

This recipe is another serendipitous exception to the rule of leavening cornmeal breads with baking soda or baking powder. Then again, it has a lot more than just cornmeal in it.

> 1 cup milk, whole or skim
> ¼ cup honey
> 1 egg
> 2 tablespoons unsalted butter or canola
>   oil
> ½ cup millet seed
> 2 cups unbleached all-purpose flour
> 1 cup cornmeal
> ½ to 1 teaspoon salt to taste
> 1½ teaspoons active dry yeast

Pour the milk and honey into the baking pan of your bread machine, break in the egg, and add the butter or canola oil, the millet, flour, cornmeal, salt, and yeast, following the directions that came with your machine for incorporating the leavening.

This loaf is best baked on your machine's regular cycle.

Millet Bread

Millet is sometimes added whole to breads to add a bit of interest to otherwise dull-textured loaves. In this particular bread, however, the millet is used in flour form, with flaxseed adding the snap.

The resulting loaf is a nice nutty-flavored one, sunny yellow in color, with a distinctively patterned crust. Toasted or plain, it's great for summer BLTs.

SMALL	LARGE
1 cup milk, whole or skim	1 1/2 cups milk, whole or skim
1 tablespoon unsalted butter or canola oil	2 tablespoons unsalted butter or canola oil
1/4 cup unsulphured molasses	1/3 cup unsulphured molasses
1 egg	2 eggs
1 1/4 cups unbleached all-purpose flour	2 cups unbleached all-purpose flour
1 cup millet flour	1 1/2 cups millet flour
1 cup uncooked oatmeal (not instant)	2 cups uncooked oatmeal (not instant)
1/2 cup flaxseed	1 cup flaxseed
1/2 to 1 1/2 teaspoons salt to taste	1 to 2 teaspoons salt to taste
1 1/2 teaspoons active dry yeast	2 teaspoons active dry yeast

Pour the milk into your bread machine pan and add the butter or canola oil, molasses, and egg or eggs. Measure in the all-purpose and millet flours, the oatmeal, flaxseed, salt, and yeast, unless your machine has a separate dispenser for the leavening, in which case add the yeast there. If the leavening is to be placed in the bottom of the baking pan for the bread machine you have, however, reverse the order in which you incorporate the liquid and the dry ingredients.

Bake the loaf on your machine's quick cycle.

Four-Grains Breakfast Bread

Old-fashioned harvests of the fields are encountering an amazing revival in the grain-and-fiber-conscious nineties, particularly at breakfast time. Oatmeal, once plebeian, is in vogue. Bran muffins abound as never before. And ancient grains like amaranth and quinoa are in demand.

Unfortunately, the popularity of these edibles sometimes simply proves the power of fad over taste. However healthy they might be, certain of them have all the flavor of recycled cardboard.

But here's a loaf that packs the nutrition of four different grains and a whole lot of flavor besides. There's a hint of cinnamon in the air when it's baking.

The amaranth flour in the recipe includes among its benefits the amino acids lysine and methionine, elements largely absent in most other flours. High in fiber and rich in iron, it contains as much as 16 percent protein.

> *1 cup milk, whole or skim*
> *1 tablespoon honey*
> *1 egg*
> *2 tablespoons unsalted butter or canola oil*
> *1 teaspoon vanilla extract*
> *1 cup unbleached all-purpose flour*
> *½ cup semolina flour*
> *½ cup amaranth flour*
> *½ cup uncooked oatmeal (not instant)*
> *1 teaspoon cinnamon*
> *½ teaspoon ginger*
> *¼ to 1 teaspoon salt to taste*
> *1½ teaspoons active dry yeast*

Pour the milk into your baking pan, unless the instructions that came with your bread machine call for starting with the yeast, in which case you will need to reverse the order in which the liquid and the dry ingredients are incorporated. Spoon the honey into the pan, break in the egg, and add the butter or canola oil and the vanilla extract. Then measure in the all-purpose, semolina, and amaranth flours and the oatmeal. Last, add the cinnamon, ginger, salt, and yeast. If your machine has a separate dispenser for leavening, the yeast should be placed there.

Use a quick bake cycle for this bread.

Sunflower Bread

In Sweden they make a sunflower-seed loaf called sunshine bread that uses apple cider as its liquid base. Cider can be substituted for the buttermilk in this recipe as well; it will give the loaf a fruitier bouquet. But, personally, I like the creamy texture the buttermilk lends the bread; somehow it complements perfectly the taste burst of the sunflower seeds.

Nutritious and flavorful, the sunflower seeds contribute contrast and interest besides, and they do so without the expense associated with those other celebrated providers of protein-rich sustenance, nuts. For a real treat, try slices of this bread with a smooth spreadable cheese like Brie or even a fragrant Limburger.

1 cup buttermilk or cider
2 tablespoons olive oil
1 tablespoon unsulphured molasses
½ cup hulled sunflower seeds
1½ cups unbleached all-purpose flour
1½ cups whole-wheat flour
¼ to 1 teaspoon salt to taste
1½ teaspoons active dry yeast

Pour the buttermilk or cider into the baking pan of your bread machine and spoon in the olive oil and molasses. Add the sunflower seeds, the all-purpose and whole-wheat flours, and the salt. Follow the directions that came with your particular machine for incorporating the yeast.

Use a quick cycle in baking this loaf.

Flaxseed Bread

Flaxseed is a rich source of protein, and this is a bread I developed early in my bread machine experiments for our vegetarian daughter Genevieve. The first couple of loaves I baked contained all whole-wheat flour, no white, as well as millet. They also boasted honey, garlic, and olive oil. I was striving for an all-around health loaf here.

Genevieve dutifully took a bite, chewed, and commented, "They actually gave you a recipe for this?"

"Well, no, I was experimenting."

With a smile that made me realize how truly beyond verbal description is the renowned expression of the Mona Lisa, she placed the slice, one bite missing, gently at the far edge of her butter plate.

Half a dozen modifications and simplifications later, the recipe included here evolved, and everyone liked the end result. The loaf is a squarish one unusual in flavor, good and crusty and distinctively flecked with the mahogany-colored flaxseed. Slices of it go particularly well, I've found, with liverwurst and thinly sliced onions or a delicately carved smoked ham, both combinations that rather contradict the original high-protein-vegetarian intent of the bread but that nevertheless make a delightful meal.

½ cup flaxseed
1½ cups scalded milk, whole or skim,
* still hot*
3 tablespoons olive oil
1½ cups unbleached all-purpose flour
1½ cups whole-wheat flour
2 teaspoons dry mustard
½ to 1 teaspoon salt to taste
1½ teaspoons active dry yeast

Put the flaxseed in your bread machine pan and cover with the hot milk. Let cool about fifteen minutes or until tepid before adding the other ingredients. Then measure in the olive oil, all-purpose and whole-wheat flours, dry mustard, and salt. Here as elsewhere, salt is very much a matter of individual taste, but this loaf seems to require a bit more than most to bring out its full flavor. Scatter the yeast over the dry ingredients, or spoon it into the yeast dispenser if your machine has one.

Use a regular full baking cycle for this bread.

Ezekiel Bread

Ezekiel bread is one of those exceptionally wholesome breads that sometimes result from the blending of a number of different and, in this case, somewhat unusual flours. The recipe, and its name, can be traced to a Biblical injunction found in Ezekiel 4:9: "Take thou also unto thee wheat, and barley, and beans, and lentils, and millet, and spelt, and put them in one vessel, and make thee bread thereof."

Simplifying the modern bread maker's life, at least one company I know of, King Arthur Flour, listed as a source in the back of the book, makes available a premixed Ezekiel flour. The blend even includes spelt, a primitive and not readily available wheat whose chaff does not separate from the grain in threshing. Spelt is always used in a blend because of its proclivity toward clinging to the chaff. I'd suspect that 100 percent spelt flour would pack a lot of straw with it. I know fiber is a prized constituent in the diet of the au courant today, but enough is enough.

This Ezekiel-based recipe produces a compact, nutty, slightly chewy loaf with a keeping quality better than that of many machine-baked breads.

> 1 cup buttermilk
> 1/4 cup honey
> 1 tablespoon olive oil
> 2 1/2 cups Ezekiel mix
> 1/4 to 1 teaspoon salt to taste
> 1 1/2 teaspoons active dry yeast

Pour the buttermilk, honey, and olive oil into the baking pan of your bread machine, add the Ezekiel mix, the salt, and, if the instructions for your machine so direct, the yeast. If your machine has a separate dispenser for leavening, spoon the yeast into the dispenser after all the other ingredients have been measured into the baking pan. Remember that if your machine has no separate dispenser and the yeast is to be placed in the pan first, the dry ingredients should be added next, before the liquids.

Bake on your machine's full cycle.

7 · Sourdough Breads

SOURDOUGH IS ASSOCIATED in many people's minds with cowboys and the wild West or gold panning in Alaska, but it's far older than that. Archaeologists have uncovered evidence of sourdough baking in ancient Egypt some six thousand years ago.

A sourdough culture can be started simply by capturing some rogue yeast from the wild. That's easy enough. All you have to do is to put a starchy liquid out to sour, or ferment. It can be potato water, corn mash, even leftover spaghetti in its cooking water. Whatever you use as bait, you'll catch something.

But there's a snag to this seemingly innocent endeavor. Wild yeasts do add flavor to a sourdough — sometimes a very strange flavor. And you never know until you've used the starter what that flavor is going to be like. I've encountered some dillies; one native yeast I garnered turned the inside of a bread loaf into a sodden stringy mess.

This is in no way meant to discourage you from making your own sourdough starter. You could well end up with a culture yummy enough to become an heirloom, passed on for generations as sourdough was in the days of yore. But I'd advise at least bringing the operation in from the wilds and taming it a bit.

The simplest approach to starting a sourdough indoors is to set out, in a warm spot, a glass or stainless steel bowl into which you've poured a cup of milk with a cupful of unbleached all-purpose flour and a teaspoonful of sugar beaten into it. The back of the stove or an oven warmed by a pilot light will serve admirably as a resting place for this concoction.

After some 24 to 38 hours, your starter should have begun to foam a bit. It should also have acquired a reasonably strong sour smell. Let it stand undisturbed until the bubbles froth up, which will probably take several days. Then refrigerate the sour, as it's often called, until needed.

If the sourdough turns pink at some point in its fermentation, you have a slime culture. Throw it out and start over.

A less chancy technique is to heat a cupful of milk to wrist temperature, beat in a cupful of unbleached all-purpose flour, and add a couple of tablespoonfuls of yogurt to seed the mixture. Cover the batter tightly with plastic wrap to keep wild yeasts out. Within a few days you should have a nice bubbly sour.

The least problematical course of all is to pick up a packet of dry granular sourdough starter at a health-food store or get it by mail order — or from a tourist trap in San Francisco — and follow the accompanying instructions.

Whichever method you use, once you have a satisfactory sour, there are two keys to continued success with it. First, the starter needs to be at room temperature before use. It wouldn't hurt to take it out of the refrigerator the night before you plan to bake a sourdough loaf. Second, the started mother lode needs to be replenished every time you draw on it. Add equal parts warm milk and unbleached all-purpose flour, beaten together, equivalent in volume to the amount of starter removed for baking.

Real, honest-to-goodness sourdough bread uses no yeast in the traditional sense. The sour itself, after all, is a yeast. But when using a bread machine, a little extra leavening may be helpful, since some sours are not potent enough to leaven a batch of dough within the somewhat condensed and artificially timed period allotted by the machine for bread making.

On the other hand, some sours will produce magnificent loaves, at least of white if not the heavier whole-wheat and rye breads, all on their own. The only way to find out what your starter can and cannot do is to try it with and without — or perhaps I should say without and with — yeast.

Incidentally, timed overnight baking is probably not to be recommended for sourdough breads. While the extra hours of rest would certainly give the sour a longer interval in which to leaven the dough, there's always the possibility that it might levitate the bread right out of the pan while you slept.

You'll notice that the order in which the ingredients for the sourdough breads are listed is different from that of most of the other recipes in this book. The reason for the change in sequence is the problem of cavitation, discussed in the chapter called "Tips and Tricks for Electronic Baking."

White Sourdough Bread

The most familiar sourdough breads this side of the Atlantic are the long baguettes and Italian loaves made famous by San Franciscans. The recipe given here uses yeast as well as sourdough for leavening. While that's definitely cheating a bit, it lends to the formula a reliability that a yeastless version simply could not supply.

Using yeast to help loft the loaf also mediates the tartness of the sourdough, resulting in a bread with just a pleasant hint of sour.

Myself, I prefer my sourdough bread truly sour. If you do too, let me recommend the all-sourdough recipe. It's very sour.

Whichever recipe you choose, don't expect from your bread machine the kind of crust that shatters at the touch of the knife the way that of an old-time hearthstone-baked loaf does. The crust of this bread, though good, will not have the same remarkable crispness.

> 1¾ cups unbleached all-purpose flour
> 2 cups sourdough starter, at room
>   temperature
> 1 tablespoon honey
> 2 tablespoons unsalted butter or canola
>   oil
> ¼ to 1 teaspoon salt to taste
> 1 teaspoon active dry yeast

Measure the flour into the baking pan of your bread machine first, then add the sourdough starter, honey, butter or canola oil, salt, and yeast. If your model has a separate dispenser for the yeast, spoon it in there.

You can use a quick cycle for this loaf, since the sour and the yeast should, between the two of them, raise the dough on that shorter cycle with no difficulty.

Sourdough Whole-Wheat Bread

Sourdough whole-wheat bread is heartier than its white counter-part, yet not as dense as a sourdough rye. The recipe given here yields a fine sandwich loaf. Leftovers, if there are any, make choice bread crumbs for casserole toppings.

> *3 cups whole-wheat flour*
> *1½ cups sourdough starter, at room*
> *temperature*
> *½ cup warm water*
> *2 tablespoons olive oil*
> *¼ to 1 teaspoon salt to taste*
> *1 teaspoon active dry yeast*

Measure the flour into the baking pan for your bread machine, then pour in the starter and water and add the olive oil and salt. Distribute the yeast according to the instructions provided with your machine.

This loaf can be baked on a quick cycle, since it does not rely on the sourdough alone for leavening power.

Sourdough Rye Bread

This comes close to the real thing in the old European tradition. The sours in Europe were always based on rye flour, which has a tendency really to ferment. However, to keep your starter from getting out of hand, I would recommend replenishing it with milk and unbleached all-purpose flour even if you regularly use it for making rye bread. A sour based on fermented rye flour tends to be too strong for all but the most fanatical devotees.

> *1½ cups rye flour*
> *1½ cups whole-wheat flour*

1½ cups sourdough starter, at room
  temperature
½ cup warm water
1 tablespoon olive oil
2 tablespoons unsulphured molasses
1 cup unbleached all-purpose flour
2 tablespoons instant espresso
1 tablespoon caraway seeds
1 tablespoon dehydrated minced onion
  (optional)
¼ to 1 teaspoon salt to taste
1 to 1½ teaspoons active dry yeast

Measure the rye and whole-wheat flours into the baking pan of your bread machine first, then add the sourdough starter, water, oil, and molasses, followed by the all-purpose flour, espresso, caraway seeds, onion if desired, salt, and yeast, placing the yeast in its own dispenser if your machine has such.

Use a full bake cycle for this bread. Even with the addition of yeast, the heavy flours called for make it a slow-rising loaf.

Sourdough Buckwheat Bread

Buckwheat flour, like cornmeal, is quintessentially American. Unlike corn, however, buckwheat is not native to these shores. Its cultivated origins lie somewhere in what is now China, and it has been grown in Europe, where it is served hulled and cooked in the form of kasha, for hundreds of years. Even so, as a flour it has never achieved the popularity on the Continent or in the Far East that it acquired in the States, where during the 1700s and 1800s it was a kitchen staple, particularly for making the buckwheat cakes immortalized in the song "Oh, Susannah."

The recipe given here makes a pleasant loaf of bread — if you like the earthy taste of buckwheat. Personally, I can take it or leave it. But I do have to admit that there's something especially warming about a buckwheat loaf served with a hearty stew on a cold winter's day. Maybe that's why buckwheat is so popular in Siberia.

1 cup unbleached all-purpose flour
2 cups buckwheat flour
2 cups sourdough starter, at room
 temperature
2 tablespoons olive oil
2 tablespoons honey
½ to 1 teaspoon salt to taste
1 teaspoon active dry yeast

Place the all-purpose and buckwheat flours in the baking pan of your bread machine first thing, then measure in the sourdough starter, and on top of that the oil, honey, and salt. Add the yeast, placing it in the yeast dispenser if your machine has one.

Use a quick bake cycle for this loaf.

All-Sour Sourdough Bread

H ere's a loaf that depends completely on its sour for leavening. Its success will stand and fall with the strength of the particular sourdough starter you have bubbling.

To help ensure a happy outcome, first of all, your starter should have the consistency of a tender pancake batter, the kind achieved from using one part flour to one part milk. If you consistently replenish your starter in those proportions, it should remain consistently dependable.

The second key to successful baking with sourdough as your sole leavening agent is to make sure that the sour has been standing unrefrigerated and bubbling, preferably in an oven with a pilot light, for at least 12 hours before being incorporated into the dough it is intended to leaven.

Third, remember to set your bread machine on its full cycle, the one that takes roughly four hours from start to finish, when using sourdough alone for leavening power. A short cycle won't allow enough time for the sour to work its magic; an overnight cycle will almost guarantee your waking to the sound of your smoke alarm and spending the morning chipping burned dough out of your bread machine.

While the recipe given here should work with most sours, you may need to add or withhold half a cupful of the measure of sour indicated, to make your bread rise more or less, respectively. Be prepared for the occasional mishap of a too heavy or an overflowing dough, for sourdough starter can be as unpredictable as a teenager.

This bread is a perfect foil for sliced salmon, tuna, sardines, and other seafood. Toasted, it invites a tangy, coarse-cut orange marmalade.

> 2 cups unbleached all-purpose flour
> 2 cups sourdough starter, at room
>   temperature or warmer
> 2 teaspoons honey
> 2 tablespoons canola oil
> 1/4 to 1 teaspoon salt to taste

Place the flour in the baking pan of your bread machine first, then add the sourdough starter, honey, oil, and salt.

Remember to set your machine on full cycle for this bread.

8 · Crusty Concoctions

"A CRUST OF BREAD" is one of those ambivalent expressions that can convey meanings ranging from derogatory to scrumptious. Then there's the "upper crust," whose reference to the highest ranks of society derives not from its physical position in a loaf of bread but from the fact that it used to be the portion placed before the most honored guest at a table. On the other hand, a "crusty" character has been an ill-tempered one ever since Achilles in Shakespeare's *Troilus and Cressida* called out to Thersites, "Thou crusty batch of nature, what's the news?"

As connotations differ, so do tastes. Myself, I love a good crust, either chewy or crisp. The *eckhaus,* or "corner house," as it's known in German, is my favorite part of a loaf, and I can think of no finer meal than a generous crust of pumpernickel or a fresh baguette spread with sweet butter and served with cheese. Revell, on the other hand, prefers the soft center slices with the least crust. The crusts he saves for fishing.

The breads represented in this section are flavorful delights, but they are particularly so for those who like a good crust. Note that I specified a good crust, not a great crust. The fact is that nothing yet devised has succeeded in duplicating the conditions of the stone hearth for baking bread, and no electronic bakery yet produced for the home can yield the huge free-form loaves of crusty white Italian bread or dark Bavarian pumpernickel found where the baker plies his trade and shapes his dough by hand. Then again, no stone hearth and no manual labor can produce good basic bread at the mere press of a button.

Country Bran Bread

Here's a rough-hewn country loaf chock-full of bran and right up to the latest health-food standards. Truth to tell, the bran phase of our family's diet consciousness was relatively short-lived. After all, one can eat only so many bran muffins, and much else presumably enriched by the light brown flakes loses rather than gains in flavor. During the height of the bran fad, I actually saw an ad for oat-bran and honey ice cream. . . .

But this simple recipe puts bran to both healthy and enjoyable use. Not sweet like bran muffins, the bread has a wonderful crust outside, a soft, silky texture inside. The flavor is hearty, nutty, and so pleasant that one would never suspect the loaf of being as highly nutritious as it in fact is. It makes splendid toast and, in the summertime, abetted by sun-warmed tomatoes fresh from the garden, wickedly wonderful BLTs.

SMALL
1 cup water or vegetable broth
2 tablespoons olive oil
2 cups unbleached all-purpose
  flour
1 1/4 cup unprocessed wheat bran
1/2 to 1 1/2 teaspoons salt to taste
1 teaspoon active dry yeast

LARGE
1 1/2 cups water or vegetable broth
3 tablespoons olive oil
3 cups unbleached all-purpose
  flour
1 1/2 cups unprocessed wheat bran
1 to 2 teaspoons salt to taste
1 1/2 teaspoons active dry yeast

Remember that if the instructions accompanying your bread machine call for the yeast to be placed in the baking pan first, the flour, bran, and salt should be added before the water or broth and the oil. Otherwise, pour the water or vegetable broth into your pan, spoon in the olive oil, then add the flour, bran, salt, and yeast, reserving the leavening for its own separate dispenser if your machine has one.

Set the machine to its quick cycle to bake this loaf.

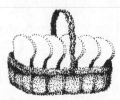

Flaky Bread

While whole-grain breads, acclaimed for their nutrition and roughage, have become staples in the kitchens of the health-conscious, not everyone likes chewy and/or crunchy kernels in his or her bread. However, flakes like those of the familiar oatmeal and the lesser-known wheat, barley, and rye available at health-food stores provide a commendable enough amount of roughage and nutrition per slice of the bread they enrich without as much chew as the whole-grain loaves present. The flakes also add a nubby interest to the crust, "the best part of this loaf," according to Susan. Brush the loaf with a simple egg glaze (a recipe for which is in the chapter "Topping It All Off") after baking and scatter some extra barley flakes over it for a crowning touch.

SMALL	LARGE
3/4 cup milk, whole or skim	*1 3/4 cups milk, whole or skim*
1 tablespoon canola oil	*2 tablespoons canola oil*
1 tablespoon honey	*2 tablespoons honey*
1 egg	*1 egg*
1 3/4 cups unbleached all-purpose flour	*3 cups unbleached all-purpose flour*
1/2 cup barley flakes	*1 cup barley flakes*
1/2 cup rye flakes	*1 cup rye flakes*
1/2 to 1 1/2 teaspoons salt to taste	*1 to 2 teaspoons salt to taste*
1 1/2 teaspoons active dry yeast	*2 teaspoons active dry yeast*

Pour the milk into your baking machine pan and spoon in the canola oil and honey. Break the egg into the pan and add the flour along with the barley and rye flakes; then measure in the salt and yeast, placing the leavening in its own dispenser if your machine is equipped with such. If the directions for your machine specify that the yeast is to be placed in the bottom of the pan, remember to reverse the order in which you incorporate the liquid and the dry ingredients.

This loaf is best baked on your machine's quick cycle.

Whole-Wheat Crunch Bread

H ere's a delightful loaf literally bursting with flavor. Millet is underutilized in our cuisine, and here the tiny seeds, firm and crisp, surprise one with their lilliputian nuggets of taste scattered throughout the loaf.

SMALL

1 cup sour cream or yogurt, regular or low-fat

2 tablespoons unsalted butter or canola oil

1 cup whole-wheat flour

3/4 cup unbleached all-purpose flour

1/2 cup millet seed

1/2 to 1 1/2 teaspoons salt to taste

1 1/2 teaspoons active dry yeast

LARGE

1 3/4 cups sour cream or yogurt, regular or low-fat

1/4 cup unsalted butter or canola oil

1 1/4 cups whole-wheat flour

1 1/4 cups unbleached all-purpose flour

3/4 cup millet seed

1 to 2 teaspoons salt to taste

2 teaspoons active dry yeast

Scoop the sour cream or yogurt into your bread machine baking pan and add the butter or canola oil. If you are making the large loaf and have opted for the butter in preference to the oil, cut it into chunks if taking it cold from the refrigerator, for easier blending. Measure the whole-wheat and all-purpose flours into the pan, then add the millet, salt, and yeast. For placement of the yeast, follow the directions provided with the particular bread machine model you have.

Bake the loaf on your machine's quick cycle.

Buckwheat Bread

The distinctive, earthy taste of buckwheat seems to be gaining renewed approbation in culinary circles, and here's a recipe for a handsome flat-topped loaf made with it that can only further its prestige.

SMALL
½ cup plus 1 tablespoon water
2 teaspoons canola oil
2 teaspoons unsulphured
  molasses
1 egg
2 cups unbleached all-purpose
  flour
¼ cup buckwheat flour
½ to 1 teaspoon salt to taste
1½ teaspoons active dry yeast

LARGE
1 cup water
1 tablespoon canola oil
1 tablespoon unsulphured
  molasses
1 egg
3 cups unbleached all-purpose
  flour
½ cup buckwheat flour
1 to 2 teaspoons salt to taste
2 teaspoons active dry yeast

Pour the water into your bread machine baking pan, unless the directions that came with the model you have instruct that you place the leavening in the pan first, in which case the other dry ingredients should be added before the liquids. Measure in the canola oil and molasses and break the egg into the pan. Add the all-purpose and buckwheat flours, the salt, and the yeast, placing the leavening in its own dispenser if a separate container is provided for it on your machine.

Set the machine on either its quick or its regular cycle to bake this loaf.

Barley Bread

Barley breads are celebrated for their moistness and denseness. However, even when fully baked, the loaves often remain slightly sticky, with a vaguely undercooked feel to them. Here's a recipe that avoids that problem, because the millet flour somehow absorbs the stickiness.

Like most barley bread recipes, this one calls for a considerable proportion of regular flour. Barley flour alone will give you a loaf whose heft is reminiscent of the Mesopotamian building bricks found in the region where the grain was first cultivated.

This bread is firm and sweet, with a golden crust. It makes superb dry toast.

SMALL	LARGE
¾ cup water or vegetable broth	1½ cups water or vegetable broth
1 tablespoon canola oil	4 teaspoons canola oil
1 egg	2 eggs
1½ cups unbleached all-purpose flour	3 cups unbleached all-purpose flour
¾ cup barley flour	1¼ cups barley flour
¼ cup millet flour	½ cup millet flour
1 tablespoon dark brown sugar	2 tablespoons dark brown sugar
½ to 1½ teaspoons salt to taste	1 to 2 teaspoons salt to taste
1½ teaspoons active dry yeast	2 teaspoons active dry yeast

Unless directed by the instructions for your particular machine to scatter the leavening over the bottom of your baking pan before measuring in the other dry ingredients and then the liquids, pour the water or vegetable broth into your bread pan, followed by the canola oil, and break the egg or eggs into it. Add the all-purpose, barley, and millet flours, the brown sugar, and the salt. Scatter the yeast over the dry ingredients, or, if your machine has a separate dispenser for the leavening, spoon it in there.

Use the machine's quick cycle to bake this loaf.

Apulian Bread

To recreate this crusty 3- to 5-pound Italian loaf, you'd need a really mammoth bread machine, not to mention a coal-fired one. So any comparison of the loaf presented here with the real thing would find it wanting. Still, it's a very good bread, with a silky texture and a crust that somehow manages to be both crisp and chewy. The almost imperceptible sour taste and aroma deriving from the starter used are wonderful. Thick slabs or chunks broken from the loaf are the perfect complement to a hearty stew.

To make the starter, called *biga* in Italy, pour half a cupful of warm water into a glass bowl prewarmed by rinsing in hot water. Add a pinch of sugar and ¼ teaspoon yeast, stir briefly, and let the mixture stand for 10 minutes or so in a warm spot, say above a pilot light on the stove, until it looks creamy and bubbly. Then mix in a cupful of flour and another half cupful of water.

This concoction should then be allowed to ferment, covered with plastic wrap, anywhere from 6 to 24 hours or more, the time depending on the temperature. On a really hot day, the starter will tend to ferment very quickly. In a cooler clime, the process may take a full day or so.

The longer the starter ferments, the stronger will be the flavor it imparts to the bread. But there can be too much of a good thing. If the mix separates noticeably and a clear liquid settles to the bottom, it's reaching the outer limits of its serviceability. If the starter begins to turn pink, don't use it. Start a new batch.

You'll find that you have more starter than you need, even for a large loaf of this bread. But the starter freezes well. If you divide the extra into separate portions matching the quantity called for in the recipe and freeze each as a separate block, then all you'll need to do when you decide to make up another loaf of the bread is to remove the premeasured cube of starter from the freezer and give it about three to four hours of room temperature in which to become bubbly again before using it.

SMALL	LARGE
¾ cup water or vegetable broth	*1½ cups water or vegetable broth*
¼ cup starter	*⅓ cup starter*
1¾ cups unbleached all-purpose flour	*3¾ cups unbleached all-purpose flour*
½ to 1½ teaspoons salt to taste	*1 to 2 teaspoons salt to taste*
½ teaspoon active dry yeast	*1 teaspoon active dry yeast*

Pour the water or vegetable broth into your baking pan and add the starter, flour, salt, and yeast. If the instructions that came with your bread machine call for starting with the yeast, however, you'll need to remember to reverse the order of ingredients.

Use the regular full-cycle setting on your bread machine for this loaf, to take maximum advantage of both the starter's leavening power and its distinctive flavor.

9 · Herb and Spice Breads

 THERE'S NO AROMA from the kitchen more tempting than that of a freshly baked loaf of bread — unless it's that from a freshly baked loaf of herb bread. The combined fragrances of a rich yeasty dough and herbs like dill and caraway send the taste buds into a frenzy of anticipation.

Herb breads are a good place to dispose of broths left from cooking up vegetables. Herbs and vegetables have a natural affinity for each other, after all. And why use plain water for your bread when there's a tasty and nutritious broth sitting in the refrigerator? Just remember to take it out to reach room temperature before using, or warm it in a pan.

Basque Shepherd's Bread

This is a very light, open-textured, simple bread that is pleasant indeed fresh from the electronic bakery. It doesn't keep very well, but then, considering that the Basque shepherds of northern Spain from whom it derives its name would prepare the dough each morning for that evening's meal, one can well understand that keeping quality was not high on the list of necessary attributes for the bread.

The shepherd would place the dough in a covered iron pot and bury it in the coals of his Pyrenees campfire before setting out each day to tend his flock. On his return in the evening, a warm pot of bread would be waiting for him. Traditionally, the top of the bread was slashed to form a cross before the meal, and the first piece of each loaf was always given to the herder's trusty sheepdog.

The similarity in shape between the shepherd's ancient iron kettle and the modern pan one buries in the electronic campfire of one's bread machine suggested the suitability of this particular loaf for the automated home bakery.

SMALL
¾ cup water
1 tablespoon olive oil
1¾ cups unbleached all-purpose
  flour
1 tablespoon sugar
1 teaspoon dried sage
½ to 1 teaspoon salt to taste
1½ teaspoons active dry yeast

LARGE
1¼ cups water
2 tablespoons olive oil
3 cups unbleached all-purpose
  flour
4 teaspoons sugar
2 teaspoons dried sage
1 to 2 teaspoons salt to taste
2 teaspoons active dry yeast

Pour the water and olive oil into the baking pan of your bread machine and add the flour, sugar, sage, salt, and yeast, placing the leavening in its own separate dispenser if your machine has such. Remember, however, that if the instructions accompanying the model you have call for placing the leavening in the bottom of the pan first thing, then the other dry ingredients should be added next, before the water and oil.

Bake the loaf on your machine's quick cycle.

Casserole Batter Bread

This loaf, as its name implies, was originally baked in a casserole. That factor gives its traditional form a natural affinity to the rounded loaves produced in a bread machine. It's a nice soft loaf with a very even texture and a puffed crown. Considering the flavoring ingredients, I was not surprised when our kids took to spreading slices of it with tomato sauce and mozzarella and popping them into the toaster oven for a quick snack.

> 1 cup milk, whole or skim
> 2 tablespoons unsalted butter or canola
>   oil
> 2½ cups unbleached all-purpose flour
> 2 tablespoons sugar
> 1 teaspoon dried basil
> 1 teaspoon dried oregano
> ½ teaspoon garlic powder or 1 clove of
>   fresh garlic, pressed
> ¼ to 1 teaspoon salt to taste
> 1½ teaspoons active dry yeast

Put the milk and the butter or canola oil in the baking pan of your bread machine, add the flour, sugar, basil, oregano, garlic, and salt, then measure in the yeast, unless the instructions that came with your machine call for reversing the order in which the yeast and the milk and butter or oil are incorporated.

Bake on either the regular or the quick cycle of your machine, and prepare to sample a truly flavorsome bread.

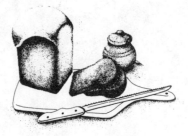

Stuffing Bread

This loaf started out to be homemade stuffing bread for chicken and turkey, the idea being to freeze it up so as to have it ready on short notice. The idea works fine in principle, but the bread is so fragrant that soon after its removal from the electronic oven, one is apt to find whole slices of it missing. All the same, even two half loaves rescued for their original purpose, safely diced and tucked away in the freezer before they too slip away under slabs of a sharp cheese or, yes, enveloping chicken salad, will do the average small bird nicely.

SMALL

1 cup water or vegetable broth
2 teaspoons olive oil
1 teaspoon unsulphured molasses
2 cups unbleached all-purpose flour
1/2 cup uncooked oatmeal (not instant)
1/2 cup cornmeal
2 tablespoons dehydrated parsley
1 tablespoon dehydrated minced onion
1 teaspoon dried rosemary
1 teaspoon dried sage
1/2 teaspoon dried thyme
1/2 teaspoon pepper
1/4 teaspoon garlic powder or 1 clove fresh garlic, pressed
1/2 to 1 1/2 teaspoons salt to taste
1 1/2 teaspoons active dry yeast

LARGE

1 1/2 cups water or vegetable broth
1 tablespoon olive oil
2 teaspoons unsulphured molasses
3 cups unbleached all-purpose flour
3/4 cup uncooked oatmeal (not instant)
3/4 cup cornmeal
3 tablespoons dehydrated parsley
4 teaspoons dehydrated minced onion
1 1/2 teaspoons dried rosemary
1 1/2 teaspoons dried sage
1 teaspoon dried thyme
1 teaspoon pepper
1/2 teaspoon garlic powder or 2 cloves fresh garlic, pressed
1 to 2 teaspoons salt to taste
2 teaspoons active dry yeast

Pour the water or vegetable broth into your bread machine baking pan and add the olive oil and molasses, unless the instructions that came with your machine call for placing the yeast in the bottom of the pan and reserving the liquids till last, adding them after the dry ingredients. Measure in the flour, oatmeal, cornmeal, parsley, onion, rosemary, sage, thyme, pepper, garlic, salt, and yeast. If your machine has a separate dispenser for leavening, spoon the yeast in there.

Use the rapid-bake setting on your machine for this loaf.

Rosemary Bread

Mediterranean country cooking is often redolent with the pungent, earthy scent of rosemary. The herb goes well with many hearty foods, from roast pork and lamb to robustly flavored seafood such as bluefish. But it's also an excellent flavoring in more delicate cuisine. The light bread to which it adds its subtle seasoning here complements chowders and rich vegetable soups wonderfully. I'm always reminded of the area around Camargue in southern France when the fragrant, sunny loaf emerges from its pan.

You'll notice a liberal quantity of olive oil in the recipe for this bread. If you can lay your hands on a flask of the dark, extra-virgin cold-pressed variety, by all means use it for the additional flavor and color it will contribute.

SMALL	LARGE
½ cup milk, whole or skim	*⅔ cup milk, whole or skim*
¼ cup water or vegetable broth	*⅓ cup water or vegetable broth*
¼ cup olive oil	*⅓ cup olive oil*
2 cups unbleached all-purpose flour	*3 cups unbleached all-purpose flour*
1 tablespoon dried or 3 tablespoons fresh rosemary	*2 tablespoons dried or ⅓ cup fresh rosemary*
¼ teaspoon dried sage	*½ teaspoon dried sage*
½ to 1½ teaspoons salt to taste	*1 to 2 teaspoons salt to taste*
1½ teaspoons active dry yeast	*2 teaspoons active dry yeast*

Pour the milk, water or vegetable broth, and olive oil into your bread machine baking pan, unless the instructions for your machine direct you to put the yeast into the pan first, followed by the other dry ingredients and then the liquids. Add the flour, rosemary, sage, salt, and yeast, placing the leavening in its own separate dispenser if your machine has one.

Bake the loaf on your machine's quick cycle.

Dill Scallion Bread

When a friend of mine, Chi Chiu-lang, was a student in New York City, he seemed to use scallions in almost everything I saw him cook, including scrambled eggs. Bread isn't all that common in Taiwan, not being part of traditional Chinese cuisine, but on the strength of his culinary example I once decided to toss some scallions into a loaf I was putting together. Adding dill, one of my own favorite herbs, I ended up with this tall, open-textured loaf that is superb with tuna salad.

The cottage cheese found in this recipe, as in others in the book, contributes to the tenderness of the bread. Perhaps I should also alert you to the fact that it makes the loaf extra filling.

> *½ cup water or vegetable broth*
> *1 egg*
> *½ cup cottage cheese, regular or low-fat*
> *½ cup minced fresh scallions*
> *2 cups unbleached all-purpose flour*
> *1 cup whole-wheat flour*
> *1 tablespoon sugar*
> *1 tablespoon dill seed*
> *¼ to 1 teaspoon salt to taste*
> *1½ teaspoons active dry yeast*

Pour the water or vegetable broth into the baking pan of your bread machine, break the egg into it, and scoop in the cottage cheese and the scallions. Add the all-purpose and whole-wheat flours, the sugar, dill, salt, and, following the directions for your particular machine, the yeast.

Bake on full cycle.

Minty Oat Groats Bread

O at groats have been hearty breakfast fare in this country since colonial times. But they make wonderful breads as well. Boiling water is needed to soften the groats before they can be used in bread baking, however. As yet there is no cycle for such a preliminary step on the bread machines' control panels, although at least one make does double as a rice cooker. So unless your machine has a separate yeast dispenser, add an extra 15 minutes or so to the preparation time for this loaf, as the groat mush must be permitted to cool to lukewarm before you proceed with the recipe. If you try to throw all the ingredients in at once, the heat from the boiling water will kill the yeast.

The lecithin you'll note in the recipe is included because as a natural emulsifier it helps solid whole-grain breads to rise and hold together. The resulting loaf is hearty but not heavy.

> 1 cup oat groats
> 1½ cups boiling water
> ¼ cup honey
> 2 tablespoons olive oil
> 1½ cups whole-wheat flour
> 1 cup rye flour
> 2 tablespoons nonfat dry milk
> 1 tablespoon lecithin
> 1 teaspoon dried mint
> ½ to 1 teaspoon salt to taste
> 1½ teaspoons active dry yeast

Put the groats in the baking pan of your bread machine and pour the boiling water over them. If your machine features a separate dispenser for yeast, you can proceed with the recipe at this point. Otherwise you will need to wait 15 minutes or so until the groat mixture has cooled to a lukewarm temperature before continuing. Add the honey, olive oil, whole-wheat and rye flours, dry milk, lecithin, dried mint, and salt to the batter. Scatter the yeast over the dry ingredients or add it to the yeast dispenser if your machine has one.

Bake this loaf on a regular full cycle.

Poppy Seed Burst

Poppy seeds are indisputably a matter of taste. A dusting of these slightly bitter decorative seeds over the top of a roll makes a visual statement without much gustatory accent. A large quantity of them, on the other hand, inspires either genuine pleasure or strong aversion.

I well remember my grandmother's strudels. She would stretch the phyllo dough into a paper-thin membrane with her hands and elbows, something I've never been able to accomplish, and fill it with one of a thousand delights — apples, cherries, mulberries, nuts, even cabbage. Then there was poppy seed strudel. Luckily, my father, for whom the very thought of this strudel was enough to arouse ecstasy, would surreptitiously and without fail eat my piece whenever this so-called delicacy was served.

Yet here's a bread I really like that's chock-full of poppy seeds. An attractive, hearty, nutty-flavored loaf, it goes well with venison and robust stews.

SMALL
¾ cup milk, whole or skim
1 tablespoon unsalted butter or canola oil
2 tablespoons honey
1 tablespoon lemon juice
2 cups unbleached all-purpose flour
2 tablespoons dark brown sugar
2 tablespoons poppy seeds
¼ to 1 teaspoon salt to taste
1½ teaspoons active dry yeast

LARGE
1½ cups milk, whole or skim
2 tablespoons unsalted butter or canola oil
2 tablespoons honey
1½ tablespoons lemon juice
3½ cups unbleached all-purpose flour
¼ cup firmly packed dark brown sugar
3 tablespoons poppy seeds
½ to 1½ teaspoons salt to taste
2 teaspoons active dry yeast

Pour the milk into your bread machine pan, unless the instructions for the machine you have specify that the yeast is to be placed in the pan first, the other dry ingredients next, and the liquids last. Add the butter or canola oil, honey, lemon juice, flour, brown sugar, poppy seeds, salt, and yeast. If your machine has a separate dispenser for leavening, spoon the yeast into its slot after all the other ingredients have been measured into the baking pan.

Set your machine to its quick cycle to bake the loaf.

Moroccan Anise Bread

Morocco, home of this bread, is a country of brilliant sunshine, verdant mountains, and vast deserts. The merest whiff of anise drifting past me brings back memories of the once black 1934 Citröen sedan my college friend Abe and I, temporarily diverted from the pursuit of our mortarboards, bought from a certain Ahmad in a Tangiers alley. Some few days later, it expired on the pastel desert beyond the Atlas Mountains, about 50 kilometers from Ksar es Souk, leaving us with but the proverbial bit of bread and water for sustenance. Sample this loaf with lamb shish kebab, and you can't help but hear the *Sheherazade.*

SMALL	LARGE
¾ cup water	*¾ cup water*
½ cup milk, whole or skim	*⅔ cup milk, whole or skim*
1½ cups unbleached all-purpose flour	*2 cups unbleached all-purpose flour*
1¼ cups whole-wheat flour	*1½ cups whole-wheat flour*
1 teaspoon sugar	*2 teaspoons sugar*
2 tablespoons sesame seeds	*3 tablespoons sesame seeds*
1 tablespoon aniseed	*2 tablespoons aniseed*
½ to 1½ teaspoons salt to taste	*1 to 2 teaspoons salt to taste*
1½ teaspoons active dry yeast	*2 teaspoons active dry yeast*

Pour the water and milk in your bread machine baking pan and add the all-purpose and whole-wheat flours, the sugar, sesame seeds, aniseed, salt, and yeast, reserving the leavening for its own separate dispenser if your machine has one. However, if the instructions for the model you have direct you to place the leavening in the bottom of the pan first thing, then you will need to remember to reverse the order in which you add the liquid and the dry ingredients.

Use your machine's rapid-bake cycle for this loaf.

Scandinavian Limpa

Limpa is a Scandinavian rye bread redolent of anise or fennel, caraway, and orange. The exact combination and proportions of the flavorings vary from country to country and even from town to town. There are also fancy versions of the bread for the Christmas holidays.

The taste of a thick slice of limpa spread with butter and *messmör*, a soft sweet Swedish goat cheese, will always be one of my fondest childhood memories. *Messmör* has the consistency of peanut butter and, in fact, is Sweden's popular equivalent of that all-American spread. It is hardly ever available in the States, but many specialty cheese stores carry a Norwegian hard version called *gjetost*. If you grate this cheese and beat it with heavy cream to a smooth consistency, you come close to the *messmör* of my childhood.

In like fashion, the recipe given here approximates the limpa I remember, though it's not the same. I'd blame this on the bread machine were it not for the fact that I've never been able to duplicate that now distant loaf by traditional methods either. Maybe you just can't bake home again.

> 1 1/2 cups milk, whole or skim
> 2 tablespoons canola oil
> 2 tablespoons unsulphured
>   molasses
> 2 cups unbleached all-purpose flour
> 1 cup rye flour
> 2 tablespoons dark brown sugar
> 1 tablespoon cocoa
> 1 tablespoon grated orange rind
> 1 teaspoon aniseed, lightly crushed
> 1/2 teaspoon caraway seeds
> 1/4 to 1 teaspoon salt to taste
> 1 1/2 teaspoons active dry yeast

Pour the milk into the baking pan of your bread machine and measure in first the oil, then the molasses, unless the instructions for your machine specify that the yeast is to be put in the bottom of the pan, followed by the other dry and then the liquid ingredients. Add the all-purpose and rye flours, the brown sugar, cocoa, orange rind, aniseed, caraway seeds, and salt. Distribute the yeast as directed for your machine.

Bake on a quick cycle.

10 · Savory Breads

IT'S AMAZING what-all is stuffed into breads these days. In some cases the results go, if you'll pardon the near pun, against the grain. Blueberry bagels, for instance — nice alliteration that, but as a concept the combination just doesn't strike me right. If bagel dough is to be filled with anything, surely it should be something savory, not sweet.

The traditional savory breads are a category of the staff of life unto themselves, usually incorporating some form of meat, fish, or dairy protein to supply a more balanced diet. Simply spread with butter, their slices are like a flavorful sandwich all made up and ready to go.

Cheddar Semolina Bread

A light bread with a subtle taste of cheese, this loaf, like most cheese breads, achieves its maximum flavor when it has just cooled to room temperature after its spell in the oven. The semolina flour, normally associated with pasta, and available from health-food stores and ethnic markets, adds a nice, slightly nutty accent. The potato adds lightness and keeping quality. Whenever you cook up potatoes, incidentally, save the water they boiled in for this or another loaf.

Leftovers of this bread, if there are any, make great croutons for minestrone and other full-bodied soups. They're also excellent scattered over a spinach salad.

¾ cup plain or potato water
2 tablespoons unsalted butter or canola
    oil
¾ cup shredded cheddar cheese
½ cup mashed boiled potato
½ cup unbleached all-purpose flour
1½ cups semolina flour
1 tablespoon sugar
¼ to ½ teaspoon salt to taste
1½ teaspoons active dry yeast

Unless directed by the instructions for your particular bread machine to reserve the moist ingredients for adding last, pour the water into your baking pan and add the butter or canola oil, the cheddar cheese, and the mashed potato. Measure in the all-purpose and semolina flours, the sugar, and salt to taste. Add the yeast as directed for your machine.

This loaf is best baked on full cycle.

Blue Cheese Bread

Our son, Revell, has a rather exotic cheese palate for a ten-year-old, his two favorites being blue and Asiago. For years now he's been alternating Asiago with peanut butter and tuna salad sandwiches in his school lunch box. Blue cheese, however, was always a bit too crumbly to stay between the bread slices, and so did not feature in his lunch menus. Enter, I thought, my blue cheese bread.

As it turns out, this loaf, almost overwhelmingly redolent of blue cheese while baking, has a rather more subtle taste once cooled. The texture is really lovely, and though dense, the bread is not heavy. Slathered with butter, it makes an excellent appetizer to serve with beer or a hearty red wine.

1 cup milk, whole or skim
1 egg
1 tablespoon unsalted butter or canola
  oil
1/2 to 1 cup crumbled blue cheese to
  taste
1 1/2 cups unbleached all-purpose flour
1 cup whole-wheat flour
2 tablespoons nonfat dry milk
1 tablespoon sugar
1/4 to 1/2 teaspoon salt to taste
1/2 teaspoon white pepper
1 1/2 teaspoons active dry yeast

Pour the milk into your baking pan, break in the egg, and add the butter or canola oil and the blue cheese. Then measure in the all-purpose and whole-wheat flours, the dry milk, sugar, salt, pepper, and yeast. If the instructions for your machine call for putting the yeast in the pan first, follow it with the dry ingredients before adding the milk, egg, butter or oil, and cheese.

Bake on full cycle, using a light setting, if available, for a golden, not too dark crust.

Cottage Cheese Bread

Cottage cheese adds a certain texture and moisture to bread, helping to create a tall, tender loaf that is also filling. In the recipe given here, its powers are augmented by the lecithin, which in its capacity as a natural wetting agent and emulsifier assists in the mixing of the ingredients and interacts with the gluten of the flour to increase the elasticity and rising potential of the dough.

Any cheese bread is at its most flavorsome about an hour after baking, when it has set. But this is the only loaf I know of that tastes better the next day.

½ cup water
¼ cup honey
1 egg
*2 tablespoons unsalted butter or canola
   oil*
¾ cup creamy cottage cheese
2 cups unbleached all-purpose flour
¼ cup nonfat dry milk
2 tablespoons lecithin
¼ to 1 teaspoon salt to taste
1½ teaspoons active dry yeast

Pour the water into the baking pan of your bread machine and add the honey, egg, butter or canola oil, and cottage cheese, unless the directions for your machine specify that the yeast is to be placed in the pan first, in which case you will need to reverse the order in which you add the dry and the liquid ingredients. Measure in the flour, dry milk, lecithin, salt, and yeast, following the instructions for the leavening provided with your machine.

Bake on a quick cycle.

Bulgarian Cheese Bread

There's a Bulgarian cheese called *sirene* that in its native country is often stuffed between layers of dough to make, when baked, a delicious cheese-filled triple-decker loaf traditionally served with tea. I've been unable to find *sirene* in the United States. But it's very similar to the Greek cheese feta, which is readily available.

A substitution more difficult to effect than that of replacing *sirene* with feta in a recipe is inducing a bread machine to bake the equivalent of a layered loaf. Short of using the device simply to mix and knead the dough and then shaping the loaf by hand and baking it in a conventional pan in a conventional oven — something which if I'm going to do I'll usually do without using the bread machine at all — there's no way of making this traditional *Tootmanik s gotovo testo* in the electronic oven. But the machine-made loaf that results from the recipe given here is a very tasty adaptation of the original bread, with a supremely silky crumb.

SMALL	LARGE
¾ cup buttermilk	1¼ cups buttermilk
1 teaspoon unsalted butter or olive oil	2 teaspoons unsalted butter or olive oil
1 teaspoon honey	2 teaspoons honey
6 ounces feta cheese	8 ounces feta cheese
2 cups unbleached all-purpose flour	3 cups unbleached all-purpose flour
½ to 1½ teaspoons salt to taste	1 to 2 teaspoons salt to taste
1½ teaspoons active dry yeast	2 teaspoons active dry yeast

Remember that if the instructions that came with your bread machine call for the yeast to be placed in the baking pan first, the flour and salt should be added before the liquids and the feta. Otherwise, pour the buttermilk into your pan and add the butter or olive oil, honey, feta cheese, flour, salt, and, if the instructions for your machine so direct, the yeast. If your machine has a separate dispenser for leavening, spoon the yeast into it after all the other ingredients have been measured into the baking pan.

Set the machine to its rapid-bake cycle for this loaf.

Pepperoni Bread

More meat loaves have bread in them than bread loaves have meat. But there are a number of prepared meats, particularly sausages, that blend well into a loaf of bread. Pepperoni, with its distinctive spicy flavor, is one of them.

If you have leftover broth from cooking vegetables or potatoes in the past couple of days, this is an excellent place to dispose of it. Such a savory bread can only benefit from the extra flavor and nutrition it will add.

A favorite with the kids more than myself, our pepperoni bread inevitably ends up as thick slices in the toaster oven bearing slabs of cheese, usually cheddar and mozzarella, the latter for stretch, but often also strewn with grated Asiago or Romano for extra zest.

1 cup water or vegetable broth
2 tablespoons unsalted butter or canola
  oil
½ cup pepperoni, cut into ¼-inch
  chunks
2 cups unbleached all-purpose flour
½ cup rye flour
1 tablespoon sugar
1 teaspoon dried oregano
¼ to 1 teaspoon salt to taste
1½ teaspoons active dry yeast

Pour the water or vegetable broth into the baking pan of your bread machine and add the butter or canola oil, pepperoni chunks, all-purpose and rye flours, sugar, oregano, and salt. Last, add the yeast, unless the instructions for your bread machine call for putting it in first, in which case the dry ingredients should be added before the water, butter or oil, and pepperoni.

This loaf does well on a quick bake cycle.

Caper Anchovy Bread

A nchovies and capers are two of those highly distinctive objects of taste that allow little room for indifference: they are approached with either relish or disgust. In our household I'm outvoted on both; no one else will touch either one of them, although the kids do eat Susan's delightful remoulade sauce with smoked fresh-caught bluefish every fall, apparently oblivious of its contents.

This bread incorporates both problematical ingredients and will presumably appeal only to anchovy and caper fanatics. Still, it's a nice moist loaf with an unusual flavor.

Note that the recipe calls for neither oil nor salt. There's plenty of both in a can of anchovies.

1½ cups water
¼ cup capers, drained

1 2-ounce can anchovies, including oil
2 cups unbleached all-purpose flour
1 cup rye flour
½ cup cornmeal
1½ teaspoons active dry yeast

Pour the water into the baking pan of your bread machine, unless the instructions for your particular machine specify that the leavening is to be placed in the pan first and the liquids last. Add the capers, anchovies, all-purpose and rye flours, and cornmeal. Distribute the yeast according to the instructions for your machine.

Bake on full cycle.

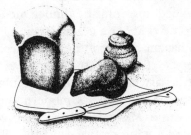

11 · Breads from the Garden

 ZUCCHINI BREAD no doubt owes its origins to the incredibly fecund nature of its vegetable component. As anyone who has grown this squash can attest, a couple of plants soon overwhelm a family's appetite unless the vegetables are consistently devoured in their most petite form — as is fashionable, for perhaps understandable reasons.

Moving the zucchini from the dinner menu to the bread basket provides welcome relief at a certain stage of summer. At the same time, zucchini has much to contribute to bread in the way of flavor and smoothness of texture. This is true of vegetables, and their cooking water, as a whole. And their usefulness doesn't end with the growing season, for today's modern supermarket provides a "garden" year-round. Many dried or frozen vegetables make admirable additions to a winter's loaf as well.

Vegetable breads tend to be richer and more filling than their plainer counterparts. So they are more often found in the company of one-pot meals like stews and soups — another reason why they make wonderful winter breads — than at the side of a full-course meal.

Almost endless variations on vegetable breads can be conceived. Those represented among the recipes in this chapter include some that readers might naturally expect to find here and some that are more startling. The aforementioned zucchini loaf will be found among the quick-bread recipes.

Hungarian Potato Bread

Potato bread began as an adulteration. Clean, pure wheat flour remained for centuries both expensive and hard to come by. Accordingly, millers and tradesmen used everything from talcum powder to ground bleached bones to stretch their salable supply of flour.

It's not surprising, then, that when the potato made its way to European shores, a mealed version of it was forthwith utilized to help eke out the merchants' stores of flour. What did come as a surprise was the way in which the addition of potato to the wheat flour actually improved the baked goods resulting from the mix.

In a family of five such as ours, as often as not there's a leftover potato or two to be found hiding in the refrigerator. Here's a great use for such strays. If none are to be found on the day you decide to bake this loaf and you boil up a potato just for the bread, by all means save the water in which the potato cooks to use in the dough as well.

Soft, light, and very open-textured, this bread makes superlative toast. It also makes a delightful sandwich with ham or salami — Hungarian, naturally — tucked between its slices and crisp sour pickles on the side. If the caraway seeds are omitted from the recipe, the loaf, sliced thick, makes wonderful French toast.

1 cup potato or plain water
½ cup mashed potatoes
2 cups unbleached all-purpose flour
1 tablespoon sugar
2 teaspoons caraway seeds (optional)
¼ to 1 teaspoon salt to taste
1½ teaspoons active dry yeast

Pour the potato water or, lacking that, plain water into the baking pan of your bread machine and add the mashed potato, flour, sugar, caraway seeds if desired, salt, and yeast, following the directions for leavening that came with your particular machine.

Use a quick bake cycle for this loaf.

Italian Potato Bread

Pasta, of course! Risotto, even. But potatoes — do they even have potatoes in Italy? That was the question I couldn't help asking myself when I first heard about Italian potato bread. Somehow I'd always thought of potatoes as a staple more or less exclusive to northern Europe.

I've since learned that they grow some very nice potatoes in Italy, and they use them in bread much as the Hungarians do. But they don't put any caraway in their loaves, and the bread contains a minimal amount of liquid. You'll find no water in this recipe beyond that contained in the boiled potatoes themselves. A little olive oil provides the only additional moisture.

Because of the dryness of the ingredients, the dough starts out crumbly, looking as if it will never hold together. Eventually, however, moisture is squeezed from the potatoes and the dough begins to resemble a stiff biscuit batter. It makes a delicious loaf, "so tender," Susan remarked, "that the only thing holding it together is the crust."

Boil the potatoes, if you don't happen to have some left over in the refrigerator, and roughly mash enough of them to fill your measuring cup. Regular Maine boiling potatoes work best. If you use the drier Idaho baking potatoes, you may need to add a couple of tablespoonfuls of water from the pot in which they were boiled to help soften the dough. Check the bread pan in your machine after the first ten minutes or so of mixing to see how the dough is forming. If it is really dry and crumbly, add a little potato water to soften it.

SMALL	LARGE
1 cup mashed potatoes	2 cups mashed potatoes
2 tablespoons olive oil	1/4 cup olive oil
1 1/2 cups unbleached all-purpose flour	2 cups unbleached all-purpose flour
1/2 to 1 teaspoon salt to taste	1 to 2 teaspoons salt to taste
1 1/2 teaspoons active dry yeast	2 teaspoons active dry yeast

If the instructions for your machine call for the yeast to be placed in the bottom of the baking pan, the flour and salt should be added before the potatoes and olive oil. Otherwise, scoop the mashed potatoes into your bread machine pan and add the olive oil, then the flour, salt, and yeast. If the machine you have features a separate yeast dispenser for leavening, add the yeast there.

The rapid-bake setting on your machine is the one to use for this loaf.

Light Onion Bread

O nion breads in this country tend to be dark. An exception is the bialy, the roll originally from the town of Bialystok in Poland. But throughout the low countries of Europe, light onion loaves, combining the once supposed social refinement of white flour with the zest of an oniony peasant bread, are very popular.

The bread presented here retains its light color while incorporating a bit of rye for added flavor. It goes particularly well with sweet butter and a hearty garden-fresh vegetable soup. Start the potatoes for the soup early, and you can borrow a little of the potato water for the bread.

SMALL	LARGE
1 cup plain or potato water	1 1/2 cups plain or potato water
2 teaspoons canola oil	1 tablespoon canola oil
1 egg	2 eggs
2 cups unbleached all-purpose flour	3 cups unbleached all-purpose flour
1 cup rye flour	1 1/2 cups rye flour
1 to 2 tablespoons dehydrated minced onion to taste	2 to 4 tablespoons dehydrated minced onion to taste
1/2 to 1 1/2 teaspoons salt to taste	1 to 2 teaspoons salt to taste
1 1/2 teaspoons active dry yeast	2 teaspoons active dry yeast

Unless directed by the instructions for the particular bread machine you have to reserve the liquids and moist ingredients for your bread dough till last, pour the water into your baking pan and add the canola oil, egg or eggs, all-purpose and rye flours, onion, and salt. Add the yeast as directed for your machine.

The rapid-bake cycle on your electronic oven is the best one for this bread.

Spinach Bread

Although the kids disparagingly call it "Popeye bread," this unusual marbled loaf is a tasty, quickly and easily made conversation starter for any adult gathering. Using your electronic oven's delayed baking mode, it is even possible simply to unwrap a package of frozen spinach and plop the verdant ice block right into the pan along with the rest of the ingredients. But in that case allow plenty of time, 4 to 6 hours, for defrosting. You want the spinach to be soft before the batter is mixed. If the greens are still frozen when the machine's agitator starts its job, the nonstick finish on your bread pan may become scratched.

This method doesn't work with machines requiring you to put the yeast in the bottom of the pan with the other ingredients on top of it. The spinach water will filter down to the leavening as it slowly thaws, activating it too soon.

Whether you use the spinach frozen, thawed, or zapped by your microwave, the liquid from the package is the only moisture provided for the bread. So if you plan to defrost the spinach beforehand, make sure you reserve all the liquid to add to the pan with the greens themselves.

For a slightly milder, sweeter loaf, brown the garlic called for in an extra tablespoonful of olive oil before adding it to the other ingredients.

SMALL	LARGE
1 10-ounce package frozen spinach, thawed, with liquid	2 10-ounce packages frozen spinach, thawed, with liquid
1 tablespoon olive oil	2 tablespoons olive oil
1 clove garlic, minced, and browned if desired in 1 tablespoon olive oil	2 cloves garlic, minced, and browned if desired in 1 tablespoon olive oil
2 cups unbleached all-purpose flour	4 cups unbleached all-purpose flour
1/2 teaspoon sugar	1 teaspoon sugar
1/4 teaspoon grated nutmeg	1/2 teaspoon grated nutmeg
1/2 to 1 teaspoon salt to taste	1 to 2 teaspoons salt to taste
1 1/2 teaspoons active dry yeast	2 teaspoons active dry yeast

Place the spinach with its water in your baking pan, spoon in the olive oil, and add the garlic, flour, sugar, nutmeg, salt, and yeast, following the directions that came with your machine for incorporating the leavening.

Bake the loaf on your machine's quick cycle. If the spinach was placed in the pan frozen and you are using the delayed-baking mode, remember to allow four to six hours for defrosting when setting the timer.

Olive Bread

I was putting a loaf of this silky-textured bread on the cooling rack when Revell, covered waist-down with mud from frog catching, wandered into the kitchen.

"And what's this one, Dad?" His tone was suspicious. The day before, I'd been working on a caper loaf — the recipe for which, probably to everyone's relief, is not included in this volume — and he now approached the tasting of each new bread with a certain reservation.

"Never mind," I replied, using a phrase I have repeatedly admonished the kids not to use.

"Come on!"

"Well, it's an olive loaf."

"You're pushing it, Dad, you're really pushing it."

Perhaps, from his perspective, that was so. The flavor of olives in this bread is subtle but definitely present, and olives seem to be an acquired taste. All the same, olive bread is a lovely foil for thinly sliced sharp Italian cheeses.

Speaking of cheese, the cream cheese — what else with olives? — in the recipe provides some of the required moisture. Cut it into small chunks for less laborious blending when the machine is kneading the dough.

SMALL

¼ cup water or olive liquid reserved from draining the olives

1 tablespoon olive oil

1 tablespoon honey

1 egg

2 ounces cream cheese, chunked

½ cup drained green pimento-stuffed olives

2 cups unbleached all-purpose flour

½ to 1½ teaspoons salt to taste

1½ teaspoons active dry yeast

LARGE

⅓ cup water or olive liquid reserved from draining the olives

1 tablespoon olive oil

2 tablespoons honey

2 eggs

4 ounces cream cheese, chunked

1 cup drained green pimento-stuffed olives

3 cups unbleached all-purpose flour

1 to 2 teaspoons salt to taste

2 teaspoons active dry yeast

Unless the instructions that came with your machine call for placing the yeast in the very bottom of the pan, followed by the other dry ingredients and then the liquids, pour the water or reserved olive liquid into your baking pan and add the olive oil, honey, egg or eggs, cream cheese, and olives. Measure in the flour, salt, and yeast, reserving the last for its own separate dispenser if your machine has one.

Use the machine's rapid-bake cycle for this loaf.

Quick Tomato Bread

This particular loaf of bread has a full-bodied tomato taste that goes well with stews and hearty winter soups. It also has olives in it. They come under the category of optional ingredients.

Needless to say, the kids have taken to making grilled cheese sandwiches from this bread. Myself, I like to toast a thick slice, cover it with anchovy fillets, and dribble olive oil lightly over them.

"What can you expect," the rest of the family observes, "from someone who likes anchovies on pizza?"

1 cup sour cream
1 egg
1 teaspoon olive oil
1 6-ounce can tomato paste
½ cup pitted black olives, well drained
   (optional)
2 cups unbleached all-purpose flour
½ cup whole-wheat flour
½ cup cornmeal
1 teaspoon sugar
1 teaspoon garlic powder or 2 cloves
   fresh garlic, pressed
1 teaspoon dried basil
1 teaspoon white pepper
½ to 1 teaspoon salt to taste
1½ teaspoons active dry yeast

Pour the sour cream into the baking pan of your bread machine, break in the egg, and add the olive oil. Scoop the tomato paste into the pan, toss in the olives if desired, and add the all-purpose and whole-wheat flours, the cornmeal, sugar, garlic, basil, white pepper, salt, and yeast, following the directions for leavening that came with your machine.

Bake on a quick cycle.

Cheese-Tomato Bread

Yuppie bread, the kids call it. And I guess that now somewhat disparaging adjective befits this bread. On the other hand, sun-dried tomatoes and sharp Italian cheeses were around for centuries before their eighties' new debut in the media style pages. Certainly they are a great combination.

This bread is for hearty winter stews and hot soups. It's also good with cheese, naturally, or simply drizzled with olive oil.

SMALL	LARGE
½ cup heavy cream	¾ cup heavy cream
2 tablespoons olive oil	3 tablespoons olive oil
2 eggs	3 eggs
½ cup sun-dried tomato slices, reconstituted according to the package instructions	¾ cup sun-dried tomato slices, reconstituted according to the package instructions
¼ cup chopped scallions	½ cup chopped scallions
2 large cloves garlic, crushed	3 large cloves garlic, crushed
¾ cup grated sharp Italian cheese such as Parmesan, Romano, or Asiago	1 cup grated sharp Italian cheese such as Parmesan, Romano, or Asiago
2 cups unbleached all-purpose flour	3½ cups unbleached all-purpose flour
½ to 1½ teaspoons salt to taste	1 to 2 teaspoons salt to taste
1½ teaspoons active dry yeast	2 teaspoons active dry yeast

Pour the cream and olive oil into your bread pan, unless the instructions for your machine direct you to place the yeast in the bottom of the pan first thing, in which case the other dry ingredients should be added next, the liquids last. Break in the eggs and add the tomato slices, scallions, garlic, grated cheese, flour, and salt. Measure the yeast into its own dispenser if your machine has one. If not, scatter it over the other dry ingredients.

Bake the loaf on your machine's quick cycle.

Tex-Mex Corn Bread

This bread is Mexican more in imagination than in reality. One evening as I was making our family's version of cheese quesadillas, stuffed to overflowing with Monterey Jack, peeled whole green chilies, and sour cream and slathered extravagantly with piquant tomato sauce, we found ourselves with unexpected company when one of Revell's friends stayed for dinner. To stretch the meal, I flicked the bread machine to its quick cycle and concocted what I hoped would be a suitable corn bread.

The dinner being a spicy south-of-the-border one, corn seemed a natural ingredient for the loaf. So did the red peppers, whose pieces one bites into unexpectedly. Don't ask me how the wheat germ crept into the recipe, that particular ingredient being more regional to Bemidji, Minnesota, than Baja California. The yeast, used instead of the baking powder commonly associated with corn breads in this country, contributes to the smoothness of the loaf.

If you peek into your bread machine early in the mixing of this bread, you'll note that the dough seems too dry. Leave it alone. Once the kneading process has been completed, the moisture squeezed from the corn kernels will have added enough liquid to make a smooth, silky, stiff dough. The final loaf is substantial, with a very even, moist crumb.

Because the bread was an afterthought to the original menu, even though we delayed dinner for half an hour we ended up trying to slice the loaf hot from the pan, which meant that it crumbled. Really hot bread does not slice well. Not only does the crust crumble, but the center of the loaf tends to compact and become sticky. Better to break the bread into chunks in such circumstances. Besides, there's something pleasingly primitive about tearing off a hunk of steaming fresh bread. Also chunks are twice as efficient as slices at mopping up extra sauce.

SMALL

1 11-ounce can of corn with
  liquid
1 tablespoon unsalted butter or
  canola oil
1 tablespoon unsulphured
  molasses
2 cups unbleached all-purpose
  flour
1/3 cup wheat germ
1 1/2 teaspoons crushed red
  peppers
1/2 teaspoon coriander
1/4 to 1 teaspoon salt to taste
1 1/2 teaspoons active dry yeast

LARGE

1 16-ounce can of corn with
  liquid
2 tablespoons unsalted butter or
  canola oil
2 tablespoons unsulphured
  molasses
3 1/2 cups unbleached all-purpose
  flour
1/2 cup wheat germ
2 teaspoons crushed red peppers
1 teaspoon coriander
1/2 to 1 1/2 teaspoons salt to taste
2 teaspoons active dry yeast

Pour the corn with its liquid into your bread machine baking pan and add the butter or canola oil and the molasses. Then measure in the flour, wheat germ, crushed red peppers, coriander, and salt. Place the yeast in its own separate dispenser if your machine has one. If it doesn't, scatter the leavening over the other dry ingredients. However, if the instructions for the model you have specify placing the leavening in the pan first thing, add the other dry ingredients next and end with the liquids.

Set your machine to its rapid-bake cycle for this loaf.

Garbanzo Bread

Garbanzos, or chick-peas, those light brown marble-sized staples of the salad bar, can also be useful in bread making. The starch of these legumes, like that of potatoes, produces a loaf lighter, softer, and better-keeping than many made from grain flours alone. The garbanzos also add a very nice nutty flavor to the bread. This recipe makes a medium-sized loaf, slices of which are delightful with vichyssoise and other cold vegetable soups in the summertime.

It is occasionally possible to buy garbanzo flour from specialty markets. But with a bread machine, it's just as easy to use the whole beans, as the machine does an excellent job of mincing them.

You can either soak dried garbanzos overnight in water — half a cup of dry garbanzos will yield a full cup of the beans after soaking — and then boil them until tender, or you can simply buy the chick-peas cooked and canned and ready to use. In either case, reserve the liquid to use in the bread as well. If there isn't enough liquid to make the full cup called for, eke it out with water.

> 1 cup water reserved from draining
>   canned garbanzos or cooking dried
>   ones
> 1 tablespoon olive oil
> 1 cup canned or freshly cooked garban-
>   zos
> 3 cups whole-wheat flour
> 2 tablespoons nonfat dry milk
> 1 tablespoon dark brown sugar
> 1/2 teaspoon pepper
> 1/4 to 1 teaspoon salt to taste
> 1 1/2 teaspoons active dry yeast

Pour the garbanzo water into the baking pan of your bread machine and add the olive oil, the garbanzos themselves, then the flour, dry milk, brown sugar, pepper, and salt. Distribute the yeast according to the directions given for the particular bread machine you have.

Bake on full cycle.

Carrot Bread

Here's a lovely saffron-colored loaf flecked with orange that makes a delightful accompaniment to a consommé or an omelet. The carrot taste is subtle, but lends a nice background flavor to this moist, sunny, high-domed bread.

My wife, Susan, upon reading this manuscript, asked why there were basil and onion in a carrot bread recipe. The answer is simple: I like basil and onions with my carrots. Since there were no leftovers when I baked this loaf, I assume the combination has general appeal. If your tastes are more traditional, you might want to substitute a teaspoon and a half of dill for the basil and onion.

But then sometime do try a loaf with the basil and onion; it really is tasty.

Note that in this recipe there is relatively little liquid, only ½ cup of water to 2 cups of flour. That's because the carrots contain a surprising amount of moisture, and a more normal measure of liquid will cause the dough to overflow the pan onto the heating element. I speak from some very messy experience here.

½ cup water
1 tablespoon honey
2 tablespoons unsalted butter or canola
*   oil*
1 cup coarsely shredded raw carrots,
*   well packed*
2 cups unbleached all-purpose flour
2 tablespoons nonfat dry milk
1 teaspoon dried basil or, if preferred,
*   1½ teaspoons dried dill*
1 teaspoon dehydrated minced onion
*   (omit if using dill)*
¼ to ½ teaspoon salt to taste
1½ teaspoons active dry yeast

Place the water, honey, and butter or canola oil in your baking pan and shake in the shredded carrots, unless the instructions for your machine specify that the liquid ingredients are to be added last and the yeast first. Next add the flour, dry milk, basil and onion, or dill if preferred, and salt. Measure in the yeast, following the instructions for the specific model of bread machine you have.

This loaf is best baked on a quick cycle with a light setting if your machine provides such a choice, as the heavier crust produced with the darker setting detracts somewhat from the delicacy of the bread.

Creamy Pumpkin Bread

In the country, the squash family turns into a cornucopia of over-abundance during the summer and fall months. Pumpkins, especially when one is trying to produce a mammoth specimen for the front porch by Halloween, as we do every year, lead to wretched excess. It's true, of course, that, properly stored, they do keep well into the wintertime. But there's only so much space one can devote to the things.

On the other hand, pumpkin is a splendid addition to bread, adding nutrition and flavor as well as moisture and texture — not that one could ever bake enough loaves to deplete significantly the likes of the 82-pound orange monster that a vine next to our barn produced last year, and certainly not with this recipe, which calls for a mere half cupful of the stuff.

Those without rampaging pumpkin vines in their gardens are spared the dilemma of disposing of excess pumpkin creatively. Pie-ready canned pumpkin works just as well in bread as pumpkin fresh from the field, cooked at home.

The absence of liquid in the recipe given here is no mistake. Pumpkins are 98 percent water, and the sour cream listed among the ingredients provides all the additional moisture needed. In fact, if you dump the sour cream and the pumpkin into your pan in one fell swoop and try to weigh them down with the other ingredients, the mixing blade, once engaged, will go round and round in the soft mush at the bottom, never drawing down the flour. To assure a proper mixing and kneading of this batter, the sour cream and pumpkin must be incorporated alternately with dry ingredients.

> 1 cup sour cream
> 2 cups unbleached all-purpose flour
> 1/2 cup canned or freshly cooked and
>   mashed pumpkin
> 2 tablespoons unsulphured molasses
> 2 tablespoons unsalted butter or canola
>   oil
> 1/2 cup buckwheat flour
> 1 teaspoon pumpkin pie spice
> 1/4 to 1 teaspoon salt to taste
> 1 1/2 teaspoons active dry yeast

Spoon half a cupful of the sour cream into the baking pan of your bread machine, add half a cupful of the all-purpose flour, then the rest of the sour cream followed by another half cupful of flour. Next, add the pumpkin and the remaining cupful of all-purpose flour. Then measure in the molasses and butter or canola oil, the buckwheat flour, pumpkin pie spice, salt, and yeast. If your machine has a separate dispenser for leavening, the yeast should be placed there.

Bake on a quick cycle.

12 · Breads from the Orchard

A LOAF OF BREAD, a jug of wine, and thou" — the words were surely penned advisedly. Whether as wine or juice, the sweet, smooth quality of fruit in its liquid form complements the fibrous texture of grains. Then too, the natural sugars in fruit aid yeast in leavening bread.

I particularly like to step out to the old orchard in what is now our back pasture to gather apples on a summer morn. The horses have stripped the bark off half the trees, and insects seem to have scavenged the other half. The fruit is scabby and not particularly attractive — it's impossible to grow picture-perfect apples anymore without massive spraying — but oh, what flavor! I bring the apples into the kitchen, Susan makes a wonderful pink applesauce, and I slip the ingredients for a batch of spiced apple granola bread into the electronic oven before the heat of the day sets in.

With the variety of fresh produce available just about everywhere these days, one needn't have an orchard of one's own in order to harvest the benefits of newly plucked fruit. For that matter, dried fruits make wonderful winter breads, traditional cold-weather pick-me-ups rich in vitamins and flavor.

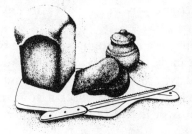

Apple Granola Bread

Here's a healthy loaf that from a cursory glance at the recipe might seem to have just too many things in it. All too often as the ingredients in a recipe increase in number, the taste and texture of the finished result abate. This bread is a notable exception. Everything from the granola and the sour cream to the honey and fragrant cinnamon enhances its flavor. Molly, a school friend of Tanya's staying with us at the time when the baking for this book was in full swing and inundated with bread along with the rest of the family, rated it one of her favorite loaves.

The dough starts out quite stiff, and it's a good idea to peek into the bread pan about five to ten minutes into the initial mixing cycle to see if the sides need scraping down with a rubber spatula, particularly if you are baking the large loaf.

The granola I generally use happens to be the Erewhon version of the cereal, but other brands work well too.

SMALL	LARGE
1 cup sour cream or yogurt, regular or low-fat	1½ cups sour cream or yogurt, regular or low-fat
1 tablespoon unsalted butter or canola oil	2 tablespoons unsalted butter or canola oil
½ cup honey	⅔ cup honey
1 egg	1 egg
1 unpeeled apple, diced	1½ unpeeled apples, diced
1 cup granola	2 cups granola
1½ cups unbleached all-purpose flour	2½ cups unbleached all-purpose flour
½ cup whole-wheat flour	½ cup whole-wheat flour
1 teaspoon cinnamon	1½ teaspoons cinnamon
½ teaspoon grated nutmeg	1 teaspoon grated nutmeg
¼ to 1 teaspoon salt to taste	½ to 2 teaspoons salt to taste
1½ teaspoons active dry yeast	2 teaspoons active dry yeast

Scoop the sour cream or yogurt into your baking pan along with the butter or canola oil, honey, and egg. Add the apple, granola, all-purpose and whole-wheat flours, cinnamon, nutmeg, and salt. Place the yeast in its own dispenser if your machine has one; otherwise scatter it over the rest of the ingredients. If it is to be placed in the bottom of the pan first thing instead, don't forget to reverse the order in which you add the liquid and the dry ingredients.

Bake the bread on your machine's quick cycle.

Apple Wheat Loaf

We put a couple of big baskets filled with apples on the bay windowsill in our bedroom every fall. For sleeping, I like a cold bedroom (and a warm goose down comforter), so the apples keep well into December. The whole room is redolent with their fragrance, which Susan likes as much as I do. She doesn't necessarily feel the same way about the nighttime temperatures in our sleeping quarters.

The time comes, however, when all the winter storage apples are gone — eaten out of hand or sliced into pies, the culls devoured to the last seed by the hens. Then we forage for the dried variety at the supermarket. Dried apples add a refreshing burst of flavor as well as nutrition to a winter loaf. The aroma of this one as it's baking is superb.

SMALL	LARGE
¾ cup buttermilk	1¼ cups buttermilk
2 tablespoons unsalted butter or canola oil	3 tablespoons unsalted butter or canola oil
2 tablespoons unsulphured molasses	3 tablespoons unsulphured molasses
¼ teaspoon lemon extract	½ teaspoon lemon extract
1 cup dried apples, packed	1½ cups dried apples, packed
1¼ cups unbleached all-purpose flour	1¾ cups unbleached all-purpose flour
1 cup whole-wheat flour	1¼ cups whole-wheat flour
1 teaspoon ground cinnamon	1½ teaspoons ground cinnamon
½ to 1 teaspoon salt to taste	1 to 1½ teaspoons salt to taste
1½ teaspoons active dry yeast	2 teaspoons active dry yeast

Pour the buttermilk into your bread machine baking pan and add the butter or canola oil, molasses, and lemon extract, unless the instructions that came with your machine specify that the yeast is to be placed in the bottom of the pan first thing, in which case these liquid ingredients should be added after the dry ones. Toss the dried apples into the pan, then measure in the all-purpose and whole-wheat flours. Add the cinnamon, salt, and yeast, spooning the leavening into its own dispenser if a separate container is provided for it on your machine.

Use your machine's rapid-bake setting for this loaf.

Serve slices of the bread warm from the electronic oven with sweet butter, honey, or maple butter.

Applesauce Bread

Come January or February, when the gardens here in New England are frozen so solid that even parsnips can't be pulled anymore, we really begin to long for spring and the white orchards of apple blossoms. But if there are no crisp apples left in the cold cellar, still there's always applesauce. Used in bread, it yields a hearty country loaf fragrant and welcome indeed on a cold winter's morning. Molly's response to it was, "Mmmmm. This is my favorite."

SMALL	LARGE
1 cup applesauce, sweetened or unsweetened	1½ cups applesauce, sweetened or unsweetened
2 tablespoons unsalted butter or canola oil	3 tablespoons unsalted butter or canola oil
1 tablespoon honey	2 tablespoons honey
½ cup raisins	1 cup raisins
½ cup almonds, coarsely chopped	1 cup almonds, coarsely chopped
2 cups unbleached all-purpose flour	3 cups unbleached all-purpose flour
¼ teaspoon cinnamon	½ teaspoon cinnamon
⅛ teaspoon mace	¼ teaspoon mace
½ to 1½ teaspoons salt to taste	1 to 2 teaspoons salt to taste
1½ teaspoons active dry yeast	2 teaspoons active dry yeast

Spoon the applesauce into the baking pan of your bread machine, unless the directions for the model you have instruct you to put the leavening in first, the liquids last. If you are making the large loaf and using butter straight from the refrigerator, cut it into chunks for more even blending, as it will be cold and hard, before next adding it to the pan. If you are using canola oil, it can be added as it comes from its container. Measure in the honey, raisins, almonds, flour, cinnamon, mace, and salt. Place the yeast in its own dispenser if your machine has one. If not, scatter it over the rest of the dry ingredients.

Use the machine's quick cycle to bake the loaf.

Pumpkin-Pie-Spice Loaf

This is one of those loaves whose components lend themselves to being loaded into the bread machine in the morning, with the timer set to produce a fresh, fragrant loaf as one walks in the door at the end of the day, without fear of the ingredients spoiling on even the warmest of days.

It's a simple, unpretentious loaf, light-textured and subtle in flavor, just a little spicy, just a little reminiscent of the apples of summer, just a little sweet, but mostly just a good homey bread.

SMALL	LARGE
1 cup unsweetened chunky applesauce	1 1/3 cups unsweetened chunky applesauce
2 tablespoons unsalted butter or canola oil	3 tablespoons unsalted butter or canola oil
2 cups unbleached all-purpose flour	3 cups unbleached all-purpose flour
1/2 cup wheat bran	3/4 cup wheat bran
2 tablespoons dark brown sugar	3 tablespoons dark brown sugar
1 1/2 teaspoons pumpkin-pie spice	2 teaspoons pumpkin-pie spice
1/2 to 1 teaspoon salt, to taste	1 to 2 teaspoons salt, to taste
1 1/2 teaspoons active dry yeast	2 teaspoons active dry yeast

Spoon the applesauce into the baking pan of your bread machine and add the butter or canola oil, flour, wheat bran, brown sugar, pumpkin-pie spice, salt, and yeast. Remember, however, to follow the directions that came with your particular machine in incorporating the leavening. If the yeast is to be placed in the pan first thing, then the applesauce and butter or canola oil should be reserved till last, and if the machine has a separate dispenser for leavening, that's where the yeast should go.

Select the machine's rapid-bake cycle for this bread. If desired, set the timer for a loaf whose just-baked fragrance will lift the spirits of any weary homecomer.

Orange Barley Malt Bread

There's nothing quite like the tang of freshly grated lemon or orange peel, and there are times when I will settle for nothing less in my cooking. But I find it handy to have some citrus oil, available in gourmet shops and by mail order, around as well. It does keep the refrigerator crisper from filling up with unsightly bald lemons and oranges whose flavorful skin has been rasped off. By all means feel free to substitute grated orange or lemon zest for the oil in the recipe given here.

SMALL	LARGE
½ cup heavy cream	*⅔ cup heavy cream*
3 tablespoons barley malt syrup	*¼ cup barley malt syrup*
2 teaspoons orange oil or grated orange or lemon zest	*1 tablespoon orange oil or grated orange or lemon zest*
1 egg	*2 eggs*
2 cups unbleached all-purpose flour	*3 cups unbleached all-purpose flour*
½ cup millet flour	*¾ cup millet flour*
½ to 1½ teaspoons salt to taste	*1 to 2 teaspoons salt to taste*
1½ teaspoons active dry yeast	*2 teaspoons active dry yeast*

Pour the cream into your bread machine baking pan and add the barley malt syrup, orange oil or zest, and the egg or, if you are making the large loaf, eggs. Next add the all-purpose and millet flours, salt, and yeast. Remember, however, to follow the directions that came with your particular machine for incorporating these ingredients; if the yeast is to be placed in the pan first thing, then the liquids should be reserved till last.

The rapid-bake setting on your machine is the one to use for this loaf.

Citrus Cherry Bread

Citrus oils allow you to add most of the flavor of freshly grated lemon, lime, or orange peel without the knuckles. Personally, I still prefer my zest fresh from the fruit most of the time. But if I'm out of the fruit or baking in a hurry, particularly with a bread machine, being able to reach for a bottle of orange or lemon oil is a real convenience.

Dried cherries are another item I try to keep on the shelf. They don't always remain there unless hidden behind jars of capers or cans of olives, commodities to which the kids haven't yet taken the same gourmet shine they've taken to the cherries, but I do try.

My favorite among the dried cherries is the Montmorency, sweet yet tangy, and ever so munchable. As Revell remarked, picking the red bits out of a slice of bread before eating the bread itself, "These cherries are great!" I'd agree, adding only that the bread is too.

SMALL	LARGE
½ cup sour cream	¾ cup sour cream
¼ cup unsalted butter or canola oil	⅓ cup unsalted butter or canola oil
1 egg	2 eggs
½ teaspoon orange or lemon oil	1 teaspoon orange or lemon oil
¾ cup dried cherries	1¼ cups dried cherries
2 cups unbleached all-purpose flour	3½ cups unbleached all-purpose flour
⅓ cup firmly packed dark brown sugar	½ cup firmly packed dark brown sugar
½ to 1½ teaspoons salt to taste	1 to 2 teaspoons salt to taste
1½ teaspoons active dry yeast	2 teaspoons active dry yeast

Scoop the sour cream into your bread machine pan and add the butter or canola oil, unless the directions for the model you have instruct you to place the leavening in the very bottom of the pan first, the other dry ingredients next, and the liquids last. If you are using butter straight from the refrigerator, it will be cold and hard, so, because you are using a sizable quantity, it should be cut into chunks before being placed in the pan, as otherwise it will fail to blend into the dough evenly. Break the egg or eggs into the pan and add the orange or lemon oil, cherries, flour, brown sugar, salt, and yeast, placing the yeast in its own separate dispenser if your machine has such.

Set the machine to its rapid-bake cycle for this loaf.

Prune Bread

Prunes have bad press in the United States, relegated as they are largely to plain stewed compotes served the elderly for a number of health reasons. But in the Old World prunes are much esteemed, featuring in such gustatory delights as lekvar, the delicate plum butter of central Europe, and slivovitz, the fiery brandy distilled around the Adriatic — and, in days gone by, in my grandmother's Viennese kitchen.

Here's a solid dark bread that makes a substantial breakfast for those who have only a slice of toast and coffee as their morning meal. Try it with cream cheese for extra sustenance and smoothness.

Be sure your machine is set to its quick cycle when you bake this bread. The regular, or long, cycle is apt to produce a bread the color of the prunes themselves.

SMALL	LARGE
1 cup milk, whole or skim	1½ cups milk, whole or skim
2 tablespoons unsalted butter or canola oil	¼ cup unsalted butter or canola oil
2 tablespoons lemon juice	¼ cup lemon juice
1 cup pitted whole dry prunes	2 cups pitted whole dry prunes
1 cup unbleached all-purpose flour	1¾ cups unbleached all-purpose flour
1 cup semolina flour	1½ cups semolina flour
½ cup uncooked oatmeal (not instant)	1 cup uncooked oatmeal (not instant)
½ teaspoon ground cloves	1 teaspoon ground cloves
½ to 1½ teaspoons salt to taste	1 to 2 teaspoons salt to taste
1½ teaspoons active dry yeast	2 teaspoons active dry yeast

Pour the milk into your baking pan and add the butter or canola oil, unless the directions for your machine instruct you to start with the yeast, followed by the dry and then the liquid ingredients. If you are making the large loaf and using butter straight from the refrigerator, cut it into chunks before placing it in the pan, so it will blend more easily with the other ingredients. Add the lemon juice, prunes, all-purpose and semolina flours, oatmeal, cloves, and salt. Then measure the yeast into its own dispenser if your machine has a separate container for leavening; otherwise, scatter it over the rest of the ingredients.

Use the machine's quick cycle for baking this bread.

Raisin Bread

There was one whole week shortly after first bringing home a bread machine during which I baked nothing but raisin bread, sometimes two or three loaves a day. This was not because we are inordinately fond of raisin bread, but because I was striving for a loaf with whole raisins in it.

The batter blade at the bottom of a bread machine pan stirs and kneads the dough rather fiercely. This hyperactivity is a technological compromise between applying enough motion to the dough to render it elastic and pliant and keeping the size of the blade small enough so that the baked loaf is not torn asunder when pulled out of the pan.

Unfortunately, the violent motion shreds chunky ingredients like raisins to puny pieces in the machine's regular cycle, which is the one it utilizes automatically unless instructed otherwise. I tried everything I could think of to keep the raisins whole, from freezing them beforehand to candying them. Nothing worked.

But why, you might ask, if it's only in the regular cycle that the raisins are mashed, didn't I simply bake the bread on the quick cycle?

Good question. The fact is that if you bake raisin bread on a quick cycle, as the instruction manual tells you to do, you will get bread with whole raisins. However, you cannot use the quick cycle and the timer together, and if you want freshly baked bread in the morning, you have to use the timer. My problem was that I think of raisin bread as something one eats in the morning, and wanted it for breakfast.

That still unsolved conundrum aside, the recipe given here makes a very tasty raisin bread — with plenty of whole raisins, clearly visible and bursting with flavor.

1 cup milk, whole or skim
1 tablespoon unsalted butter or canola
oil
1 cup raisins
2 cups unbleached all-purpose flour
2 tablespoons dark brown sugar
1½ teaspoons cinnamon
¼ to 1 teaspoon salt to taste
2 teaspoons active dry yeast

Pour the milk into the baking pan of your bread machine and add the spoonful of butter or canola oil and the raisins, unless your machine has a mix cycle permitting you to add the raisins separately, for greater fullness, after the other ingredients have been blended. Measure in the flour, brown sugar, cinnamon, salt, and yeast. For placement of the yeast, follow the directions provided with your bread machine.

Bake this loaf on a quick cycle.

Sour Cream Raisin Bread

Because the dough for this bread is fairly dense, the raisins tend to become smashed, insinuating themselves into the overall texture of the loaf rather than remaining plump islands of flavor in its expanse. If you want your bread replete with whole raisins, you need to wait to add them until the machine has nearly finished kneading the dough. Since I seem seldom to be around at the right moment for that, I simply accept mushed raisins. And if it's the raisin flavor you're after, this almost cakelike loaf accented with the subtle tartness of sour cream is a lovely addition to any baker's repertoire.

SMALL	LARGE
1 cup sour cream or yogurt, regular or low-fat	*1½ cups sour cream or yogurt, regular or low-fat*
1 tablespoon canola oil	*2 tablespoons canola oil*
1 cup raisins	*1½ cups raisins*
2 cups unbleached all-purpose flour	*2¾ cups unbleached all-purpose flour*
1 tablespoon dark brown sugar	*2 tablespoons dark brown sugar*
1 teaspoon cinnamon	*2 teaspoons cinnamon*
½ teaspoon ground cloves	*1 teaspoon ground cloves*
½ to 1½ teaspoons salt to taste	*1 to 2 teaspoons salt to taste*
1½ teaspoons active dry yeast	*2 teaspoons active dry yeast*

Put the sour cream or yogurt, canola oil, and raisins in the baking pan of your bread machine and add the flour, brown sugar, cinnamon, cloves, and salt. If your machine has a separate dispenser for leavening, spoon the yeast in there. Otherwise, scatter it over the other dry ingredients. However, if the instructions that came with your machine call for placing the yeast in the very bottom of the pan first thing, you will need to remember to reverse the order in which you add the liquid and the dry ingredients.

Bake the loaf on your machine's quick cycle.

Apricot Bread

Apricots bring to mind, for me, scenes from the movie version of *Lost Horizons*, set somewhere in Hunza land, where eternal youth springs from this stone fruit in alliance with lots of yogurt. They also recall my grandmother's homemade *marillenbrand*, an apricot brandy that, while it might not extend life, certainly made it seem eternal.

Today, fresh apricots have more or less vanished from my experience. Oh, I know they can be bought in supermarkets, but the hard, dry, tart spheroids found there have very little in common with the sun-warmed taste bursts I remember picking ripe from the trees, always checking first for yellow jackets, which loved them as much as I did.

Surprisingly, the dried apricots likewise available in supermarkets still make a great nibble, and also a good sweet bread that adds a sumptuous touch to an afternoon tea, not to mention a nutritious boost to a child's after-school snack. For an even more tempting loaf, give it an apricot jam glaze such as the one found among the recipes in the chapter "Topping It All Off."

SMALL	LARGE
1 cup milk, whole or skim	1½ cups milk, whole or skim
1 tablespoon walnut oil	2 tablespoons walnut oil
2 tablespoons unsulphured molasses	3 tablespoons unsulphured molasses
1 cup dried apricots, halved	1½ cups dried apricots, halved
2 cups unbleached all-purpose flour	3¼ cups unbleached all-purpose flour
1 cup unprocessed wheat bran	¾ cup unprocessed wheat bran
¼ to 1 teaspoon salt to taste	½ to 1½ teaspoons salt to taste
1½ teaspoons active dry yeast	2 teaspoons active dry yeast

Place the milk, walnut oil, and molasses in your machine's bread pan, add the apricots, and measure in the flour, wheat bran, and salt. Last, unless the instructions that came with your machine call for reversing the order in which the leavening and the liquids are incorporated, spoon in the yeast, using the separate dispenser for it if your machine has one.

Bake the loaf on your machine's quick cycle.

Three Nuts Apricot Bread

Nuts and apricots seem somehow to have a natural affinity for each other. Certainly in this loaf, Susan's favorite for cream cheese sandwiches, they are a magnificent combination.

Following personal preference, I make this bread with an assortment of the tree nuts such as almonds, hazelnuts, pecans, and walnuts. But groundnut fans can successfully substitute peanuts, reducing the salt in the recipe if the nuts are salted, for any or all of the nuts listed, cupful for cupful.

It's simplest to add the nuts and the apricots whole. Besides, with this method one bites into good-sized chunks of the rich nuts and fruit hidden in unexpected corners of the loaf. But if you prefer a more uniform loaf with fewer surprises, quarter the apricots and use chopped nuts.

SMALL	LARGE
1 cup milk, whole or skim	1½ cups milk, whole or skim
1 tablespoon unsalted butter or walnut oil	2 tablespoons unsalted butter or walnut oil
1 tablespoon honey	2 tablespoons honey
1 egg	1 egg
½ cup dried apricots, quartered if desired	1 cup dried apricots, quartered if desired
½ cup blanched almonds, whole or chopped, or ½ to 1½ cups peanuts, replacing some or all of the other nuts listed	¾ cup blanched almonds, whole or chopped, or ¾ to 2¼ cups peanuts, replacing some or all of the other nuts listed
½ cup pecan halves or pieces	¾ cup pecan halves or pieces
½ cup walnut halves or pieces or whole or chopped hazelnuts	¾ cup walnut halves or pieces or whole or chopped hazelnuts
1¾ cups unbleached all-purpose flour	2¾ cups unbleached all-purpose flour
¾ cup unprocessed wheat bran	1 cup unprocessed wheat bran
½ to 1 teaspoon salt to taste	1 to 2 teaspoons salt to taste
1½ teaspoons active dry yeast	2 teaspoons active dry yeast

Unless the instructions for your machine specify putting the yeast into the baking machine bread pan first thing and covering it with the other dry ingredients before adding the liquids, pour the milk into your pan, add the butter or walnut oil and the honey, and break the egg into the pan. Toss in the apricots, almonds or peanuts, and the pecans and walnuts or hazelnuts if you are using those in your mix. Then measure in the flour, wheat bran, salt, and yeast. If your machine has a separate dispenser for the leavening, place the yeast there.

The rapid-bake cycle on your machine is the best setting for this bread.

Plum Pecan Bread

Toward the end of the summer, small dark purple Italian prune plums make their way to market. To my mind these are really the best of baking plums, being juicy yet firm, and they go particularly well with nuts like pecans. But any ripe plums can be used in making this bread.

The flavorsome loaf is very tender, even when cooled. So it will need to be sliced thick, country fashion.

SMALL
¾ cup unsweetened prune juice
¼ cup unsalted butter or canola oil
1 egg
1 cup chopped pitted plums
½ cup pecan halves
2½ cups unbleached all-purpose flour
½ to 1½ teaspoons salt to taste
1½ teaspoons active dry yeast

LARGE
⅞ cup unsweetened prune juice
5 tablespoons unsalted butter or canola oil
1 egg
⅔ cup chopped pitted plums
¾ cup pecan halves
4 cups unbleached all-purpose flour
1 to 2 teaspoons salt to taste
2 teaspoons active dry yeast

Pour the prune juice into your baking machine bread pan and add the butter, cut into small pieces for better blending if taken cold from the refrigerator, or canola oil if preferred. Break in the egg and add the plums, pecans, flour, salt, and yeast, positioning the yeast as directed for your particular machine. If the instructions that came with the model you have call for starting with the yeast, the other dry ingredients should be added before the liquid and moist ones. To bake the loaf, use your machine's quick cycle.

French Walnut Bread

As taste and texture go, walnuts have a rather soft crunch, and in a bread machine, the kneading blade chops the pieces for you, so don't hesitate to use whole halves. The recipe given here produces a dense, nut-brown loaf with a fine, pebbly texture. The bread is rich and earthy and goes well with Neufchâtel and other soft cheeses.

½ cup milk, whole or skim
1 egg
4 tablespoons walnut oil
1½ cups walnut halves or large pieces
2 cups unbleached all-purpose flour
1 teaspoon sugar
¼ to 1 teaspoon salt to taste
1½ teaspoons active dry yeast

Unless the instructions that came with your machine specify that the yeast is to be placed in your baking pan first, followed by the dry and then the liquid ingredients, pour the milk into the pan and break the egg into it. Add the walnut oil and the walnuts, then the flour, sugar, salt, and yeast.

Use a quick bake cycle for this loaf.

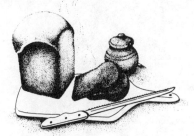

Sweet Almond Bread

O f all the nuts used in cooking, almonds are, I think, the best in
bread and pastries. When it comes to cakes, there's nothing
like Susan's walnut *gâteau*, which contains no flour, just grated
walnuts. In pies, pecans surely reign supreme. But for breads and
pastries, almonds have no rival. Try this sweet almond bread and
see if you don't agree.

SMALL	LARGE
½ cup milk, whole or skim	*¾ cup milk, whole or skim*
2 teaspoons canola oil	*5 teaspoons canola oil*
1 egg	*1 egg*
1 teaspoon almond extract	*2 teaspoons almond extract*
½ cup blanched almonds,	*¾ cup blanched almonds,*
coarsely chopped	*coarsely chopped*
2 cups unbleached all-purpose	*3 cups unbleached all-purpose*
flour	*flour*
¼ cup firmly packed dark brown	*½ cup firmly packed dark brown*
sugar	*sugar*
¼ to 1 teaspoon salt to taste	*½ to 1½ teaspoons salt to taste*
1½ teaspoons active dry yeast	*2 teaspoons active dry yeast*

Pour the milk into the baking pan of your bread machine, unless
the instructions that came with the model you have call for starting
with the yeast, in which case the dry ingredients should be added
before the liquids, and measure in the canola oil. Break the egg into
the pan and spoon in the almond extract. Add the almonds, flour,
brown sugar, salt, and yeast, placing the leavening in its own separate dispenser if your machine has that feature.

Use your machine's rapid-bake cycle for this loaf.

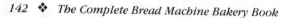

13 · Quick Breads

THE BREAD MACHINES were designed to bake yeast breads. But baking powder is another useful leavening agent, and the breads raised with it are quite different in many ways from their yeast-raised cousins.

To make something like Irish soda bread or a quick bran loaf by using baking powder but adding yeast for additional leavening, as the instructions included with the bread machines suggest, really isn't cricket. It's a matter not so much of principle as of taste. I love a yeasty loaf, but not if I'm eating soda bread.

It is quite possible to make a baking-powder bread in the electronic oven if the recipe is properly adapted. However, try as I might, I've never had a real baking-soda-only bread work in the machine.

Breakfast Bran Bread

This is the loaf version of the classic bran muffin. A low loaf, it's crumbly and soft, so cut it in slabs rather than thin slices.

> 2/3 cup milk, whole or skim
> 1/2 cup unsulphured molasses
> 1 egg
> 1/4 cup solid vegetable shortening
> 1 cup unbleached all-purpose flour
> 1 cup unprocessed wheat bran
> 1/4 cup firmly packed dark brown sugar
> dash salt
> 1 tablespoon double-acting baking
>   powder

Measure the milk and molasses into your bread pan, break in the egg, and add the shortening. Then toss in the flour, wheat bran, brown sugar, salt, and baking powder.

This baking-powder bread is best baked on a quick cycle.

Mock Boston Brown Bread

I've always liked steamed Boston brown bread. All the good fresh coffee beans that have become available in the last decade have been a boon to coffee aficionados, but not to the baked-beans-and-Boston-brown-bread set: I find we no longer have a reliable supply of coffee cans in which to steam breads and puddings.

I've called this bread a mock Boston brown bread because to my mind real Boston brown bread can be achieved only through hours of steaming in a coffee tin old enough to be just beginning to rust at the seams. All the same, this version adapted for bread machine baking, if not as moist and puddingy as the real thing, is still very tasty, and, due to the characteristic shape of bread machine pans, it's, well, almost round.

I've made this loaf with buttermilk. But running out of that commodity one day, I substituted sour cream diluted with water. The results were rewarding enough that I've stayed with the sour cream version ever since. The recipe works equally well without the raisins, a note I add for those oversaturated with plumped raisins in fruitcakes and other confections in their youth.

> 1 cup sour cream
> 1/2 cup water
> 1/2 cup unsulphured molasses
> 1 egg
> 1 cup raisins (optional)
> 1 cup unbleached all-purpose flour
> 1/2 cup whole-wheat flour
> 1 1/2 cups unprocessed wheat bran
> 1/2 cup cornmeal
> 1/4 to 1 teaspoon salt to taste
> 1 teaspoon baking soda
> 2 teaspoons double-acting baking
>   powder

Scoop the sour cream into the baking pan of your bread machine, add the water and molasses, and break in the egg. If you like raisins in your brown bread, toss in a cupful of them here. Because this bread is baked on a quick cycle, whole raisins will survive the kneading process relatively intact. If your machine has an interruptible mix cycle, the raisins can be added separately instead, after all the other ingredients have been blended together. Measure in the all-purpose and whole-wheat flours, the wheat bran and cornmeal, and the salt. Scatter the baking soda and baking powder more or less evenly over these dry ingredients.

Bake on your machine's quick cycle.

Zucchini Bread

This recipe doesn't use enough zucchini to solve the surplus problem for those with zucchini in their summer gardens. But the presence of the vegetable among the ingredients ensures a moist and flavorful bread. Raisins, pecans, or walnuts can be added for extra goodness. I'd vote for the pecans.

You might note that, beyond the honey and eggs, no liquid is called for. The zucchini, being 99 percent water, supplies plenty.

> 1/2 cup honey
> 2 eggs
> 1/2 cup unsalted butter
> 1 teaspoon vanilla extract
> 1 cup zucchini, finely chopped
> 1 cup raisins, pecans, or walnuts
> (optional)
> 2 cups unbleached all-purpose flour
> 1/2 teaspoon cinnamon
> 1/4 to 1 teaspoon salt to taste
> 1/2 teaspoon baking soda
> 1 teaspoon double-acting baking
> powder

Place the honey and eggs in your bread machine's baking pan and add the butter, cut into small chunks if it's hard, since you are using a sizable quantity, so that it will blend with the other ingredients better. Then add the vanilla extract, the chopped zucchini, and the raisins or nuts if desired. Next, add the flour, cinnamon, salt, baking soda, and baking powder, taking care to sprinkle the last two over the other ingredients rather than spooning them into one spot, so they will be distributed uniformly throughout the dough.

Use a quick bake cycle for this loaf.

Irish Currant Bread

Here's a lovely tea bread that's brimming with currants. A festive version of Irish soda bread, this loaf uses baking powder. Now before I get a bushel of letters remonstrating that real Irish soda bread is made with baking soda alone, none of this fancy baking-powder stuff, thank you, let me say that no one is more aware of this discrepancy than I.

In point of fact, for quite some time I had a whole row of diminutive rock-hard loaves aspiring to be Irish soda bread lined up by the "brick factory," as our daughter Tanya dubbed my bread machine the week the queue began forming at the rear of the kitchen counter. They were the result of a fortnight of trying to devise an all-soda Irish soda bread recipe that would work in a bread machine. It couldn't be done.

Soda doesn't have much staying power as a leavening agent, and even the shortest cycle of a bread machine is such that by the time baking begins, the soda is no longer generating any carbon dioxide to raise the dough. If you increase the quantity of soda in a recipe to the point where it works — well, barely, anyway — in a bread machine, the loaf emerges smelling like old fish.

So, strictly speaking, the bread presented here is not a genuine Irish soda bread, simply because it is not leavened by soda. In all else, however, it is true to its heritage, right down to the tea.

The designation of this particular loaf as a tea bread derives not from the happenstance that the bread is often served with the proverbial Irish cuppa, but from the fact that the liquid used in it really is tea. Tea is acidic, and is what in the original recipe, designed for conventional baking, sent the baking soda on its bubbly way. Here, it still adds flavor and color. And the loaf, baking powder notwithstanding, is still delicious.

To continue the tradition of tending a soda bread to its proper conclusion, let the loaf cool on a rack. Then wrap it in a just-damp linen towel and let it set overnight. Slice very thin and serve with sweet butter.

> 1 cup tea, room temperature to tepid
> 1 egg
> 1 cup dried currants
> 2 cups unbleached all-purpose flour
> ½ cup firmly packed dark brown sugar
> ¼ to 1 teaspoon salt to taste
> 1½ tablespoons double-acting baking
>   powder

Pour the tea into the baking pan of your bread machine, break the egg into it, and toss in the currants, making sure they're not all stuck together. Add the flour, brown sugar, salt, and baking powder.

Bake on your machine's quick cycle.

Teff Nut Bread

Teff is an ancient grain grown in the highlands of Ethiopia, where it has been used for centuries to make bread. Traditionally esteemed for its reputedly rich nutritional value and high iron content, it makes a terrific ultra-fine-grained bread. The flour is available in this country from sources listed in the back of the book.

At first, buying flour from Ethiopia seemed to me like arrogantly robbing the starving of their last means of sustenance. Then I realized that teff flour is probably one of that poverty- and war-ravaged country's few exportable items and a means of earning desperately needed foreign exchange. So, with a clearer conscience, I began experimenting. This teff nut bread recipe is a notable result.

In many parts of North Africa, nomadic peoples have been known to live for months on dates and camel's milk alone. The combination, as it so happens, is an almost perfect diet nutritionally. Camel's milk is in rather short supply in the part of Connecticut where we live, but the addition of whole cow's milk, dates, and nuts to the already nutritious teff flour results in a loaf that is truly a meal in itself.

Teff flour looks like a light-colored cocoa powder, so it's not surprising that bread made from it is very dark even when baked on a light machine setting. Don't be disappointed to see a smallish, quite compact loaf the color of a chocolate bar emerge from your pan; it will not be burned. You'll find the texture unbelievably silky for a bread. Superb spread with just sweet butter or a mild, soft cheese, delicate slices of it make an excellent selection for an old-fashioned high tea.

1 cup whole milk
1 egg
¼ cup unsalted butter or canola oil
½ cup pecans, coarsely chopped
½ cup dates, chopped
1½ cups teff flour
½ cup firmly packed dark brown sugar
1 teaspoon cinnamon (optional)
¼ to 1 teaspoon salt to taste
½ teaspoon baking soda
*2 teaspoons double-acting baking
   powder*

If a preliminary bread-mixing setting is available on your machine, the nutmeats and dates in this recipe can be reserved and added separately, after the initial blending of the other ingredients, to remain as chunkier bits in the finished loaf. Otherwise, place the milk and egg in the baking pan of your bread machine and add the butter, first cutting it into small chunks if it's hard so it will blend with the other ingredients better, or substitute canola oil if you prefer. Add the chopped pecans and dates next, then the flour, brown sugar, cinnamon if desired, and salt. Scatter the baking soda and baking powder evenly over the other ingredients for better blending.

Use a quick bake cycle for this bread.

Peanut Butter Bread

A peanut butter bread might seem to be overdoing things a bit. But there's a good nutritional reason for combining peanuts with the wheat of flour. Peanuts, besides being a good source of the B vitamin niacin, not to mention fiber, are an excellent protein. However, their protein is incomplete, lacking several important amino acids. Wheat and dairy products, on the other hand, provide the missing amino acids and thus complement the peanuts admirably.

Besides, if the peanut butter is already in the bread, as our ever-practical child Revell observed while putting up his school lunch one day, "all you need is the jelly."

Peanut butter is ordinarily salty enough so that no additional salt is needed for this bread. However, if what you have around the house is the unsalted variety, as is true in our home, you might want to add a dash or two of salt, though I don't.

> 1 cup milk, whole or skim
> 1 egg
> 2/3 cup smooth peanut butter
> 1 1/2 cups unbleached all-purpose flour
> 1/4 cup firmly packed dark brown sugar
> 4 teaspoons double-acting baking
>   powder

Pour the milk into your baking pan, break the egg into the milk, and ladle in the peanut butter, followed by the flour, brown sugar, and baking powder.

Set your machine on quick bake for this bread.

Banana Bread

M y first attempts to turn out a satisfactory banana bread using a bread machine were quite sticky endeavors. The customary recipes for this traditional bake-sale and potluck-supper standard, which produce golden, moist loaves from an ordinary oven, consistently produced from the electronic oven a loaf with a soft, gooey — in fact, soggy — spot at top center. On the other hand, the recipes to be found in any of the bread machine booklets I perused yielded coarse loaves tasting as if banana skins, rather than the fruit pulp itself, had been used for flavoring.

Looking at the baking process in a bread machine from an engineering point of view — oh, all right, from the point of view of a year's worth of mostly forgotten college physics, if the truth must be known — I decided that the kind of rich, velvety loaf characteristic of traditional banana bread required a denser, moister dough than the machine was designed to deal with. That meant either redesigning the machine or modifying one of my recipes to compensate for the persistence of a relatively cool spot at the center top of the pan during the baking process. A smaller, squatter loaf should work. It did.

The recipe given here makes a modestly sized loaf, but an exceedingly tasty one. As with any banana bread, one of the secrets of success is to have on hand bananas that are truly ripe. Their skins should be well flecked with brown. But the loaf itself takes literally only a minute or two of preparation time.

> ¼ cup buttermilk
> 1 egg
> ¼ cup unsalted butter or canola oil
> 1 teaspoon vanilla extract
> ½ cup mashed ripe banana
> 1 cup unbleached all-purpose flour
> ½ cup sugar
> ¼ to 1 teaspoon salt to taste
> ¼ teaspoon baking soda
> 2 teaspoons double-acting baking
>   powder

Measure the buttermilk into the baking pan of your bread machine, break the egg into it, and add the butter, cutting it into chunks if it's hard so it can more easily be mixed with the other ingredients, or substitute canola oil, if you prefer. Then add the vanilla. Scoop in the mashed banana, add the flour, sugar, and salt, and scatter the baking soda and baking powder over the dry ingredients.

Bake on your machine's quick cycle.

14 · Mix Masters and Other Instant Flavors

CAKE MIXES HAVE BEEN AROUND since the 1930s, but it's only in the last couple of decades that their sales have really taken off. As I heard the story, people considered the original mixes just too easy. It was necessary only to dump a mix into a bowl, add water, ladle the concoction into a cake pan, and bake it. Surely something that simple couldn't be that good.

Then one astute packager came up with the idea of having the consumer add the eggs and milk to the mix. This would lend the customer a certain sense of accomplishment while adding a wholesome fresh image to the product.

In today's hurried lives, I'm not sure much of anything can be made too simple. Assuming you feel the same, here's a clutch of recipes for breads whose flavor derives largely from packaged premixed ingredients readily available on supermarket shelves.

Wheatena Bread

Hearty breakfast breads can be created from the many multi-grain cereal mixes on the market. The particular loaf presented here, however, relies on a single cereal for its unusual flavor, and while it's rare that I tout a specific brand, I know of no generic form of Wheatena, the key flavoring ingredient.

An attractive, evenly shaped loaf with a nutty taste and an unexpected snap, this bread should not be limited to breakfast time simply because it's cereal based. All the cold cuts that go well with mustard are nicely complemented by it.

SMALL

1 cup milk, whole or skim
1½ cups unbleached all-purpose
   flour
½ cup uncooked Wheatena
3 tablespoons dark brown sugar
⅛ teaspoon mace
½ to 1½ teaspoons salt to taste
1½ teaspoons active dry yeast

LARGE

1½ cups milk, whole or skim
3 cups unbleached all-purpose
   flour
1 cup uncooked Wheatena
⅓ cup firmly packed dark brown
   sugar
¼ teaspoon mace
1 to 2 teaspoons salt to taste
2 teaspoons active dry yeast

Pour the milk into the baking pan of your bread machine and add the flour, Wheatena, brown sugar, mace, and salt. Then, unless the instructions that came with the model you have call for reversing the order in which the yeast and the milk are incorporated into the dough, either scatter the yeast over these ingredients or spoon it into its own separate dispenser if that feature is provided on your machine.

Bake the loaf on your machine's quick cycle.

Spud Bud Bread

Potato bread is one of those great-tasting breads not often made anymore. I suspect its neglect can be traced to the shortage of leftover potatoes in fridges nowadays, what with so many quick-fix dinners being consumed, plus the lack of time to cook up a whole fresh potful of potatoes in lieu of them, all for a mere loaf of bread. But here's a modified Hungarian potato bread that uses instant potato "buds," or flakes, and thus can easily be made any time it's wanted. I like the loaf the traditional way, with caraway. The rest of the family prefer it plain. Bake yours to suit.

SMALL	LARGE
3/4 cup water	*1 cup water*
1 tablespoon unsalted butter or canola oil	*2 tablespoons unsalted butter or canola oil*
1 1/2 cups unbleached all-purpose flour	*2 cups unbleached all-purpose flour*
1/2 cup instant mashed potato buds	*3/4 cup instant mashed potato buds*
1 tablespoon sugar	*2 tablespoons sugar*
2 teaspoons caraway seeds (optional)	*1 tablespoon caraway seeds (optional)*
1/2 to 1 1/2 teaspoons salt to taste	*1 to 2 teaspoons salt to taste*
1 1/2 teaspoons active dry yeast	*2 teaspoons active dry yeast*

Measure the water and butter or canola oil into the baking pan of your bread machine. Then add the flour, instant mashed potato, sugar, caraway seeds if desired, salt, and yeast, following the directions that came with your particular machine for incorporating the leavening, as for some models the order in which the ingredients are placed in the pan should be reversed.

Use the quick baking cycle on your machine for this loaf.

Onion Soup Bread

Certain so-called prepared foods dominate contemporary cuisine, often replacing in both our memories and our loyalties the original dishes they set out to imitate. Oreo cookies come immediately to mind. So does canned tomato soup.

Perhaps none of these concoctions more typifies the culinary shortcut than dehydrated onion soup. Packets of it are dumped into everything from meat loaves to sour cream. For many people, dehydrated onion soup has become the third most-used spice after salt and pepper.

It should come as no surprise, then, that in due course I decided to try dumping a packet of dehydrated onion soup into a bread dough I was assembling. It should come as no surprise, either, that it worked very well.

Considering the convenience of bread machines, dehydrated onion soup is a natural timesaving ingredient. It also yields a very moist, tasty, nicely oniony loaf, even if the onions themselves do not remain very visible.

This loaf is highly aromatic both during baking and afterward. It's one of those breads I call real estate specials: if you're trying to sell a house, put the ingredients for this loaf into your bread machine pan and set the timer so it will finish baking just when the prospective buyer is expected to arrive. A kitchen redolent with its scent could well sell the house by itself.

A packet of dehydrated onion soup contains plenty of salt, and most people will probably find no more is needed in the recipe. But if you like a salty bread, by all means add a dash.

The soup packets themselves range in size from 1½ to 2½ ounces. Use whatever size you have handy; anything in this range works well.

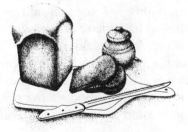

1 ¼ cups buttermilk
2 tablespoons unsulphured molasses
2 tablespoons unsalted butter or canola
  oil
1 packet dehydrated onion soup
2 cups unbleached all-purpose flour
½ cup cornmeal
dash salt (optional)
1½ teaspoons active dry yeast

Pour the buttermilk into the baking pan of your bread machine and add the molasses, butter or canola oil, onion soup mix, flour, cornmeal, and salt if desired. Distribute the yeast according to the instructions given for the particular bread machine you have.

Bake on a quick cycle.

Ranch Bread

This loaf has nothing to do with campfires and chuck wagons along the Chisholm Trail — unless the name of the popular creamy salad dressing used in it is somehow related to the frontier days of the last century, but I've been unable to determine any such relationship. It simply occurred to me while experimenting with recipes one day that creamy salad dressings have all the ingredients of a loaf of bread except the flour and the yeast. So I added them, with quite satisfactory results.

In making the larger loaf, I diluted the dressing with sour cream for a somewhat lighter, milder bread. If you find the flavor of the small loaf overwhelming — some may, although my family liked its piquancy — try using half a flask of dressing and half a cup of sour cream instead of the dressing alone.

Thick slices of the dense, rich loaf just spread with butter make a meal in themselves. The bread is at its aromatic best served as hot from the electronic oven as good slicing will allow. Any leftovers can be diced and toasted for flavorsome croutons.

SMALL	LARGE
1 8-ounce flask (1 cup) ranch salad dressing, regular or low-fat, or ½ flask (½ cup) dressing and ½ cup sour cream	1 8-ounce flask (1 cup) ranch salad dressing, regular or low-fat
2 cups unbleached all-purpose flour	½ cup sour cream
¼ cup cornmeal	3 cups unbleached all-purpose flour
1 tablespoon dark brown sugar	⅓ cup cornmeal
½ to 1½ teaspoons salt to taste	2 tablespoons dark brown sugar
1½ teaspoons active dry yeast	1 to 2 teaspoons salt to taste
	2 teaspoons active dry yeast

Unless the instructions that came with your machine call for placing the yeast in the bottom of the pan, followed by the other dry ingredients and then the liquids, put the salad dressing or dressing and sour cream into your baking pan. Add the flour, cornmeal, brown sugar, salt, and yeast, reserving the leavening for its own dispenser if your machine has one.

Bake the bread on your machine's quick cycle.

Dijon Rye Bread

Mustard and rye are two hearty tastes that go exceptionally well together. Their affinity inspired this bread, whose name derives from the type and origin of the mustard used, not from any ascribed birthplace of the loaf itself. I've never seen mustard rye bread in Dijon. On the other hand, I'm sure the epicurean sensibilities of that municipality's city fathers would not be offended by such a flavorful namesake.

By all means use a grainy version of the mustard for extra piquancy. For both visual and gustatory accent, add a mustard glaze. This bread makes a great accompaniment to spit-roasted chicken or a hearty bean soup.

1 cup water or vegetable broth
2 tablespoons olive oil
2 tablespoons unsulphured molasses
⅓ cup prepared Dijon mustard
1 cup unbleached all-purpose flour
1 cup whole-wheat flour
1 cup rye flour
1 tablespoon instant coffee, regular
or decaffeinated, or Postum
½ teaspoon dried thyme
½ to 1 teaspoon salt to taste
1½ teaspoons active dry yeast

G L A Z E

1 teaspoon prepared Dijon mustard
1 teaspoon unsulphured molasses
1 teaspoon warm water

Pour the water or vegetable broth into the baking pan of your bread machine and add the oil, molasses, and mustard, unless the instructions for your machine specify that the yeast is to be placed in the bottom of the pan, followed by first the dry and then the liquid ingredients. Measure in the all-purpose, whole-wheat, and rye flours, the instant coffee or Postum, and the thyme and salt. Add the yeast according to the directions for your particular machine.

Bake on full cycle. To glaze the loaf, mix together the teaspoonful of mustard, molasses, and warm water and, while the loaf is still hot from the pan, brush this mixture over its crown with a pastry brush. The glaze will cool to a rich gloss.

Pesto Bread

Maybe it was reading Dr. Seuss's *Green Eggs and Ham* to my children too many times, maybe it was the pestofication of so many dishes during the yuppie eighties, maybe it was the fact that an exceptionally gray winter was dragging, oh, so slowly into spring that I was actually longing to have a little green in my life again — whatever the case, one day I concocted a pesto bread.

Pestos are mixtures of herbs and/or other ingredients such as olives or sun-dried tomatoes blended with oil into a paste. Traditionally, their concoction involved the use of a mortar and pestle. Hence the name. Today, most pestos are made in a blender or a food processor, and as long as the grinding cycle is not prolonged or hurried enough to heat the mixture appreciably, there's really no difference in flavor between a pesto so produced and the pounded variety.

Specialty-food stores usually carry a variety of pestos. For the recipe given here, I used a standard basil version purchased ready-made at the supermarket. The resulting bread did not emerge from its pan green enough to mitigate my winter mood. However, it proved its worth as a hearty, compact, different-tasting herb bread with a mild bite nicely complementing, say, a rich vegetable soup.

> *½ cup milk, whole or skim*
> *1 egg*
> *1 tablespoon olive oil*
> *3 tablespoons basil or other pesto*
> *2 cups unbleached all-purpose flour*
> *¼ to 1 teaspoon salt to taste*
> *1½ teaspoons active dry yeast*

Measure the milk into the baking pan of your bread machine and break the egg into it. Add the olive oil, pesto, flour, salt, and, last, unless otherwise directed in the instructions for your particular machine, the yeast.

Use a quick bake cycle for this loaf.

Salsa Bread

Mexican fare, albeit modified and highly stylized sometimes, seems about to become as "American" as pizza, which as found in this country bears equally little resemblance to the Italian original, and salsa is everywhere these days. Now I remember from my youthful travels in Mexico many a tasty meal of *molé* and goat meat wrapped in corn tortillas. But salsa, that current culinary craze, does not feature in my recollections.

Our kids snack their way through a large jar of salsa in no time. I once jokingly remarked that the saucy stuff would soon replace peanut butter as the spread of choice in our family. It was shortly thereafter that I concocted this loaf.

Tomato orange in color, salsa bread with its distinctive piquant flavor is a good foil for cold cuts in summer sandwiches. Salt is not needed, as there's plenty of spicing in the sauce. Choose the mild, medium, or hot variety to suit your taste.

SMALL

1 cup thick salsa
2 cups unbleached all-purpose
   flour
½ cup cornmeal
1½ teaspoons active dry yeast

LARGE

1⅔ cups (1 16-ounce jar) thick
   salsa
3 cups unbleached all-purpose
   flour
1 cup cornmeal
2 teaspoons active dry yeast

Scoop the salsa into your baking machine pan and add the flour, cornmeal, and yeast, following the directions that came with your particular machine for incorporating the leavening, as some machines specify reversing the order in which the ingredients are placed in the pan.

To bake the loaf, set your machine on its quick cycle.

Refried Bean Bread

Instant refried bean mixes are available at most health-food stores these days. Dehydrated flakes of precooked pinto beans seasoned with onion, salt, and spices, they are supposed to be reconstituted with boiling water. However, they also serve admirably as the flavoring agent for a quick and unusual bread.

Cold sliced chicken, mayonnaise, and a sprinkling of fresh cilantro are marvelous sandwiched between toasted pieces of this bread. So are salsa — but of course — and cheddar or Monterey Jack cheese grilled to a melt atop a slab of it, topped just before serving with shredded lettuce and sour cream.

1¼ cups buttermilk
2 tablespoons unsalted butter or
canola oil
1½ cups unbleached all-purpose
flour
½ cup instant refried bean mix
1½ teaspoons active dry yeast

1¾ cups buttermilk
3 tablespoons unsalted butter or
canola oil
2⅓ cups unbleached all-purpose
flour
1 cup instant refried bean mix
2 teaspoons active dry yeast

Put the buttermilk and butter or canola oil into your bread machine baking pan and add the flour and refried bean mix, unless the instructions that came with your machine call for reversing the order in which the leavening and the liquids are incorporated into the batter. Then either spoon the yeast into its own separate dispenser, if your machine has that feature, or scatter it over the other ingredients.

Bake the loaf on your machine's quick cycle.

Teriyaki Bread and Other Flavorsome Rice Oddities

Considering the circumstance of the bread machine's Oriental origins, itself odd enough in view of that vast region's scarcity of breads, I suppose the concept of teriyaki bread is not all that strange. This loaf materialized because I was looking for ways to expand the machine's horizons while staying within the limits of what these electronic ovens do best, which is to bake visually rather similar but gustatorily quite different breads with the barest of effort on their owners' part, when an array of quick-cooking rice dishes on the supermarket shelf caught my eye. I picked up a few.

My initial assortment included teriyaki, broccoli au gratin, and chicken and cheese. Although the contents of the boxes varied from 4.5 to 6 ounces among the sundry brands, I found they could be interchanged quite successfully in the basic recipe given here.

When using these mixes, however, it's a good idea to open the lid of your electronic oven a couple of minutes into the kneading cycle to check the dough. It should be forming into a ball that the mixing blade of your machine can batter around. If the dough is too soft, sticking to the edges of the pan and acquiring a bowl shape, add extra flour a little at a time until the dough rolls up.

The rice grains scattered throughout the baked loaf will be quite al dente, but not more so than they are in some of the upscale restaurant dishes presently in vogue. The firm grains contribute nice contrast and a good crust to the bread.

SMALL

1 cup water or vegetable broth
1 tablespoon canola oil
1 4.5- to 6-ounce box quick-cooking teriyaki or other rice mix
1½ cups unbleached all-purpose flour
1½ teaspoons active dry yeast

LARGE

1½ cups water or vegetable broth
2 tablespoons canola oil
1 4.5- to 6-ounce box quick-cooking teriyaki or other rice mix
3 cups unbleached all-purpose flour
2 teaspoons active dry yeast

Pour the water or vegetable broth into the baking pan of your bread machine, followed by the canola oil and the teriyaki or other rice mix. Add the flour and the yeast, remembering, however, to follow the directions that came with your particular machine for incorporating the leavening; if the yeast is to be placed in the pan first thing, then the water or broth and the oil should be reserved till last.

Use your machine's rapid-bake cycle for this loaf.

Falafel Bread

Falafel, the piquant Middle Eastern fare made from garbanzos, or chick-peas, yellow peas, wheat germ, and spices from the Oriental bazaars, has always been a favorite staple of desert travelers because of the ease with which the lightweight mix could be prepared into a nutritious, protein-rich meal. That same ease of preparation makes falafel an ideal ingredient for bread machine baking. Instead of being reconstituted and rolled into the traditional small balls for nibbling, the falafel mix is simply incorporated into the bread dough. Because the blend is already highly seasoned, no additional salt is needed.

The aroma of this bread while baking, exotic and enticing, makes it difficult to resist pulling the loaf from the electronic oven before the finishing beep. Try a slice slathered with tahini, the traditional sesame seed butter that so often accompanies falafel in the Middle East. The spread can be found in the same Oriental shops and health-food stores that carry the falafel mix.

SMALL	LARGE
1 cup water or vegetable broth	1¼ cups water or vegetable broth
3 tablespoons olive oil	⅓ cup olive oil
1½ cups unbleached all-purpose flour	2 cups unbleached all-purpose flour
½ cup whole-wheat flour	¾ cup whole-wheat flour
½ cup unreconstituted falafel mix	1 cup unreconstituted falafel mix
1½ teaspoons active dry yeast	2 teaspoons active dry yeast

Pour the water or vegetable broth into the baking pan of your bread machine, unless the instructions that came with the model you have call for starting with the yeast, in which case you will need to reverse the order in which the liquid and the dry ingredients are incorporated into your batter. Add the olive oil, all-purpose and whole-wheat flours, falafel mix, and yeast. If your machine has a separate dispenser for leavening, spoon the yeast in there.

Set your machine to its rapid-bake cycle for this loaf.

15 · No Gluten, No Cholesterol, and Other No-Nos

ONE PLACE where bread machines really shine is in custom baking for those with special dietary needs. When a loaf of bread is home baked, you know what went into it, so there's no need to worry about the wrong ingredients sneaking into your diet. At the same time, the machines are capable of handling doughs too sticky or otherwise too difficult to work by hand that apart from this hurdle make perfectly wonderful breads. I'm thinking here particularly of gluten-free bread, which at the outset of its preparation, the designation notwithstanding, more resembles a large blob of glue suspiciously like the gelatinous stuff it's supposed to be free of than a normal bread dough.

With the single exception of some kind of liquid, bread lacking any of the ingredients ordinarily considered essential — salt, sugar, even wheat — can be produced with a bread machine. Experiment with whatever a given diet might permit, and chances are you can come up with a good bread, sometimes even a great one like the saltless loaf in this chapter.

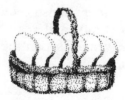

Saltless Tuscan Bread

Salt is conventionally deemed as basic an ingredient of bread as flour and a liquid are. Not only does it supply a flavor-enhancing accent to which we've become accustomed, but it slows the action of yeast, inducing smoother and more uniform leavening.

Although rare, saltless breads existed long before our diet-conscious age, in which almost any product can be purchased free of sugar, sodium, or what have you. The reason for the omission of salt in the old days had more to do with matters of finance than with health, however. Salt was a relatively expensive commodity because it was easy to tax.

The tender and flavorsome though saltless loaves of Tuscany on which the recipe given here is based are leavened by a starter similar to the one used in Apulian bread but omitting the pinch of sugar. However, because the Tuscan loaf uses far more starter, it can be baked on your machine's quick cycle.

The starter recipe given here is presented as a small batch in order to simplify visualizing the proportions of the ingredients. However, it can readily be doubled or tripled and frozen in portion-size quantities, to be defrosted three or four hours before needed.

To make the basic starter, pour half a cupful of warm water into a glass bowl prewarmed by a hot-water rinse and mix into it ¼ teaspoon of yeast. Let the mixture rest in a warm spot, such as the oven of a gas stove or the rangetop above a pilot light, until it has a creamy, bubbly look, a matter of 10 minutes or so. Then, with a wooden spoon, stir in a cupful of flour and another half cup of water.

This mixture should ferment, covered with plastic wrap, from 6 hours to a day or more. It will ferment quickly in hot weather; in cold weather it may take a couple of days.

If the mixture separates, leaving a clear liquid at the bottom, you may have to discard it. The starter should smell sour and fresh. If it's slimy, it's been left too long.

Starters do vary in consistency and strength as they grow. In some instances you may find that a dough made with the amount of starter listed in the recipe is too stiff for your machine to knead. I've encountered this problem more often with large loaves and oblong pans than in the making of smaller square or round loaves. Check the dough a few minutes into the preliminary mixing cycle, and if it's too firm, add a little extra water.

SMALL	LARGE
1 cup starter	*1½ cups starter*
½ cup water or vegetable broth	*1¼ cups water or vegetable broth*
2 cups unbleached all-purpose flour	*2¾ cups unbleached all-purpose flour*
1 teaspoon active dry yeast	*1½ teaspoons active dry yeast*

Unless the instructions that came with your baking machine call for starting with the dry leavening, place the starter and water or vegetable broth in the baking pan of your bread machine and add the flour. If your machine has a separate dispenser for the yeast, that's where it should go. If not, scatter it over the flour.

Bake this loaf on your machine's quick cycle.

No-Gluten Bread

One doesn't realize the importance of the unseen gluten present in most flours until one tries to make bread without it. Gluten adds a stretchy quality to dough that holds it together as it expands under the pressure of the carbon dioxide released by the fermenting yeast. It is gluten that turns the thousands and thousands of tiny bubbles in the dough into semipermanent balloons — the holes, or open texture, you see when slicing bread.

For those allergic to gluten, bread must include no wheat, oat, rye, or related flours. One is limited to working with rice, tapioca, potato, and other less common flours that without something to stretch them produce an inedible, bricklike bread. To lend elasticity to these glutenless flours, guar gum or xanthum gum is added. Of the two, xanthum gum is the more effective substitute, so I have used it here. A source for xanthum gum is listed at the back of this book.

The dough for this bread is extremely sticky, and I found it did not work well in a large batch. Hence the single small-loaf recipe.

The bread is a tad heavy and moist, but for a nongluten bread it has rather good flavor and crumb, especially when toasted.

1¾ cups buttermilk
1 teaspoon vinegar
4 egg whites
2 cups brown or white rice flour
1¼ cups tapioca flour
1½ teaspoons dark brown sugar
3½ teaspoons xanthum gum
½ to 1½ teaspoons salt to taste
4½ teaspoons active dry yeast

Place the buttermilk, vinegar, and egg whites in the baking pan of your bread machine. Add the rice and tapioca flours, followed by the brown sugar, xanthum gum, salt, and yeast. The order in which these ingredients are placed in the pan should be reversed if the directions for the bread machine you have specify that the dry ingredients are to be placed in the pan first, the liquids last.

Use your machine's rapid-bake setting in making this loaf. For the first five minutes or so of the mixing cycle, scrape down the sides of the baking pan with a rubber spatula to make sure the rather soft dough blends properly.

No-Fat Bread

There are many recipes for breads low in fat or at least in cholesterol. This one is altogether fat free except for what little is found in the flour and oatmeal, where it is almost an afterthought to the list of nutrients.

Fats add flavor and tenderness to bread. But flavor can be supplied by herbs or spices, and toughness is not a serious problem in fat-free loaves unless you insist on cakelike softness.

Fats also keep bread from going stale prematurely, and therein lies the real problem with most fat-free adaptations. By the time they've made their way from the baker to the store to your home, they're fit only for stuffing.

A bread machine solves this problem nicely, because you can have a loaf of bread fresh from the oven every day if you like. So for those on a fat-restricted diet, here's a tasty loaf with next to none of the forbidden ingredient. Toss everything needed for it into your bread machine before you go to bed, set the timer, and dream of the fragrant awakening you'll have.

SMALL

1 cup water

1 tablespoon unsulphured molasses

2 cups unbleached all-purpose flour

1/2 cup uncooked oatmeal

1/2 teaspoon dried basil

1/2 teaspoon dried sage

1/2 teaspoon garlic powder

1/2 to 1 1/2 teaspoons salt to taste

1 1/2 teaspoons active dry yeast

LARGE

1 1/2 cups water

2 tablespoons unsulphured molasses

3 cups unbleached all-purpose flour

3/4 cup uncooked oatmeal

3/4 teaspoon dried basil

3/4 teaspoon dried sage

3/4 teaspoon garlic powder

1 to 2 teaspoons salt to taste

2 teaspoons active dry yeast

Pour the water into your bread machine baking pan and add the molasses, flour, and oatmeal. Measure in the basil, sage, garlic, salt, and yeast, reserving the leavening for its own separate dispenser if your machine has one. If, on the other hand, the instructions that came with the model you have call for starting with the yeast, remember to reverse the order in which you add the liquid and the dry ingredients.

Your machine's rapid-bake cycle is the one to use for this bread.

Low-Lactose Milk Bread

Milk bread, that rich yellow European bakery fare so delectable for breakfast, is not exactly high on the list of acceptable foods for anyone with lactose intolerance. Here, however, is a tasty low-lactose version of the bread, using reduced-lactose milk found under the name Lactaid in the dairy cases of many supermarkets as well as in health-food stores. It's so good no one would suspect it of being a special-diet loaf.

SMALL	LARGE
½ *cup Lactaid*	¾ *cup Lactaid*
2 egg yolks	*3 egg yolks*
½ *teaspoon vanilla extract*	*1 teaspoon vanilla extract*
1½ cups unbleached all-purpose flour	*2 cups unbleached all-purpose flour*
2 teaspoons dark brown sugar	*1 tablespoon dark brown sugar*
½ *to 1½ teaspoons salt to taste*	*1 to 2 teaspoons salt to taste*
1½ teaspoons active dry yeast	*1½ teaspoons active dry yeast*

If the instructions accompanying your bread machine specify placing the yeast in the bottom of your baking pan, you will need to reverse the order in which the liquid and the dry ingredients are incorporated into the batter. Otherwise, pour the Lactaid into your bread machine pan and add the egg yolks and vanilla extract, followed by the flour, brown sugar, salt, and yeast. If you have a machine with its own dispenser for leavening, add the yeast there.

Use your machine's quick cycle to bake the loaf.

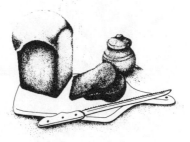

Low-Lactose Whole-Wheat Bread

This is a fine, smooth-textured loaf typical of the milk-based breads, but it uses lactose-reduced low-fat milk instead. The combination of the whole-grain proteins with those of dairy products creates food proteins more complete than those of the grains used separately and more similar to those found in meat and fish. So this is the perfect loaf for the lactose-intolerant seeking to maintain a balanced diet while reducing their intake of animal proteins.

SMALL

1 cup Lactaid

1 tablespoon canola oil

1 tablespoon unsulphured molasses

2 cups whole-wheat flour

½ cup unbleached all-purpose flour

½ to 1½ teaspoons salt to taste

1½ teaspoons active dry yeast

LARGE

1½ cups Lactaid

2 tablespoons canola oil

2 tablespoons unsulphured molasses

3 cups whole-wheat flour

1 cup unbleached all-purpose flour

1 to 2 teaspoons salt to taste

2 teaspoons active dry yeast

Pour the Lactaid into your bread machine baking pan and add the canola oil and molasses, unless the directions that came with your machine specify that the yeast is to be placed in the pan first, followed by the other dry ingredients and then the liquids. Measure in the whole-wheat and all-purpose flours and the salt. If your machine has a separate dispenser for leavening, spoon the yeast in there; if not, scatter it over the rest of the dry ingredients.

This loaf should be baked on your machine's quick cycle.

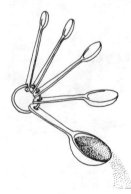

16 · Topping It All Off

NO ONE EVER CLAIMED that the aesthetics of baking with a bread machine beats, or even equals, that of creating the variegated traditional loaves adorning *boulangerie* windows and the pages of artful bakery books. Realistically, the puff-topped cubes or oblongs or cylinders with the grooves along their sides that emerge from the electronic oven are the ugly ducklings of the bread basket. Then again, look at what happened to that creature.

The fact is, these loaves are so tasty they're never around long enough for anyone to spend time contemplating their aesthetic shortcomings. Still, there are occasions when you want to share a loaf with neighbors or company and a bit of festive decoration is in order. Those are the times to put together a quick glaze.

The quintessence of a bread is revealed in its crust. The color and texture and aroma of that crown tell the tale of the whole loaf, and the flavor is at its fullest there.

Glazing in bread making evolved to highlight that crust; and garnishes, to announce the loaves' contents. Witness the tradition of rolled oats on oatmeal bread and, more obliquely, the poppy seeds that came to be the distinctive signature of an egg loaf. Accented bread may be visually more important in bread machine baking, which produces loaves quite often similar in shape and size and color, than it is in traditional baking, where the dough can be shaped in quite distinctive ways.

In conventional baking, a glaze is brushed over a loaf of bread either just before it's popped into the oven to bake or just after it's pulled from the rack, still warm and mellow. In the case of the bread machine bakery, only the latter option is available. Still, most glazes work splendidly on loaves fresh from these compact electronic ovens, and they do add that visual finishing touch that somehow, even though it's not crucial, makes the bread taste even better.

Glazes are matters of personal preference. I wouldn't use a molasses glaze or put rolled oats on an egg bread. Let me amend that: I wouldn't put rolled oats on an egg bread, and I've never used a molasses glaze on it, either. But, come to think of it, a nice mahogany molasses glaze might go rather well with an egg bread. Maybe I'll give it a try.

Where the boundary between glazes and frostings lies I've never been sure. Powdered sugar mixed with water or warm milk and drizzled over a Danish ring as an underlay for extra nuts really seems to me to be a frosting, yet is considered a glaze. Then again, a Danish coffee cake, the "cake" in its name notwithstanding, is actually a very rich bread, not a cake. So maybe the dividing line between glaze and frosting has more to do with the one between bread and cake than with anything else.

Semantics aside, in today's innovative world of breads anything goes — well, almost anything. I'd still have to think about rolled oats some before I tried them on that egg bread. But experiment to see what works for you.

Basic Egg Glaze

The most basic of all glazes is the egg glaze. Small seeds adhere to it well and accent the crown of a loaf. Flakes of the grains used in a bread are another option, oftentimes giving a signature, so to speak, to the loaf. Oats flecking the crust of an oatmeal bread or barley flakes on the crown of a barley loaf herald the contents of the bread beneath.

> *1 egg*
> *1 tablespoon water or milk, whole or*
> *skim*
> *small seeds for garnish — caraway,*
> *mustard, poppy, sesame — or grain*
> *flakes such as oats or rye*

Break the egg into a small bowl and whip in the water or milk. Then when you take a loaf of bread hot from your electronic oven, close the lid of the machine to keep the interior warm and, using a pastry brush, paint the crown of the hot loaf with this glazing mixture. In the case of a bread that promises to be difficult to shake loose from the pan, knock the loaf out, then slip it right back into the container before proceeding with your glazing.

Sprinkle plenty of the small seeds or flakes you've chosen over the glaze and return the pan to the bread machine to bake the glaze on. In 2 or 3 minutes it will have turned to a pretty gloss dotted with the little seeds.

Salt Wash

Used primarily on a crusty white bread, and normally brushed onto a loaf before baking, a simple salt wash adds a little extra savor even when applied to a finished loaf.

> *¼ cup hot water*
> *1 teaspoon salt*

Dissolve the salt in the water and brush this briny wash over your bread as it comes hot from the oven. Then put the loaf back into the warm bread machine for a few minutes to dry the glaze.

Crunchy Salt Glaze

This one's for pretzel lovers and other salt enthusiasts to add to the darker multigrain breads.

> 1 egg
> 1 1/2 teaspoons honey diluted with 1 1/2
>   teaspoons warm water
> 1 tablespoon coarse sea or kosher salt

Beat the egg and diluted honey together in a bowl. As soon as you take your bread from the bread machine, close the lid of the machine to keep the oven warm. Knock the bread from its pan to make sure it will slide out easily after glazing, then put it right back into the pan.

Stir the salt into the egg and diluted honey and, working quickly, brush this mixture over the top of the loaf. You'll need a reasonably stiff pastry brush to lift the salt crystals out of the bowl along with the egg mix.

Pop the pan back into the still-warm baking machine for 2 to 3 minutes to allow the residual oven heat to bake the glaze on. When you remove the bread the second time, you'll have a sparkling loaf that looks as if it's covered with tiny diamonds.

Molasses Glaze

Molasses adds a dark sheen to hearty ryes, pumpernickels, and raisin breads. Use it with restraint, however, lest it remain too sticky.

> 1 tablespoon unsulphured molasses
> 1 tablespoon hot water
> dehydrated onion flakes or small seeds
>   for garnish (optional)

Stir the molasses and water together briskly and spread liberally over the top of your bread with a soft brush as soon as the loaf is removed from your electronic oven. In the case of a solid loaf such as a country rye or pumpernickel, knock the loaf out of its pan first to ensure that it won't give you trouble later, then return it to the container before applying the glaze.

Sprinkle dehydrated onion flakes or some other attractive garnish such as black sesame seeds or flaxseed over the molasses if you'd like. Then return the loaf to the still-warm bread machine briefly to firm the gloss on.

Oil Wash

O il washes are used predominantly on herb and savory breads to give them a soft luster. Fresh, bright herbs, finely minced and sprinkled over them, add a finishing sparkle to most loaves in either category.

> *1 egg*
> *1½ to 2 teaspoons olive oil*
> *fresh herbs, chopped fine (optional)*

Break the egg into a small bowl and whip till frothy. Add slowly, beating lightly between additions, enough olive oil to make a smooth blend. Brush this mix over your bread while it's still hot from the oven and, if desired, sprinkle herbs over it to garnish the loaf. Return the bread, in its pan, to the hot bread machine briefly to set the glaze.

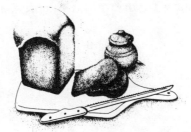

Confectioners' Sugar Glaze

More than an everyday glaze, less than a frosting, a powdered sugar gloss adds a delicate confectionery touch to a loaf of bread. Sweet glazes are usually reserved for coffee breads and cakes, but they occasionally grace a plain milk bread intended for a festive brunch.

> *1 cup confectioners' sugar*
> *2 to 3 tablespoons water or warm milk,*
> *whole or skim*

Sift the powdered sugar into a small bowl and add the liquid a few drops at a time, beating until smooth and dribbly. Drizzle over warm bread just out of its baking pan. Spiral and crisscross patterns are becoming.

Flavored Sugar Glazes

A sugar glaze is capable of almost infinite variation. Substitute a few drops of vanilla or almond extract for part of the milk or water in the preceding basic confectioners' sugar glaze, or dispense with the suggested liquids altogether and use coffee or rum or brandy instead if one of those flavorings would suit the bread and your taste. Replace a couple of spoonfuls of the powdered sugar with cocoa if appropriate, or add a dash of cinnamon or nutmeg or some other spice if it would bring out the flavor of the loaf. Just don't let your glaze overpower the bread it's meant to merely accent.

A Sugar Dusting

A dusting of powdered sugar is technically not, by itself, a glaze. But if you keep a shaker can of confectioners' sugar within easy reach of your bread machine, it takes only a second to turn a scrumptious almond loaf or a delectable banana bread into a visual delight as well. A feathery dusting of pure white sugar, maybe even shaken through a lace doily for an intricate pattern against the background of a golden crust, has almost irresistible appeal.

Apricot Jam Glaze

Wonderful with milk breads, this glaze is also the natural signature for an apricot loaf. It complements many of the nut breads nicely as well.

⅓ cup apricot jam
1 teaspoon water
1 teaspoon lemon juice

In a small pan, stir the apricot jam, water, and lemon juice together and heat. Once the mixture is hot, brush it onto the top and the upper half of the sides of a loaf of sweet bread removed from its pan but still warm from the electronic oven. Don't brush the sticky glaze all the way down to the bottom of the loaf, or you'll have nothing to hang on to when slicing the bread.

Honey Glaze

Here's a sweet glaze that goes well with chocolate and fruit breads. Triple the recipe, and you can use the leftovers as a spread. When slicing a glazed bread, one never gets enough of the topping.

1 tablespoon honey
1 tablespoon lemon juice
1 tablespoon triple sec

Spoon the honey, lemon juice, and triple sec into a small pan and stir over low heat until warm. Brush the glaze over the top and partway down the sides of your loaf of bread as soon as you've taken it from its pan.

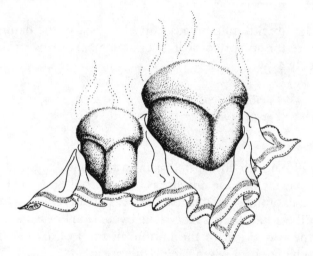

17 · Shaped Breads — The Designer Touch

ON THE WHOLE, I expect the bread machine to do it all — mix the ingredients for a good loaf of bread, monitor the rising, punch the dough down, monitor the second rise, bake the loaf, and buzz to let me know it's done. This last step is really superfluous, though, since the aroma of freshly baked bread wafting through the house usually has me hanging around the kitchen checking the machine's timer to see how long it has to go.

Some breads simply can't be wedged into this routine, however. The machine will mix the dough for, say, a Swedish cardamom bread, traditionally presented as a long golden braid, and in due course produce a utilitarian-looking but equally tasty loaf, needing at most the addition of a glaze and a sprinkling of pearl sugar. There's no way to pull off the same switcheroo with a folded-over, crisp-edged stromboli or with something like Philadelphia sticky buns, inseparable from the syrupy goo in which they traditionally nestle. Here the form is as much a part of the treat as the flavor is. So, in the recipes that follow, you'll need to add the finishing touches by hand — not much work, considering the glorious results.

Double Garlic Twists

These crisp bread sticks are wonderful with hearty winter soups redolent of rich, mellow vegetables. They also make fine pre-prandial appetizers, and as late-night video snacks they're well nigh irresistible.

The thinner the twists, the crisper they will be. Leave a little extra space in the top loops of them, and they'll double as Christmas tree ornaments, adding a whimsical homemade touch that will help to counterbalance all those holiday sweets. Kids tend to nibble on garlic twists as readily as they do candy canes.

¾ cup water
2½ cups unbleached all-purpose flour
1 cup grated sharp cheddar cheese
2 cloves fresh garlic, pressed
1 tablespoon sugar
½ teaspoon salt
2 teaspoons active dry yeast

G L A Z E

⅓ cup unsalted butter
½ cup grated Parmesan cheese
2 cloves fresh garlic, pressed

Pour the water into the baking pan of your bread machine, unless the instructions for the particular model you have specify that the leavening is to be placed in the pan first and the liquids last. Add the flour, cheddar cheese, garlic, sugar, and salt. Distribute the yeast according to the instructions for your machine. Select the dough cycle and let the machine do its job.

When the dough is ready to be worked, place it on a baking board and roll it into a log, pressing the dough gently beneath your palms. Slice the log into 16 more or less equal pieces. One at a time, roll these pieces into even, slender ropes about 14 to 16 inches long. They should be a little thicker than a pencil.

Lift the ends of each dough rope, bring them together, and cross them, forming a small loop at the top of the folded rope. Continue to twist the ropes together four or five times, being careful not to pull them lest the soft dough stretch, leaving you with large "feet" at the ends. Place the twists on greased cookie sheets.

For the glaze, melt the butter in a small saucepan set over low heat. Add the Parmesan cheese and garlic and mix well.

Brush the twists liberally with the glaze. Place the cookie sheets in a cold oven, turn it to 400 degrees F., and bake the twists for 25 to 30 minutes, the time depending primarily on how crisp you like your bread sticks. Everyone in our family prefers them on the dark side, when the bit of extra time in the oven has intensified their flavor and crunchiness.

Mini Caraway Salt Loaves

This is great company bread. Served straight from the oven, crusts crisp, centers soft, fragrant with caraway, the little individual loaves turn any meal into something special.

The pungent aromatic seeds accenting these loaves are especially popular in northern and eastern Europe, where they are used to flavor everything from classic rye breads to goulash. Sugar coated, the seeds are even used as digestive comfits, something I've pointed out to the children as persuasively as I could, all to no avail. Our kids are still less than fond of caraway, and in this they're not alone. Caraway is one of those love-it-or-leave-it seasonings. I find these small loaves somehow lacking without caraway seeds, but others much prefer them "naked." You may want to make half the batch with caraway and half without. That way you can please almost everybody.

The farina in the bread, incidentally, remains essentially uncooked, adding a crunchy roughage and texture to the loaves. The paprika adds more rosy hue than sharp flavor.

¾ cup water
2 tablespoons olive oil
2¼ cups unbleached all-purpose flour
¼ cup uncooked farina
1 tablespoon sugar
2 teaspoons paprika
¼ teaspoon salt
2 teaspoons active dry yeast

G L A Z E

1 egg
1 tablespoon cold water
caraway seeds to taste
coarse sea or kosher salt to taste

If the directions for your bread machine instruct you to place the yeast in the very bottom of the pan, you will need to reverse the order in which you incorporate the liquids and the dry ingredients. Otherwise pour the water and olive oil into your machine's baking pan and add the flour, farina, sugar, paprika, salt, and yeast, reserving the leavening for its own separate dispenser if your machine has one. Set the machine on dough cycle.

You'll find the dough that emerges when the machine beeps its readiness a very springy, resilient one. Roll it out to a log the length of your rolling pin. The log will contract once you stop rolling, but don't worry. At this preliminary stage, all you want to be able to do is to cut the dough into 8 equal pieces.

Next roll each of these 8 pieces into smaller logs 6 to 8 inches long. Flatten the individual logs to a little less than half their original thickness and place them on an ungreased cookie sheet. The flattening will provide more surface area for your glaze mixture and the caraway and salt. The mini-loaves will round up again nicely as they rise.

For the glaze, beat the egg well in a small bowl, add the cold water, and beat well again. Brush each loaf generously with the egg and water mixture, then sprinkle on the caraway seeds and salt. Don't be stingy. While we normally cook with little salt, this bread, like pretzels, really calls for that commodity, almost by definition. As to the caraway, well, I've stated my opinion on that subject.

Place the sheet of mini-loaves in a cold oven, set the thermostat to 350 degrees F., and bake the breads for 30 to 35 minutes. Serve hot from the oven.

One way of presenting these rolls that never fails to please, by the way, is to wrap them in individual napkins as part of each place setting. Not only does this keep each mini-loaf warm and toasty, but everyone has a most satisfying surprise on unrolling his or her napkin.

Stromboli

Stromboli is a Rhode Island sort of thing not found anywhere else, as far as I know. For that matter, to my knowledge the only places in Rhode Island that serve this one-dish meal are the original Stromboli's pizza restaurant and a couple of offshoots of that establishment whose owners at one time or another worked at Stromboli's. That said, the dish is not what one would call exotic, just very, very tasty.

Essentially, a stromboli is a giant calzone designed by a Greek pizza chef who decided to stuff it with everything in and around the kitchen sink. For us it's a bit of a refrigerator cleaner, the stuffing consisting of various meats, cheeses, and condiments tucked away in odd corners of the fridge.

Only two rules govern the stuffing of stromboli. One is that it must include some spicy sausage like chorizo, linguica, or pepperoni. The second is that it requires a zippy cheese such as the currently trendy Pecorino Romano or Parmigiano Reggiano. We often use Asiago, a family favorite in perennial residence in the refrigerator.

The filling ingredients listed below are those I happened to use for the last stromboli I made. They're fairly typical, though. The quantities are approximate. One hasn't always, for instance, an exact half a pound of each kind of meat stashed away in the refrigerator. The pickle slices are included because a jar of them had been sitting on the rather full bottom shelf since a summer picnic, threatening a number of times to fall off. There would have been 5 slices, but I ate 2 while putting them on the stromboli. There was no lettuce in the icebox. The traditional stromboli has shredded lettuce on top of all the other ingredients. No one in our family is particularly fond of wilted lettuce, so I simply left it out.

The list of ingredients for the stuffing starts with the bottom layer and progresses to the top, in the order in which you'd normally place the items on the shell of dough.

1 cup water
¼ cup olive oil
3 cups unbleached all-purpose flour
1 teaspoon salt
2½ teaspoons active dry yeast

F I L L I N G

½ pound cooked ham, thinly sliced
½ pound cooked pot roast, thinly sliced
½ pound salami, sliced
6 linguica sausages, sliced in half the long way
1 cup shredded Fontina cheese
½ cup grated Parmigiano Reggiano cheese
½ cup grated Asiago cheese
½ pound portobello mushrooms, sliced and sautéed in butter
12 pitted black olives, halved
3 slices bread-and-butter pickle (optional)
shredded lettuce (optional)

G L A Z E

1 egg
1 tablespoon cold water

Pour the water and olive oil into the baking pan of your bread machine and add the flour and salt. Follow the directions that came with the particular model you have for incorporating the yeast, and set the machine on dough cycle.

At the beep, dump the dough out onto a lightly floured board. It will be a little sticky at first. Flatten the ball, then stretch it into a small circle. Finally, with a rolling pin, shape it into a larger circle 14 to 16 inches in diameter.

Transfer the circle to an ungreased baking sheet and let the dough rest for 10 to 15 minutes while you raid the refrigerator.

The filling for stromboli, as opposed to its cousins pizza and focaccia, is piled on only one half of the rolled-out dough. If you're following my recipe, lay out the ham slices, then the pot roast, salami, and linguica, leaving a rim of dough clear around the outer edge of the semicircle. Scatter the Fontina on top of the meat, followed by the Parmigiano Reggiano and Asiago. Pat the mushrooms into place and add the olives and pickles, along with any other tidbits you might have found in your refrigerator that seem appropriate, including lettuce if you'd like.

Brush the outer rim of the dough circle with cold water. Then fold the bare half of the dough over the filling and crimp the edges of the stuffed circle, now a semicircle, to seal the package. Using a small sharp knife, make 4 or 5 slits, each about 3 inches long, in the top of the sealed crust to allow steam to escape while the stromboli is baking.

For the glaze, beat the egg well in a small bowl, add the cold water, and beat again. Coat the entire top of the stromboli with the beaten egg mixture, using a small pastry brush.

Place the stromboli in a cold oven. Set the temperature to 400 degrees F. and bake for 20 to 30 minutes or until golden brown.

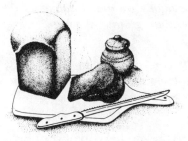

Cinnamon Buns

A ustria has its strudel, Sweden its Shrove Tuesday buns, France croissants, and America cinnamon buns. Although the key ingredient here, cinnamon, is not even produced in the United States, it's probably the most popular sweet spice in the country.

Quality counts when it comes to cinnamon. Lately a number of companies have brought out discount lines of bulk spices, and there really is a difference among cinnamons. Select with care and a discerning nose. The nutmeg in these rolls adds just the little extra twist of fragrance and flavor that makes them special.

> ¾ cup milk, whole or skim
> ¼ cup unsalted butter
> 2½ cups unbleached all-purpose flour
> ⅓ cup sugar
> ½ teaspoon salt
> 2 teaspoons active dry yeast
>
> FILLING
>
> ½ cup firmly packed dark brown sugar
> 3 teaspoons ground cinnamon
> 1 teaspoon ground nutmeg
>
> GLAZE
>
> 1 cup confectioners' sugar
> 2 tablespoons milk, whole or skim
> ½ teaspoon vanilla extract

Pour the milk into the mixing pan of your bread machine and add the butter, cutting it into small chunks if it's not soft, as otherwise, since you're using a relatively large amount, it may not blend altogether evenly into the dough. Next measure in the flour, sugar, and salt. Position the yeast according to the directions given for your machine, unless you have a model with its own dispenser for leavening, in which case the yeast should be measured into the dispenser the very last thing. Set the machine on its dough cycle.

When the machine beeps to let you know it's completed its work, set out an ovenproof glass or stainless steel pan measuring 9 by 9 by 2 inches and grease it well.

Transfer the dough from its bread machine pan to a baking board and roll it out into a 10-inch square.

For the filling, sprinkle the brown sugar all over the dough square, making sure to spoon some out to the edges. Then dust the cinnamon and nutmeg evenly over the brown sugar.

Roll the dough up tightly into a log. Some brown sugar is bound to spill out at the ends of the roll, but no matter. Simply save this extra sugar for the next step.

Slice the rolled log into 9 equal sections. Place these sections in the greased pan sliced side up, arranging them in rows of 3. The two end pieces of the log always seem to have a little less sugar and cinnamon mix left inside, so put them in the pan end up and sprinkle the reserved extra sugar over them.

Place the pan of rolls in a cold oven and set the thermostat to 375 degrees F. Bake the buns for 35 to 45 minutes, depending on how brown you like your cinnamon rolls.

When removed from the oven, the buns will be baked together into a single loaf. They'll stay fresher that way, so simply remove the loaf as a unit from the pan and place it crust side up on a wire rack to cool.

Meanwhile, prepare the glaze for the buns by beating together the powdered sugar, milk, and vanilla. Dribble this mixture over the buns while they are still quite warm so it will form a smooth, icinglike glaze.

Sticky Buns

They do things their own way in Philadelphia, as they've done since the signing of the Declaration of Independence. Take sticky buns, for instance. In no other city are the sticky buns so sticky as they are in Philadelphia, where they're the bakery equivalent of a finger-licking Southern barbecue. For all of Philadelphian propriety, there's simply no way to eat these buns without a great deal of finger licking. The secret of the true Philly sticky bun, simplistic though it may sound, is boiling water.

3/4 cup milk, whole or skim
2 medium eggs
2 tablespoons unsalted butter
3 cups unbleached all-purpose flour
1 tablespoon sugar
1 teaspoon salt
2 1/2 teaspoons active dry yeast

FILLING

2 tablespoons unsalted butter
3/4 cup sugar
2 teaspoons ground cinnamon
1/2 cup raisins

GLAZE

1/4 cup unsalted butter
1 1/2 cups firmly packed dark brown sugar
1/2 cup water

Pour the milk into the baking pan of your bread machine and add the eggs and butter, unless the instructions for your machine specify that the yeast is to be placed in the bottom of the pan, followed by first the dry and then the liquid ingredients. Measure in the flour, sugar, and salt. Add the yeast according to the directions for your particular machine. Let the bread machine do its thing on the dough cycle.

Roll the finished dough into a rectangle about 18 by 14 inches. The dough is very springy and will pull back as you roll it out. Let it rest a minute or two between rollings, so the dough relaxes, and you'll be able to stretch it out again.

Give it a final rest while you butter the sides of a 9-by-13-inch ovenproof glass or stainless steel baking pan. In this instance I definitely prefer glass, because it allows the buns to be lifted more easily when the time comes to add water to the pan. In any case, there's no need to grease the bottom of the dish, as you'll soon see.

Roll the dough out one last time, and it should hold its 18-by-14-inch shape.

To prepare the filling, melt the butter and brush it evenly over the dough. Sprinkle the sugar over the butter, spreading it out to the edges of the rectangle and patting down any lumps with the back of a spoon. Add the cinnamon in the same fashion, then scatter the raisins over the rest of the filling.

Roll the dough up lengthwise and slice the roll into 12 pieces.

Melt the butter for the glaze and pour it into your baking pan, swirling it around to coat the bottom. Spread the brown sugar over the butter, then place the rolls on top of the sugar cut side up, arranging them in 4 rows of 3 and pressing them down gently to flatten them a bit.

Place the pan in a cold oven, let sit for 15 minutes, then turn the oven to 400 degrees F. and bake the buns for 25 minutes.

Boil the water in a small pan and transfer it to a warmed measuring cup or a pitcher with a spout for easier pouring. Remove the buns from the oven and, using a wide spatula, lift them gently at one end of the pan just enough to allow you to pour half the boiling water into the pan. An oven mitt is helpful here, as the water will steam. Tip the pan a little to let the water run toward the center, then turn the pan and repeat the process at the other end.

Cover the pan loosely with a sheet of tinfoil and bake the buns for 10 more minutes.

When you take the pan from the oven, rest the buns for 5 minutes or so to allow the caramelized sugar at the bottom of the pan to thicken a little. Then invert the buns on a wire rack set over a shallow boat of aluminum foil to catch the extra syrup. Spoon this over the buns and let them cool just enough to prevent burned tongues. Do eat these sticky buns warm, however, for the greatest of gooey delights imaginable.

18 · Twice-Baked Cookies

OVEN-DRIED, OR TWICE-BAKED, rusks and cookies have a long culinary history in Europe. From the *biscotti* of Italy to the zwieback of Germany and the *skorpor* of Sweden, these traditional homely nibbles — many of them quite nutritious and low in fat for all their engaging flavor — are made from breads cut into oblong bars that are then baked a second time in a slow oven.

Melba toast, or twice-baked bread, is a practical end for your loaves. It's a noble foil for pâtés, and it suits dips well, making a flavorsome low-salt substitute for chips. Cut some firm day-old bread into slices about ¼ of an inch thick. Don't limit yourself to white. Experiment. Place the slices on an ungreased cookie sheet and bake them in an oven preheated to 325 degrees F. until they are crisp and golden. They're best served fresh — if you'll pardon my use of that term in connection with stale bread — hot from the oven.

Take the same bread and slice it a little thicker, maybe in pieces ½ to ¾ of an inch across, then cross-cut these slices into cubes. Sauté them in a mix of half butter and half olive oil until they are crisp and just one step past golden brown. Drain them on paper towels, and you have croutons, not the cardboard kind found in salad bars, but real ones, crunchy islands of flavor with which to garnish green pea and other creamy soups.

Or, while the croutons are sautéing, toss in some freshly pressed garlic. Then, at the last minute, as you pull the pan from the fire, sprinkle the cubes with Parmesan cheese, a little extra melted butter, and some finely minced parsley. These croutons are matchless for adding crunch and contrast to a salad. Try making them from pumpernickel or rye bread.

To add a little moisture and a touch of naughtiness to what is otherwise rather dry fare, *biscotti* are sometimes dipped in chocolate after the second baking. They've also been known to be dipped in a glass of the sweet Tuscan wine *vin santo*. Zwieback and *skorpor* are frequently softened by being dunked in the coffee, tea, or cocoa with which they are so often served.

Dunking isn't very proper, my mother was wont to point out. But she would indulge in it when having a little bite on her own, and, personally, I find dunking a good bread in a flavorsome beverage one of the true pleasures of life, marred only, on occasion, by a piece of the baked goods dropping off and splashing into the cup, with the inevitable result of a spotted shirt. Well, no one said dunking was neat. Perhaps that's why it tends to be a solitary endeavor. In any event, whether accompanied by an appropriate beverage or dunked in it, twice-baked cookies are a pleasure to nibble on.

Plain Rusks

Summer is a special time in the part of Sweden where I spent my childhood, the sunlit days seeming to last forever, the twilight lingering till nearly midnight. Some of my fondest memories of that time are of sitting on a large rock in the woods not far from our house on those sunny afternoons and white nights drinking *saft*, the Swedish drink of diluted fruit syrup, and eating *skorpor*, or simple rusks.

Susan's comment on first tasting these rusks was "Bland, aren't they! I can see why you'd be led to dunk them in something."

So, in the spirit of compromise, when I bake bread for rusks I now cut about 1 inch off the top and bottom of the loaf, sandwich a layer of sliced bananas between these two extremities, and cover the resulting flat cake with a melba sauce for a dessert everyone in the family likes. Then, from the center, I make plain rusks for myself.

SMALL
3/4 cup milk, whole or skim
2 tablespoons unsalted butter
1 tablespoon solid vegetable
shortening
2 cups unbleached all-purpose
flour
1/4 cup sugar
1/4 to 1 teaspoon salt to taste
1 1/2 teaspoons active dry yeast

LARGE
1 1/4 cups milk, whole or skim
3 tablespoons unsalted butter
2 tablespoons solid vegetable
shortening
3 1/2 cups unbleached all-purpose
flour
1/3 cup sugar
1/2 to 1 1/2 teaspoons salt to taste
2 teaspoons active dry yeast

Pour the milk into your bread machine baking pan and add the butter, shortening, flour, sugar, salt, and yeast, following the directions that came with your particular machine for incorporating the leavening, since some machines specify reversing the order in which the ingredients are placed in the pan.

Bake the loaf on your machine's quick cycle.

To make the rusks, cut the cooled loaf into slices approximately 3/4 to 1 inch thick. Cut these slices in turn into bars 1 or 1 1/4 inches wide. Precision doesn't really count here. In fact, the rustic look of unevenly sized pieces is a plus, adding a certain homeyness.

Place the bars on an ungreased cookie sheet and dry them in your regular oven at 350 degrees F. for 10 to 15 minutes or until golden brown, turning them once halfway through the baking time for more even toasting. Cool the rusks thoroughly on racks and store them tightly covered — if there are any left after you've sampled them.

Silver Birch Biscotti

Dipping Chocolate

Hippie remnants of the sixties are scattered throughout our contemporary culture, from Doonesbury to the revival fashions of retro rock radio. Coffeehouses reminiscent of the beatnik era — my own, I object when the kids mistakenly put me in the Woodstock set — are mushrooming across the country. So finding recently in rural eastern Connecticut what in earlier years would have passed for a flower-power coffee-shop-cum-bakery came as no surprise to me, although its clientele, ranging from high-schoolers to senior citizens in their sixties and seventies, seemed oblivious to any Haight-Ashbury connection.

But times, and pastries, change. Eclairs have gone the way of the Devil Dog, displaced by the likes of *biscotti*, although they're often dipped in chocolate. The fare at the Silver Birch Bakery, as close to a Bleecker Street coffeehouse as I could find in our area at the time, was no exception.

The California adaptation of Italian *biscotti*, on which this recipe is based, calls for pine nuts, but Carolyn Berke, proprietress of the Silver Birch Bakery, modified the recipe to bring back the more traditional European walnut. In adapting the recipe for bread machines, I added millet flour, to improve the texture, and yeast, because baking powder alone would not leaven the dough sufficiently.

SMALL	LARGE
½ cup orange juice	¾ cup orange juice
2 tablespoons unsalted butter	3 tablespoons unsalted butter
1 tablespoon solid vegetable shortening	2 tablespoons solid vegetable shortening
1 medium egg	2 medium eggs
¾ cup walnut halves	1 cup walnut halves
2 cups unbleached all-purpose flour	3 cups unbleached all-purpose flour
¼ cup millet flour	½ cup millet flour
⅓ cup sugar	½ cup sugar
½ teaspoon ground ginger	1 teaspoon ground ginger
¼ to 1 teaspoon salt, to taste	½ to 1½ teaspoons salt, to taste
1 teaspoon double-acting baking powder	2 teaspoons double-acting baking powder
1½ teaspoons active dry yeast	2 teaspoons active dry yeast

Pour the orange juice into the baking pan of your bread machine, add the butter and shortening, and break the egg or eggs, depending on the size of the loaf you are making, into the pan. Measure in the walnuts, all-purpose and millet flours, sugar, ginger, salt, baking powder, and yeast, placing the yeast in its own separate dispenser if your machine has one. The order in which these ingredients are placed in the pan should be reversed if the instructions for your bread machine specify that the dry ingredients are to be placed in the pan first, the liquids last. Bake on your machine's quick cycle.

To make the *biscotti,* cut the loaf when cool into slices approximately ¾ to 1 inch thick, then cut each slice into bars about 1 or 1¼ inches wide.

Place the bars on an ungreased cookie sheet and dry them for 10 to 15 minutes, turning them once halfway through the baking time, in an oven set to 350 degrees F. When they are lightly browned, remove them from the oven and transfer them to racks to cool.

For dipping the *biscotti,* if you're in a rush you can use one of the commercial chocolate dips, either brown or white, available in the baking section of most supermarkets. However, my own bias is very much toward making one's own chocolate dip. It really takes but a minute more, and the extra-rich chocolate flavor makes it well worthwhile.

DIPPING CHOCOLATE

*4 one-ounce squares semisweet baking
chocolate*
½ cup heavy cream

*contrasting chocolate for garnish, if
desired*

Melt the chocolate in the top of a double boiler, stirring constantly to prevent the cocoa butter from separating out, and blend in the cream. Remove from the heat.

Dip the *biscotti* into the chocolate mixture until a third or a half of each is covered. Stand them on edge to dry on a cooling rack or prop them at an angle against the rim of a platter with no chocolate touching the platter.

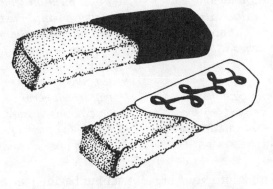

For an attractive finishing touch, once the dip has set on the *biscotti*, white chocolate can be drizzled over the dark, Jackson Pollock style. The first time I decided to try my hand at this bit of embellishment, I was temporarily stymied by the fact that, like most families, we have only one double boiler. I've tried to melt a small amount of chocolate in a regular pot. Let me tell you, it's tricky. Besides, one really needs only a couple of tablespoonfuls.

What I ended up doing was taking a small chunk of commercial white dipping chocolate and melting it in the microwave. Then with a toothpick I drizzled it in a crisscross pattern over the dark chocolate. The effect was fantastic.

Biscotti d'Anice

The Italian word *biscotti*, although now applied loosely to a broad range of cookies, means literally "twice cooked" and originally referred to those subtly and variously flavored rusks that so often accompany a hot drink or perhaps a glass of wine in their native country. Here's a recipe for the classic nut-crunchy version whose anise flavor, assuming you like that distinctive taste, goes so well with the milk-infused *caffellatte* served throughout Italy.

SMALL	LARGE
¾ cup milk, whole or skim	*1¼ cups milk, whole or skim*
zest of 1 medium lemon	*zest of 2 medium lemons*
½ teaspoon vanilla extract	*1 teaspoon vanilla extract*
½ cup blanched almonds, toasted	*¾ cup blanched almonds, toasted*
2 cups unbleached all-purpose flour	*3 cups unbleached all-purpose flour*
¼ cup sugar	*⅓ cup sugar*
2 tablespoons wheat germ	*¼ cup wheat germ*
4 teaspoons aniseed, crushed	*2 tablespoons aniseed, crushed*
¼ to 1 teaspoon salt, to taste	*½ to 1½ teaspoons salt, to taste*
1 teaspoon active dry yeast	*1½ teaspoons active dry yeast*

Pour the milk into your bread machine baking pan and add the lemon zest, vanilla extract, almonds, flour, sugar, wheat germ, aniseed, and salt. Place the yeast in its own dispenser if your machine has one; otherwise, scatter it over the rest of the ingredients in the pan. If it is to be placed in the bottom of the pan first thing instead, don't forget to reverse the order in which you add the liquid and the dry ingredients.

Bake the bread on your machine's quick cycle. Allow it to cool, then, for *biscotti*, cut it into slices roughly ¾ to 1 inch thick and cut these slices into bars about 1 to 1¼ inches wide.

Oven-dry the bars on an ungreased cookie sheet at 350 degrees F., turning them once, until they are an even, toasty brown, which will take 10 to 15 minutes. Make sure they are completely cool before storing, and keep them in a tightly covered tin or jar.

Rye Rusks

Called *kryddskorpor,* or spiced rusks, in Swedish, these dried cookies have no spices in them. They are, however, flavored with orange zest, and back in the days of my youth, which my children place somewhere between the invention of the wheel and the ascent of Bill Haley and his Comets, oranges were considered a rare and exotic spice, at least in the north country where I grew up.

To harvest this spice for the rusks, peel the zest from the orange with a sharp knife. Wide strips, like those you'd have after peeling an apple, are fine here. Just try to minimize the amount of white pith you peel off with the outer, orange part, even though a bit of it in the bread will add a touch of pleasant bitterness to the rusks. You'll notice the use of gluten flour in this recipe. It's there to help the rather heavy rye dough rise.

SMALL	LARGE
¾ cup milk, whole or skim	1¼ cups milk, whole or skim
2 tablespoons unsalted butter	3 tablespoons unsalted butter
1 tablespoon solid vegetable shortening	2 tablespoons solid vegetable shortening
1 tablespoon unsulphured molasses	2 tablespoons unsulphured molasses
zest of ½ medium orange	zest of 1 medium orange
1½ cups unbleached all-purpose flour	2¼ cups unbleached all-purpose flour
¾ cup rye flour	1 cup rye flour
¼ cup gluten flour	⅓ cup gluten flour
¼ cup sugar	⅓ cup sugar
¼ to 1 teaspoon salt, to taste	½ to 1½ teaspoons salt, to taste
1½ teaspoons active dry yeast	2 teaspoons active dry yeast

Measure the milk into the baking pan of your bread machine and add the butter, shortening, molasses, orange zest, and the all-purpose, rye, and gluten flours, followed by the sugar, salt, and, last, unless otherwise directed in the instructions for your particular machine, the yeast. If your machine features a separate dispenser for leavening, spoon the yeast in there.

Use your machine's quick cycle to bake the loaf.

For the Rye Rusks, allow the loaf to cool, then cut it first into slices about ¾ to 1 inch thick and then into bars 1 to 1¼ inches wide. You don't need to be precise about the measurements.

Place the bars on an ungreased cookie sheet and oven-dry them at 350 degrees F. for 10 to 15 minutes or until they are a rich brown, turning them once halfway through the baking time for more even toasting. Cool the rusks thoroughly before storing.

In an airtight container, I'm told, rusks will keep for a very long time. I wouldn't know. Somehow my tin is empty within days, if not hours, of being stocked.

Zwieback

Not surprisingly, the originally German word *Zwieback*, long since anglicized, is yet another term that translates literally as "twice baked." Traditional to the northern European countries, zwieback has long been a favored accompaniment to compotes and preserved fruits. The zwieback's rather bland flavor is a perfect foil for the sweet syrup of the fruit, and its dry crispness complements the soft texture of the fruit itself. Although the combination may strike some as a rather plain dessert by today's voluptuous standards, it is a remarkably refreshing one on a warm summer's eve.

In the United States, zwieback has come to be associated nearly inseparably with infants. The rusks do make good teething biscuits, and the commercial varieties almost invariably portray a smiling baby on the box. The fact is, however, that zwieback and preserved fruits are one of those simple, forgotten pleasures deserving of universal revival.

In place of regular white flour, for a loaf destined for the zwieback tin I like to use the new white whole-wheat flour developed at Kansas State University of Agriculture and Applied Science. Containing all the vitamins, minerals, and fiber of the whole-wheat kernel minus the faintly bitter accent of so many dark whole-wheat flours, it makes a "white bread" that, remarkably, is highly nutritious. The zwieback made from it is very light and open-textured.

If you don't have any white whole-wheat flour in the house, simply substitute regular unbleached all-purpose flour and reduce the yeast in the recipe by ½ teaspoon.

¾ *cup milk, whole or skim*	*1 cup milk, whole or skim*
2 tablespoons solid vegetable shortening or lard	*3 tablespoons solid vegetable shortening or lard*
2 tablespoons unsulphured molasses	*3 tablespoons unsulphured molasses*
1 medium egg	*1 medium egg*
2¼ cups white whole-wheat flour (or unbleached all-purpose flour)	*3¼ cups white whole-wheat flour (or unbleached all-purpose flour)*
½ teaspoon ground nutmeg	*1 teaspoon ground nutmeg*
¼ to 1 teaspoon salt, to taste	*½ to 1½ teaspoons salt, to taste*
1½ teaspoons active dry yeast (if using all-purpose flour, reduce to 1 teaspoon)	*2 teaspoons active dry yeast (if using all-purpose flour, reduce to 1½ teaspoons)*

Unless the instructions that came with your bread machine call for placing the yeast in the bottom of the pan, followed by the other dry ingredients and then the liquids, pour the milk into your baking pan and add the shortening or lard, molasses, egg, flour, nutmeg, salt, and yeast, reserving the leavening for its own dispenser if your machine has one.

Bake the bread on your machine's quick cycle.

To make Zwieback sticks, allow the loaf to cool, cut it into slices ¾ to 1 inch thick, then cut these slices into bars 1 to 1¼ inches wide.

Oven-dry the sticks on an ungreased cookie sheet at 350 degrees F., turning them once halfway through the baking time, until they are lightly toasted, which will take 10 to 15 minutes. Make sure they are completely cool before storing them in a tightly covered tin or jar.

Mandelbrot

In German the word *Mandel* means "almond," and *Brot* "bread." Yet I came across *Mandelbrot* in a village bakery outside of the German town of Oldenburg, not far from Denmark and the North Sea, that contained not a whit of almonds, but instead an abundance of hazelnuts. So what's in a name? These cookies are great, particularly when dipped in chocolate.

The dough is a sticky, heavy one. Check the inside of your bread machine baking pan 5 to 10 minutes into the first kneading cycle to make sure all the dough has been picked up by the mixing blade. If not, give it a little help by scraping down the sides of the pan with a rubber spatula.

Don't try to increase the ingredients to make a large loaf of this bread. The resulting dough would be more than the machine could deal with. Believe me, I know — I've tried it dozens of times.

> 6 ounces frozen orange juice concen-
>   trate
> 2 tablespoons unsalted butter
> 2 tablespoons grated lemon zest
> 3/4 cup chopped hazelnuts
> 2 cups unbleached all-purpose flour
> 1/3 cup semolina flour
> 1/4 cup sugar
> 1/4 teaspoon ground ginger
> 1/4 teaspoon ground cinnamon
> 1/4 to 1 teaspoon salt, to taste
> 2 teaspoons active dry yeast

Scoop the orange juice concentrate into your baking pan and add the butter, zest, hazelnuts, all-purpose and semolina flours, sugar, ginger, cinnamon, salt, and yeast, following the directions that came with your particular machine for incorporating the leavening, since some machines specify reversing the order in which the ingredients are placed in the pan and some models have a separate yeast dispenser.

Bake the loaf on your machine's quick cycle.

For *Mandelbrot* cookies, slice the cooled loaf into pieces about

¾ to 1 inch thick, then cut across the slices to make bars 1 to 1¼ inches wide.

Place the bars on an ungreased cookie sheet and oven-dry them at 350 degrees F. for 10 to 15 minutes or until lightly toasted, turning them once halfway through the baking time for even color. Cool them thoroughly on racks.

Dip some or all of them in chocolate if you'd like, following the instructions given with the recipes for Silver Birch *Biscotti* and Dipping Chocolate, pages 193–195.

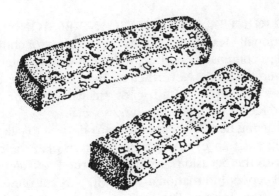

19 · Loaves for Tea and High Tea

 HIGH TEA, THE AMERICAN VERSION of which traditionally featured coffee as the beverage of choice, is making a comeback. Granted, we're not talking about a massive
social movement here. Nevertheless, more and more people are
gathering as a family or with friends, on weekends or holidays at
least, for coffee or tea and something special.

In the growing number of country inns dotting this land, teatime
has become such an event that guests often plan their arrival to
coincide with the occasion. According to the Professional Association of Innkeepers International, some 30 percent of member inns
now serve afternoon tea. For some, tea has replaced the cocktail
hour. Originally a ceremony for the British upper classes in need of
an event to fill the long afternoons, teatime today is a respite from
too few hours in which to do too much — a luxury of time, rest, and
renewal.

The bread machine helps to give you time for tea when you don't
have a butler and staff to provide it for you. The treats described on
these pages can be served straight from the electronic oven with a
simple accompaniment of sweet butter or a spread or fruit compote. For a company tea, take 10 minutes to make a fanciful pinwheel of a loaf fresh from your electronic oven sandwiched with
the spread or compote and serve it on your prettiest cake platter. It
will be an eye-catcher whose taste delights as well.

Sally Lunn

Sally Lunn is a familiar listing in the repertory of the home bakery. Butter-rich and golden from the egg yolks in it, this sweet bread is one that could easily slip unnoticed over the border into the realm of cakes.

Its name, like that of Anadama bread, has different legendary sources. It is often attributed to the French *soleil et lune,* or sun and moon, the association deriving presumably from the golden crust and white underside of the buns into which the dough was traditionally shaped. In another story, it is the namesake of an English villager who peddled her homemade cakes on the streets of Bath; a local baker was so taken with the buns that he began to bake them himself, but sold them as Sally Lunn's.

3/4 cup milk, whole or skim
2 eggs
6 tablespoons unsalted butter
2 cups unbleached all-purpose flour
1/4 cup sugar
1/4 to 1 teaspoon salt to taste
2 teaspoons active dry yeast

Pour the milk into your bread machine's baking pan and break the eggs into it, unless the instructions that came with your machine call for placing the yeast in the bottom of the pan and reserving the liquids till last, adding them after the dry ingredients. Since you're using a fair amount of butter, cut it into chunks if it's hard, so it will blend into the dough more uniformly, before adding it to the liquid ingredients. Then measure in the flour, sugar, salt, and yeast.

This attractive high loaf can be baked on your machine's quick cycle.

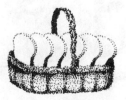

Mock Brioche

Classic brioche, with its fluted sides and little topknot and silky texture, is, like real French bread, found only rarely outside of France. Certainly a bread machine pan cannot create the distinctive flutes or the cocky topknot, nor does the kneading blade seem capable of producing the smooth grain of true brioche. I suspect that, for all its beating and crashing the dough about, a baking machine is no match for the experienced hands of a French pastry chef. All the same, the recipe given here results in a very handsome loaf, rich in butter and eggs, with a high, rounded dome.

> ¼ cup milk, whole or skim
> 3 eggs
> 10 tablespoons unsalted butter
> 2½ cups unbleached all-purpose flour
> 2 tablespoons sugar
> ½ to 1 teaspoon salt to taste
> 1½ teaspoons active dry yeast

Unless the instructions that came with your machine call for placing the yeast in your bread machine pan first and reversing the order in which the liquid and other dry ingredients are incorporated into the batter, pour the milk into your baking pan and break in the eggs. Since you are using a sizable quantity of butter, if it's not soft, cut it into chunks so it will blend more easily with the other ingredients, then add it to the pan. Measure in the flour, sugar, salt, and yeast, placing the leavening in its own receptacle if your machine has one.

Use a quick bake cycle for this bread.

Maple Oat Bread

To our good fortune, a neighbor, Chappie Rich, besides running an efficient dairy farm, graces country living for local residents and wayfarers alike with newly pressed cider from his mill, fresh fruits and vegetables, and, in early spring, rich maple syrup from his busy sugarhouse. He taps our sugar bush, as maple groves are known, and gives us gallons of beautiful syrup in return. Hence this somewhat extravagant recipe.

The loaf that results, retaining a lingering flavor of maple, is devoured with much delight by our children, who dieters would with some justification maintain add insult to injury by slathering it with maple butter! Substituting maple-flavored syrup for the real thing in the recipe not only works, but probably makes more sense if one isn't fortunate enough to have a sugar bush out back and someone nearby offering to tap it.

¾ cup water
½ cup maple or maple-flavored syrup
2 tablespoons unsalted butter or canola
  oil
2½ cups unbleached all-purpose flour
1 cup uncooked oatmeal (not instant)
¼ to 1 teaspoon salt to taste
1½ teaspoons active dry yeast

Pour the water and the maple syrup into the baking pan of your bread machine, add the butter or canola oil, then measure in the flour, oatmeal, salt, and yeast, unless directed by the instructions for your particular machine to place the yeast in the pan first, in which case the dry ingredients should be added before the liquids.

Set your machine to its full cycle for this loaf.

Light Citrus Loaf

The lightness of this loaf refers to its flavor, not to its substance. A diet cake it's not. But considering the millet and graham flours it incorporates, it's certainly not empty calories either.

The flavor and texture of the loaf are just right for creating a pinwheel cake, a lovely way to add sparkle to a late afternoon tea. The confection looks as if it took forever to make, when really it's quite simple and quick to construct.

In making a pinwheel, choose a filling for the striped vanes that will not add too much sweetness, since the tiny layers will use quite a bit of it. The rich colors of natural fruit preserves such as raspberry or blackberry add a stunning contrast. The lighter tones of apricot and peach lend the cake a quieter accent.

SMALL	LARGE
³/₄ cup buttermilk	⁷/₈ cup buttermilk
¹/₄ cup sour cream or yogurt, regular or low-fat	¹/₃ cup sour cream or yogurt, regular or low-fat
2 tablespoons canola or other light oil	2 tablespoons canola or other light oil
1 teaspoon lemon extract	1¹/₂ teaspoons lemon extract
1 teaspoon orange extract	1¹/₂ teaspoons orange extract
1 teaspoon vanilla extract	1¹/₂ teaspoons vanilla extract
1³/₄ cups unbleached all-purpose flour	2¹/₂ cups unbleached all-purpose flour
¹/₃ cup millet flour	¹/₂ cup millet flour
¹/₄ cup graham cracker crumbs	¹/₂ cup graham cracker crumbs
¹/₄ cup sugar	¹/₃ cup sugar
¹/₄ to 1 teaspoon salt, to taste	¹/₂ to 1¹/₂ teaspoons salt, to taste
2 teaspoons active dry yeast	2¹/₂ teaspoons active dry yeast

If the instructions for your machine specify that the leavening is to be placed in the bottom of your baking pan first thing, add the dry ingredients next, the liquids last. Otherwise, place the buttermilk and sour cream or yogurt in the pan, followed by the oil and the lemon, orange, and vanilla extracts. Measure in the all-purpose and millet flours and add the graham cracker crumbs, sugar, salt, and yeast. If your machine features a separate dispenser for leavening, spoon the yeast in there; otherwise, scatter it over the rest of the dry ingredients.

Bake the loaf on the machine's quick cycle.

To make a pinwheel cake, once the cake has cooled, cut away the crusts to form an oblong. Laying the loaf on one of its long sides, slice it very thin. The bread accommodates slices no more than ¼ inch across if carved gently with a sharp serrated knife.

Next, starting at one end, spread a slice of the bread with fruit preserves, bringing the filling well out to the edges. Spread the next slice and lay it over the first. Continue to the end of the loaf, finishing with a plain slice. If the filling is overflowing the edges of the bread, run a knife around the edge of the stack to even up the sides. Then cut the reassembled loaf in thirds from top to bottom.

Keeping the slices firmly in place, turn the loaf on its side again and cut it diagonally from corner to corner. Eyeing the result of your labors, you'll find that what you've created is six fat striped triangles. Now you're ready to put the pinwheel together.

Place the triangles on a round serving platter, all facing the same way, so that they meet in the center. Ideally, their stripes will form a spiral pattern. If any of them doesn't, simply flip the offending triangle over. A swirl of whipped cream or a circle of fruit added to the middle of the pinwheel is the nicest finishing touch for it.

A round loaf from a machine such as the Welbilt will produce striped semicircles instead of triangles. But it makes a lovely pinwheel all the same. It will need to have its first, thin slices run the

the length of the cylinder instead of across it. For the second slicing, lay the cylinder on its side and cut it into thirds. Then stack it back on end and make the final cut at right angles to the stripes. The pinwheel blades will truly have the effect of running in circles.

Scandinavian Cardamom Bread

A cardamom braid is my favorite coffee bread, although saffron bread is a close second on my list. I bake four long plaited cardamom loaves almost every Saturday morning during the fall and winter. By Monday after school they're usually gone — and I've not consumed more than half a dozen slices myself. Honest.

No machine-baked bread will ever replace the long golden-brown braids glistening with pearl sugar that I have associated with cardamom bread since my childhood. The aesthetic ingraining of those early years simply won't allow such a trade-in. However, with the recipe given here it is possible to capture, if not the original visual appeal, then at least the flavor and fragrance of true cardamom bread. Besides, the loaf is a handsome one even in its more modern form, its golden dome studded with pearl sugar.

Although not readily available in most local grocery shops and supermarkets, pearl sugar may be purchased through some of the catalog concerns listed in the back of this book. Granulated sugar can be substituted for it in the glaze, but it's really not the same. Pearl sugar crystals are fairly large, as their name implies, and they don't dissolve into a glaze as regular sugar does, but rather remain brilliantly white and sparkling on top of a loaf.

If possible, buy whole cardamom for your baking. This will mean peeling and grinding the seed. But the flavor of freshly ground cardamom is far more intense than the pre-ground variety, which almost always includes the flavorless paperlike husk.

½ cup light cream
1 egg
¼ cup unsalted butter
2½ cups unbleached all-purpose flour
¼ cup sugar
1 teaspoon hulled cardamom seeds,
    finely ground
dash salt
1¼ teaspoons active dry yeast

GLAZE

1 egg
1 tablespoon cold water
pearl sugar for garnish

Pour the cream into your bread machine pan and break the egg into it. Add the butter, cutting it into chunks first if it's hard, so it will blend more uniformly into the dough. Measure in the flour, sugar, cardamom, salt, and, following the instructions given for leavening for your particular machine, the yeast.

Use the short cycle, and a light loaf setting if available on your machine, for best results in baking this bread. As soon as the loaf is done, pull the pan from the machine and immediately close the lid to retain heat. Remove the loaf from its pan. Beat together the egg and water and paint the top of the loaf liberally with this mixture, using a pastry brush. Sprinkle generously with pearl sugar and gently fit the bread back into its baking container. Pop the pan back into the bread machine for another 2 minutes or so. The residual heat of the machine will bake the glaze on, causing most of the pearl sugar to adhere. Remove the loaf to its cooling rack with care.

Swedish Saffron Bread

Saffron bread is even richer and somewhat sweeter than carda-mom bread. The trick to achieving a truly saffrony loaf, both colorwise and flavorwise, is to crumble the saffron strands or, better yet, grind them with a mortar and pestle, and steep them in very hot water in a small glass or stainless steel container for 10 minutes before adding the infusion to the other ingredients.

> ½ cup heavy cream
> 2 eggs
> ¼ cup unsalted butter
> ½ teaspoon saffron strands, crumbled
>   or finely ground, infused in 1 table-
>   spoon hot water
> 2½ cups unbleached all-purpose flour
> ½ cup sugar
> dash salt
> 1¼ teaspoons active dry yeast
>
> G L A Z E
>
> 1 egg
> 1 tablespoon cold water

To save time, make the saffron infusion first thing, so it can be steeping while you assemble the other ingredients. Then pour the cream into your bread machine pan and break the eggs into it. Since you are using a fair amount of butter, if it's not soft, cut it into chunks so that it will blend better into the dough, then add it to the liquids. When the saffron has steeped for 10 minutes, pour the infusion into the pan and measure in the flour, sugar, salt, and, following the instructions for the leavening provided for your particular machine, the yeast.

Use your machine's short cycle, and a light loaf setting if available, for this bread. As soon as it has finished baking, take the pan from the machine, closing the lid of the machine again to retain heat. Remove the loaf from its pan. Beat together the egg and water and with a pastry brush paint the top of the loaf with the glazing mixture. Then put the loaf back in its pan and return it to the bread machine for 2 minutes or so. The oven's residual heat will bake the glaze on.

Sweet Greek Bread

Here's a cakelike loaf redolent of the anise of distant Greek isles, perfect for a lazy Sunday morning brunch and daydreaming. The egg yolks lend the bread a golden sunny color, the aniseed its distinctive accent. For more uniform flavor, the aniseed can be ground with a mortar and pestle or in a small electric grinder before being added to the dough. But left whole, the little seeds contribute contrast to both the texture and the taste of the bread.

SMALL	LARGE
²/₃ cup milk, whole or skim	1¼ cups milk, whole or skim
1 tablespoon canola oil	2 tablespoons canola oil
1 tablespoon honey	2 tablespoons honey
2 egg yolks	3 egg yolks
2 cups unbleached all-purpose flour	3¼ cups unbleached all-purpose flour
½ teaspoon aniseed, ground if desired	1 teaspoon aniseed, ground if desired
½ to 1½ teaspoons salt to taste	1 to 2 teaspoons salt to taste
1½ teaspoons active dry yeast	2 teaspoons active dry yeast

Remember that if the instructions accompanying your bread machine call for the yeast to be placed in the baking pan first, the dry ingredients should be added before the liquids. Otherwise pour the milk into your pan and add the canola oil, honey, egg yolks, flour, aniseed, salt, and yeast. If your machine has a separate dispenser for leavening, spoon the yeast into the dispenser after all the other ingredients have been measured into the baking pan.

Bake the loaf using your machine's quick setting.

Dutch Ginger Bread

Ginger is a key spice in Oriental cooking and, strangely enough, considering the plant's tropical origins, in northern European baking as well. Paper-thin gingersnaps grace the Christmas tables of Scandinavia, and the heavier dark ginger cookies, along with gingerbread, are as Germanic as sauerkraut.

This Dutch loaf, however, is rather different from what many of us have come to know as gingerbread. It is far less sweet, and the flavor of ginger is much more subtle. Fresh from the electronic oven on a cold winter's day, it's a wonderful accompaniment to hot chocolate or Dutch coffee, which is half strong coffee and half chocolate. The open-textured slices, if there are any left over, make great French toast.

SMALL	LARGE
1 cup milk, whole or skim	1½ cups milk, whole or skim
1 teaspoon canola oil	1½ teaspoons canola oil
1 teaspoon honey	2 teaspoons honey
1 egg	2 eggs
2 cups unbleached all-purpose flour	3½ cups unbleached all-purpose flour
2 teaspoons chopped candied orange peel	1 tablespoon chopped candied orange peel
1/16 teaspoon cinnamon	1/8 teaspoon cinnamon
1/16 teaspoon ground cloves	1/8 teaspoon ground cloves
1/16 teaspoon ground ginger	1/8 teaspoon ground ginger
1/16 teaspoon mace	1/8 teaspoon mace
1/2 to 1 teaspoon salt to taste	1 to 2 teaspoons salt to taste
1 teaspoon active dry yeast	1½ teaspoons active dry yeast

Pour the milk into your baking machine pan, unless the instructions for the model you have specify placing the yeast in the very bottom of the pan first thing, in which case the other dry ingredients should be added next, the liquids last. Spoon in the canola oil and honey and break the egg or eggs, depending on the size of the loaf you are making, into the pan. Add the flour, candied orange peel, cinnamon, cloves, ginger, mace, and salt. Spoon the yeast into its dispenser if your machine has one, otherwise scatter it over the other dry ingredients.

Use your machine's rapid-bake cycle for this loaf.

Pepparkaka (Swedish Spice Cake)

The most popular cake in the Sweden of my childhood was *sockerkaka*, a sponge cake whose name translates literally as "sugar cake." A more fragrant version of the cake, and my own favorite, was *pepparkaka*, or "ginger cake." Both used baking powder for their leavening, along with a quantity of eggs, but since a bread machine simply can't whip eggs to the proper froth, I substituted yeast in adapting an old family recipe for the machine — with notable success.

For the plainer *sockerkaka* omit the spices listed in the recipe and substitute either the grated zest of a lemon or a teaspoonful of vanilla extract, whichever your preference in flavors dictates.

Revell, the youngest of our children, likes his spice cake toasted and sprinkled liberally with cinnamon sugar. The rest of the family considers this practice wretched excess.

SMALL

1¼ cups milk, whole or skim
¼ cup unsalted butter (or canola oil)
1 medium egg
2 cups semolina flour
1½ cups unbleached all-purpose flour
⅔ cup sugar
1 teaspoon each ground ginger, ground nutmeg, ground cloves, and ground cinnamon (or 1 teaspoon vanilla extract or grated zest of 1 small lemon)
¼ to 1 teaspoon salt, to taste
1½ teaspoons active dry yeast

LARGE

1½ cups milk, whole or skim
⅓ cup unsalted butter (or canola oil)
1 medium egg
3 cups semolina flour
1¼ cups unbleached all-purpose flour
½ cup sugar
1½ teaspoons each ground ginger, ground nutmeg, ground cloves, and ground cinnamon (or 1½ teaspoons vanilla extract or grated zest of 1 large or 2 small lemons)
½ to 1½ teaspoons salt, to taste
2 teaspoons active dry yeast

Pour the milk into your baking pan and add the butter (or canola oil), unless the directions for your machine instruct you to start with the yeast, followed by the dry and then the liquid ingredients. If you are using butter straight from the refrigerator, cut it into chunks before placing it in the pan, so it will blend more easily with the other ingredients. Break the egg into the pan and add the semolina and all-purpose flours and the sugar. Add the ginger, nutmeg, cloves, cinnamon, and salt. For a plain sugar cake, substitute the vanilla extract or lemon zest for the spices and use a modest measure of salt. Spoon the yeast into its own dispenser if your machine has a separate container for leavening; otherwise, scatter it over the rest of the ingredients.

Use the machine's rapid-bake cycle for this loaf.

The aroma of a spice loaf permeates the house when it's baking, as you might have guessed from the ingredients. Serve it warm from its oven, when it's at its fragrant best. In Sweden, *pepparkaka* is a traditional accompaniment to strong black coffee for the grown-ups and *saft*, the delicately flavored fruit drink made from any number of natural fruit syrups diluted with water, for the children.

Ginger Cake

Back in the thirteenth and fourteenth centuries, when the trade in ginger was as lively as that in pepper, the sensual powers attributed to it certainly enhanced its sales. But it does seem curious that the spice most widely used in Chinese cookery should have come to be the archetypical Christmas flavor in the West. What's Christmas, after all, without gingersnaps or a gingerbread house?

Whatever the reasons for ginger's worldwide popularity, its wake-up flavor is indomitable. Slice this loaf very thin and spread it with sweet creamery butter for a quick, refreshing pick-me-up. For a more leisurely repast, try the striped gingerbread stack described below. The dark and light bands of cream cheese and lekvar, or prune butter, are striking, as is the subtle blend of flavors that results.

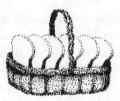

SMALL
3/4 cup milk, whole or skim
2 tablespoons heavy cream
3 tablespoons canola or other
  light oil
1 cup unbleached all-purpose
  flour
3/4 cup semolina flour
1/2 cup sugar
1 tablespoon instant coffee, regular or decaffeinated
1 1/2 teaspoons ground ginger
1 1/2 teaspoons ground cloves
1/2 to 1 teaspoon salt, to taste
1 1/2 teaspoons active dry yeast

LARGE
1 cup milk, whole or skim
1/4 cup heavy cream
1/4 cup canola or other light oil
1 medium egg
2 cups unbleached all-purpose
  flour
1 1/2 cups semolina flour
2/3 cup sugar
2 tablespoons instant coffee, regular or decaffeinated
2 teaspoons ground ginger
2 teaspoons ground cloves
1 to 2 teaspoons salt, to taste
2 teaspoons active dry yeast

Pour the milk into your bread machine baking pan and add the cream and oil, along with the egg if you are making the large loaf. If the instructions that came with your machine specify that the yeast is to be placed in the bottom of the pan first thing, however, these ingredients should be reserved to be added last, after the dry ones. Measure in the all-purpose and semolina flours and add the sugar, instant coffee, ginger, cloves, salt, and yeast, spooning the leavening into its own dispenser if a separate container is provided for it on your machine.

Bake the loaf on your machine's quick cycle.

For a striped gingerbread stack, spectacular both to behold and to taste, remove all crusts but the top crust once the loaf has cooled. Lay the loaf on its side and cut it into slices about 1/2 inch thick. The bread can be sliced into even thinner pieces, which are nice for simply buttered tea sandwiches, but here you'll be stacking the layers, and you don't want the edifice to be too precarious.

Set the top crust aside and spread the other slices alternately with cream cheese and lekvar, or prune butter. (You'll need, for either the small or large loaf, 3 or 4 ounces of cream cheese, double that if you'd like a swirl of it whipped to crown the loaf, and a 12-ounce can or jar of prune filling — you don't want to run out just short of the top of the stack.) Apple butter, which also goes well with this loaf, can be substituted for the lekvar, but only if its consistency is very firm.

Smooth the filling all the way out to the edges of the slices. It's

best to spread each slice while it's flat on your working surface and then add it to the stack, as if you were buttering an order of toast, rather than placing each slice on the stack and then spreading it with filling, as in assembling a layer cake. Don't worry about a little filling oozing over the edge of the bread.

Stack the layers like pancakes, run a knife around the perimeter of the stack to remove any excess filling and to bring out the striped pattern, and put the upper crust in place. Add a swirled topknot of whipped cream cheese as the stack's crowning glory. If the cream cheese is difficult to whip, it can be softened with about 1 tablespoon of cream or milk. Sprinkle with chopped nuts or dates if desired.

Cherries and Cheese Loaf

Cheese makes its appearance in all types of baked goods, from the cream cheese found enriching a really solid New York–style cheesecake to the pot cheese adorning a Danish. Here, ricotta is put to good use with dried cherries.

A word about dried cherries. They're expensive, but they're worth it. Dried cherries add something special to a bread, and when you consider that it takes eight pounds or so of the fresh fruit to make a pound of the dried — in our family it would probably take sixteen, since no one would be just pitting the cherries when readying them for the drying rack — the price doesn't seem all that high. The nutritional value, on the other hand, does, for the wizened cherries are fairly packed with vitamins.

I particularly like the dried Montmorency cherries from Washington State for baking. Tart, tangy, and bursting with flavor, they also sparkle like liquid rubies in a snowy-white bread. Even when simply added with the other ingredients at the outset of operations, dried cherries, unlike raisins, are firm enough to survive your bread machine's kneading relatively intact. For the largest possible splashes of color, however, wait to add them until the machine beeps for add-ins, if it performs such oratory, or until the first kneading cycle is completed.

SMALL	LARGE
¼ cup water	⅓ cup water
¼ cup unsalted butter (or canola oil)	⅓ cup unsalted butter (or canola oil)
2 medium eggs	2 medium eggs
½ cup ricotta cheese	¾ cup ricotta cheese
½ teaspoon vanilla extract	1 teaspoon vanilla extract
2¼ cups unbleached all-purpose flour	3 cups unbleached all-purpose flour
2 tablespoons sugar	3 tablespoons sugar
¼ to 1 teaspoon salt, to taste	½ to 1½ teaspoons salt, to taste
1½ teaspoons active dry yeast	2 teaspoons active dry yeast
⅓ cup dried cherries	½ cup dried cherries

Pour the water into your bread machine baking pan and add the butter (or canola oil). If you are using butter cold from the refrigerator, cut it into chunks before adding it to the pan, since otherwise it will not be incorporated uniformly into the other ingredients. Break the eggs into the pan and measure in the ricotta cheese, vanilla extract, flour, sugar, salt, and yeast, spooning the leavening into its own dispenser if your machine has one. However, should the directions for your machine specify that the yeast is to be placed in the bottom of the pan first thing, you'll need to remember to reverse the order in which you add the liquid and the dry ingredients.

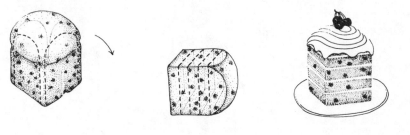

Set the machine to its quick cycle for this bread and add the cherries at the beep or after the first kneading.

When the bread is served piping hot from its pan, the cherries are still moist inside, reminding one of a fresh cherry pie. Slices are delectable spread with cream cheese, and if you're one of those who can't stay away from the cherry jar, you can always sneak some more of them into the cream cheese too.

Sour Cream Blueberry Loaf

Chantilly Cream

Not again!" was Susan's first startled remark upon cutting open my first version of this thick, dark loaf. It's true, I have on occasion come up with a loaf whose color somehow did not jibe with Western society's gustatory norms. A blue corn bread that was vividly blue comes immediately to mind. Well, here was another blue loaf. This time the color resulted from dried blueberries — and the flavor was irresistible.

When it comes to baking, dried blueberries impart far more taste per spoonful than do fresh ones, even the ones straight from our blueberry patch. Particularly in a bread-machine dough, the moisture in fresh berries limits the amount you can use, so you can achieve only a fraction of the flavor found in a loaf using dried berries.

The trick in adding the flavor without the blue is to reserve the berries to toss into your bread machine pan after the initial kneading cycle or at the beep if your machine so obliges.

SMALL	LARGE
1 cup sour cream or yogurt, regular or low-fat	1½ cups sour cream or yogurt, regular or low-fat
1 tablespoon unsalted butter or canola oil	2 tablespoons unsalted butter or canola oil
2 cups unbleached all-purpose flour	2¾ cups unbleached all-purpose flour
1 tablespoon dark brown sugar	2 tablespoons dark brown sugar
½ teaspoon ground allspice	1 teaspoon ground allspice
¼ to 1 teaspoon salt, to taste	½ to 1½ teaspoons salt, to taste
1½ teaspoons active dry yeast	2 teaspoons active dry yeast
⅓ cup dried blueberries	½ cup dried blueberries

Unless the instructions that came with your machine call for placing the yeast in the very bottom of the pan, followed by the other dry ingredients and then the liquids, spoon the sour cream or yogurt into your baking pan and add the butter or canola oil, flour, brown sugar, allspice, salt, and yeast, reserving the last for its own separate dispenser if your machine has one.

Set the machine to its rapid-bake cycle for this loaf, and don't forget to add the blueberries at the beep, or 10 minutes into the first kneading cycle if your machine doesn't beep for dried fruit.

For a tea cake that looks luscious — and is — remove the crusts from this loaf, slice it crosswise, cut the slices on the diagonal, spread them liberally with Chantilly Cream (see below) and fresh blueberries, and line them up in a row like a prism on a pretty platter. Even off the edges of the filling with the flat edge of a knife or a spatula and surround the cake with more blueberries, sugared or glazed with a little melted apple jelly if you'd like.

CHANTILLY CREAM

    1 cup heavy cream, well chilled
    1 tablespoon confectioners' sugar
    1 teaspoon vanilla extract (or ½ tea-
        spoon vanilla extract + ½ teaspoon
        almond extract)

Whip the cream, using chilled beaters and a chilled bowl, until it begins to thicken. Beat in the confectioners' sugar a little at a time. When the cream is almost stiff, add the vanilla extract (or the vanilla and almond extracts) and whip until blended. The touch of almond is scrumptious with blueberries, but vanilla alone works perfectly well.

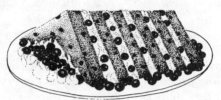

Almond Bread

We don't have a strawberry patch. We do have enough blueberry bushes to reap a bountiful harvest from them every year; our daughters, Genevieve and Tanya, used to sell the surplus from a roadside buckboard to earn extra preteen summer spending money. We also have currants and gooseberries galore, not to mention a wild bramble patch supplying an abundance of succulent raspberries and blackberries. Every spring I announce that this is the year when we're going to put in a strawberry patch, and every year we end up heading for a pick-your-own berry farm instead. There's just too much to be done around the place, I guess.

But when we head for the berry farm to pick strawberries, I toss all the ingredients for this almond loaf into the bread machine before we go and set the timer for our return. The bread has a heavenly fragrance of marzipan and a rich almond taste, and a generous square of it served warm in a bowl heaped high with strawberries and covered with cream makes a superlative shortcake. For extra verve use a dark corn syrup glaze and sprinkle with slivered almonds.

> 1 cup milk, whole or skim
> 1 egg
> 3 tablespoons unsalted butter
> 1 8-ounce can almond paste, cut into
>   about 1/8-inch slices for better
>   blending
> 2 1/2 cups unbleached all-purpose flour
> 2 tablespoons dark brown sugar

¼ to ½ teaspoon salt to taste
2 teaspoons active dry yeast

GLAZE

1 teaspoon dark corn syrup
1 teaspoon warm water
slivered almonds for garnish

Unless the instructions that came with your machine call for putting the yeast in the pan first and incorporating the liquid ingredients last, pour the milk into the baking pan of your bread machine and break in the egg. If the butter is not soft, cut it into small chunks to ensure its blending into the dough, then add it to the liquids. Next add the almond paste, sliced so it will blend better too. Measure in the flour, brown sugar, and salt, and add the yeast as directed for your bread maker.

You can use your machine's full cycle with this bread, but the quick cycle is better. If a light color setting is available, use it as well. As soon as the bread has finished baking, remove it from the machine, closing the cover again, and ease the loaf from its pan. Combine the corn syrup and warm water and brush the top of the loaf with this mixture, using a pastry brush. Sprinkle the slivered almonds over the glaze, put the bread gently back in its pan, and return it to the electronic oven for a few minutes to dry the glaze.

Bread of Two Chocolates

Peppermint Butter

B read and chocolate have been a popular combination in Europe for a long time. A rather good little Swiss movie called *Bread and Chocolate* even took its name from their amiable fraternization.

The coalition originated, I suspect, as a handy lunch among hikers. I remember being sustained on many wanderings in my youth by a couple of strips of *Landjäger,* that hard, dry German sausage that will last without refrigeration seemingly considerably longer than the teeth that chew it, a hearty hunk of rye bread, and a chocolate bar for extra energy.

The chocolate on those occasions was usually the bittersweet kind, and I inevitably ended up alternating bites of it with chunks of the firm, rough-textured bread. They went wonderfully together. I guess that, in essence, is how otherwise strange but good combinations are discovered.

This particular loaf is soft and moist. Its fine texture, due in part to the use of semolina flour, is riddled with distinct bits of tasty chocolate. The loaf is not truly sweet, and it's certainly not a cake. But try it with Nutella if you can find that concoction. This chocolate hazelnut spread from France is much loved by our children, who discovered it during a family sojourn in the village of Restinclières in the south of France. They found it quite irresistible spooned lavishly onto chunks of crisp-crusted French bread fresh from the bakery down the lane.

Lacking Nutella, try the bread with peppermint butter. The mint contributes a totally unexpected sparkle that beautifully complements tea.

1 cup milk, whole or skim
2 tablespoons unsalted butter
1 teaspoon vanilla extract
3/4 cup semisweet chocolate chips
1/2 cup walnuts, coarsely chopped
1 1/2 cups unbleached all-purpose flour
1 cup semolina flour
1/3 cup nonfat dry milk
3 tablespoons sugar
2 tablespoons cocoa
1 tablespoon instant espresso
1/4 to 1 teaspoon salt to taste
1/2 teaspoon baking soda
1 1/2 teaspoons yeast

Remember that if the instructions that came with your bread machine call for the leavening to be placed in the baking pan first, the other dry ingredients should be added next, before the liquid ingredients. Otherwise, pour the milk into the pan and measure in the butter, vanilla extract, chocolate chips, and walnuts. Add the all-purpose and semolina flours, the dry milk, sugar, cocoa, instant espresso, salt, baking soda, and, if the instructions for your machine so direct, the yeast. If your machine has a separate dispenser for leavening, spoon the yeast into the dispenser after all the other ingredients have been measured into the baking pan.

Use a quick bake cycle for this loaf.

PEPPERMINT BUTTER

½ cup unsalted butter, softened
1 tablespoon confectioners' sugar
½ teaspoon peppermint extract

Cream the butter and confectioners' sugar until smooth. Add the peppermint extract and blend well. Serve with a sprig of fresh mint from the garden.

Rum and Chocolate Bread

In my opinion, you can recommend this one for grown-ups," commented Revell. Well, not everything is for ten-year-olds.

This rich, moist loaf nicely complements a cup of strong, fragrant after-dinner coffee. Try serving thin slices of it spread with softened sweet butter flavored by a drop or two of citrus essence, either lemon or orange, and garnished with a twist of bright peel. The silky texture of the bread harmonizes well with the smoothness of the butter, and the double dose of lemon or orange from bread and spread reinforces the citrus accent.

If you read both of the following recipes, you'll notice that the one for the small loaf uses all cream, the one for the large loaf half cream and half milk. The recipe for the large loaf, however, also lists an egg, whereas that for the small loaf doesn't. These modifications balance out the fat and liquid contents for each loaf so that it will bake properly.

SMALL	LARGE
3/4 cup heavy cream	1/2 cup heavy cream
1/4 cup dark rum	1/2 cup milk, whole or skim
1 teaspoon orange oil	1/3 cup dark rum
1/2 teaspoon lemon juice	1 egg
1 teaspoon grated lemon zest	1 teaspoon orange oil
4 teaspoons chocolate syrup	1 teaspoon lemon juice
2 cups unbleached all-purpose flour	2 teaspoons grated lemon zest
2 teaspoons cocoa	2 tablespoons chocolate syrup
1/2 to 1 1/2 teaspoons salt to taste	3 cups unbleached all-purpose flour
1 teaspoon active dry yeast	1 tablespoon cocoa
	1 to 2 teaspoons salt to taste
	1 1/2 teaspoons active dry yeast

Pour the cream or, if you are making a large loaf of this bread, the cream and milk into the baking pan of your bread machine. Add the rum, and, again for the large loaf, the egg. Then measure in the orange oil, lemon juice, zest, chocolate syrup, flour, cocoa, and salt. If your machine has a separate dispenser for leavening, add the yeast there. If not, scatter it over the rest of the dry ingredients. However, if the directions for your machine specify placing the yeast in the bottom of the baking pan, remember to reverse the order in which you add the dry and liquid ingredients.

Bake the loaf on your machine's quick cycle.

Panettone

Sophisticated Italian cooking, in a variety sending into near-oblivion mere spaghetti with meatballs and tomato sauce, has grown tremendously in popularity over the past decade. To my delight, this has brought osso buco and a number of other favorite dishes of mine to restaurant tables. But I've yet to become enamored of Italian desserts. The right one for me just hasn't come along. Like many non-Italians, I find Italian desserts to be this cuisine's weakest suit. Maybe it has something to do with being a noodle- and rice-based culture. The Chinese aren't exactly renowned for their desserts either.

Still, as the entrée menu has expanded far beyond pizza and pasta bolognese, so spumoni has been superseded by *tiramisù* and other exotic sweets.

There are two Italian desserts newly popular in this country that are well served by the bread machine's talents: *panettone* and the less well known *zuccotto,* a Florentine cream-filled cake.

Panettone is particularly well suited to bread machines having a round baking pan, since the loaf's traditional shape is like a chef's hat, cylindrical and tall. But certainly a square *panettone,* while perhaps disconcerting at first to those accustomed to its more conventional manifestation, is in no wise less tasty because of its figure.

The Christmas season in Italy would be unthinkable without the consumption of countless pieces of this cross between a cake and a sweet yeast bread. From the breakfast slice served with cappuccino or *caffellatte* to the delicate portion proffered with a glass of marsala or other sweet wine after dinner to the elaborate *panettone farcito* that is probably its most impressive rendering, it is everywhere to be seen.

There are probably as many versions of *panettone* as there are bakeries in Italy. The recipe given here is one adapted for bread machines. No recipe is given for a so-called large loaf, however, because the oblong pans of machines like the Panasonic have the wrong shape for it, while large loaves of it from machines like the Hitachi are simply too tall to cut without toppling.

> *1/3 cup water*
> *1 medium egg*
> *2 egg yolks*
> *2 tablespoons unsalted butter (or*
>   *canola oil)*
> *2 tablespoons grated orange or lemon*
>   *zest*
> *1/4 cup chopped candied citron*
> *1 7/8 cups unbleached all-purpose flour*
> *1/4 to 1 teaspoon salt, to taste*
> *1 1/2 teaspoons active dry yeast*
> *1/2 cup raisins*

Remember that if the instructions that came with your bread machine call for the yeast to be placed in the baking pan first, the flour and salt should be added next, before the remaining ingredients. Otherwise, pour the water into your pan, then add the egg, egg yolks, butter (or canola oil), orange or lemon zest, citron, flour, salt, and yeast. If your machine has a separate dispenser for leavening, spoon the yeast into its slot after all the other ingredients have been measured into the baking pan.

Set your machine on its quick cycle. When it beeps a last call for ingredients, add the raisins. If your machine doesn't have a raisin alarm, add them 10 minutes into the first kneading cycle.

Panettone Farcito

It's not all that difficult to make *panettone farcito*, the legendary version of *panettone* laced with orange liqueur, stuffed with sweetened cheese, zest, and chocolate, and crowned with confectioners' sugar. It is demanding only in that it needs a few hours of undisturbed chilling in the refrigerator following its assembly. And it is something to behold! So if the loaf of *panettone* that emerges from your electronic oven happens to be perfectly shaped and fairly pleading to be treated specially, do give this creation a try.

You may be startled to note the chocolate chips, strongly associated with American baking, in this very Italian recipe. Well, if you want to hark back to the days before chocolate chips, you can substitute 2 one-ounce squares of semisweet baking chocolate, coarsely grated. But the chocolate's essentially the same, and tossing in the chips is so much easier!

After baking the *Panettone* (see above), prepare the filling.

> *1½ cups ricotta cheese*
> *¼ cup confectioners' sugar*
> *1 tablespoon grated orange zest*
> *2 tablespoons cocoa*
> *½ teaspoon vanilla extract*
> *⅓ cup semisweet chocolate chips (or 2*
> *one-ounce squares of semisweet*
> *baking chocolate, coarsely grated)*

orange liqueur for lacing the Panettone
(*approximately ¼ cup*)

confectioners' sugar for garnish

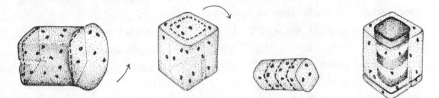

Scoop the ricotta cheese into a small bowl and, using an electric mixer, beat in the ¼ cup of confectioners' sugar. Spoon in the orange zest, cocoa, and vanilla extract and blend until the mixture is smooth and creamy. Fold in the chocolate chips (or grated chocolate).

To assemble the cake, first lay the freshly baked *Panettone* (see preceding recipe) on its side and, using a long, thin serrated knife with a good point, slice off the top crust and about an inch of the bottom of the loaf. Reserve. Then carefully cut a cylinder through the remaining bar of bread and gently remove this core, leaving a shell about 1 inch thick. Although perhaps daunting to contemplate, the maneuver is really not difficult to perform.

Cut the circular core crosswise into 4 even slices. Two of these rounds can be frozen for later use in a fondue or bread pudding. Set the other 2 aside for the moment.

Sprinkle both the reserved square cut from the bottom of the *Panettone* and the inside of the shell you've just created with about a third of the orange liqueur. Place the shell over the bottom piece to form a drum. Spoon a third of the cheese mixture into this well. Then sprinkle both sides of one of the reserved rounds with a little more of the orange liqueur and insert it to form a layer of cake over the filling. Spoon in another third of the cheese mixture, sprinkle the second cake round with orange liqueur, and place it over this layer of filling. Add the remaining filling, then sprinkle the underside of the top crust of the *Panettone* with the remaining liqueur and place it over the shell of bread as a lid.

Chill the cake in the refrigerator for 3 to 4 hours before serving. Just before bringing the *Panettone Farcito* to the table, dust the top with confectioners' sugar. Cut vertically into wedges to serve.

20 · Petits Fours and Other Frosted Treats

THERE ARE TIMES when a sweet tooth really can't be satisfied with anything less than a richly frosted sweet. There's also something visually special about a thick, swirled icing or a glossy glaze on a dessert treat.

Now, the maximum amount of frosting per piece of cake is not found on those gorgeous big round layer cakes with the splendiferous frills on top. No, for the most frosting per bite, short of licking icing from the spoon after scraping out the mixing bowl — which, of course, is the baker's prerogative — what one wants is one of those little pastries known as petits fours. Here's an assemblage of these and other frosted delights.

Kumquat Delight

Easy Semisweet Chocolate Frosting

Kumquats aren't found only in Chinese restaurants or Oriental markets anymore. They are quite often available fresh in supermarkets throughout the country come late winter and early spring. When you see them, pick some up for this delightfully spicy, color-studded loaf.

Toasted slices of Kumquat Delight spread with sweet butter and Seville orange marmalade are a real breakfast treat. Slabs of the loaf edged or iced with chocolate, the rich frosting contrasting both in flavor and appearance with the handsome loaf itself, are a lovely accompaniment to an herbal or a fruit tea.

The pepper in the recipe, incidentally, didn't slip into the list of ingredients inadvertently. It does indeed belong there, for it accents the pungency of the kumquats.

SMALL
¾ cup milk, whole or skim
1 tablespoon unsalted butter (or canola oil)
1 cup fresh kumquats, halved and pitted
2½ cups unbleached all-purpose flour
2 tablespoons dark brown sugar
1 teaspoon ground mace
¼ teaspoon freshly ground black pepper
¼ to 1 teaspoon salt, to taste
1½ teaspoons active dry yeast

LARGE
1 cup milk
2 tablespoons unsalted butter (or canola oil)
1½ cups fresh kumquats, halved and pitted
3½ cups unbleached all-purpose flour
3 tablespoons dark brown sugar
1½ teaspoons ground mace
½ teaspoon freshly ground black pepper
½ to 1½ teaspoons salt, to taste
2 teaspoons active dry yeast

Pour the milk into your baking pan and add the butter (or canola oil), kumquats, flour, brown sugar, mace, pepper, and salt. Last, add the yeast, following the instructions given for your particular machine. If the model you have features a separate dispenser for leavening, add the yeast there. On the other hand, if the instructions for your machine specify that the leavening is to be placed in the baking pan first thing, reverse the order in which you add the liquids and the other dry ingredients.

Bake the loaf on your machine's quick cycle.

For the iced version of this loaf, let the Kumquat Delight cool on a rack for about 10 to 15 minutes after you've shaken it out of its pan. When it can be handled easily, cut it into fairly thick slices and, using a thin, flexible knife or spatula, spread a liberal helping of chocolate —either a commercial or a homemade spread — around the edges of the slabs. If you're a real chocolate fancier, spread it all over the tops too. Nutella, that wonderful chocolate-hazelnut spread imported from Italy, is another scrumptious choice. A chocolate icing no sweeter than semisweet, like the one that follows, best complements the kumquat flavor.

EASY SEMISWEET CHOCOLATE FROSTING

1 cup semisweet chocolate chips
2 cups heavy cream, well chilled
1 teaspoon vanilla extract
dash salt

kumquats for garnish

Melt the chocolate chips in a heavy saucepan over very low heat or in the top of a double boiler. Let the melted chocolate cool while you whip the cream, using a chilled bowl and beaters, until it is stiff and swirled. Stir the vanilla extract and salt into the melted chocolate and fold this mixture into the whipped cream. Spread to your heart's desire.

Garnish your Kumquat Delight with slices of kumquat or maybe even a whole fruit fanned out in a bold design. For a kumquat fan, cut the fruit lengthwise in thin slices almost all the way through to the stem end. Setting the kumquat stem end down on a small lid like that of a vanilla extract bottle, as if you were placing it in an egg cup, helps you to keep from slicing too far. Then coax the slices apart sideways to open up the fan.

For a fabulous company display, cut slices of this bread in half and arrange them one edged up on the next in an overlapping row down the length of a serving platter. The bits of bright kumquat and rich chocolate on parade will be irresistible. Complete the enticement with sliced or fanned fruit as above, strewn with julienned kumquat for an extra splash of color.

Banana Almond Loaf

Basic Petit Four Icing

Here's an incredible fruit-and-nut combination. The almonds add both crunchiness and their own special flavor to this banana lover's delight, whose taste is accentuated by the extra splash of almond extract in the bread (a tip borrowed from a devastatingly rich banana cream pie Susan's mother used to make). For best results, wait until the bananas are really ripe before making this loaf.

"Ugh, they're black," Tanya once pointed out on seeing some poised on the counter by the bread machine awaiting further mellowing.

"Properly speckled to indicate ripeness," I corrected. True enough, for eating out of hand the bananas were a bit gone by. But I noticed there was no leftover Banana Almond Loaf to go stale.

Another flavor tip is to toast the almonds slightly before adding them to the dough. It's an optional step, but browning them on a cookie sheet in a 350-degree F. oven or in a dry skillet on the stovetop before using them really brings out their flavor.

You'll note from the recipe that this is a yeast-based, cakelike bread, not the more usual baking-powder banana nut bread. It makes an excellent base for petits fours.

SMALL	LARGE
¼ cup milk, whole or skim	*⅓ cup milk, whole or skim*
1 tablespoon canola or other light oil	*2 tablespoons canola or other light oil*
1 medium egg	*1 medium egg*
1 cup mashed ripe banana	*1½ cups mashed ripe banana*
1 teaspoon almond extract	*1½ teaspoons almond extract*
½ cup slivered blanched almonds, toasted if desired	*¾ cup slivered blanched almonds, toasted if desired*
2½ cups unbleached all-purpose flour	*3½ cups unbleached all-purpose flour*
¼ cup dark brown sugar	*⅓ cup dark brown sugar*
¼ to 1 teaspoon salt, to taste	*½ to 1½ teaspoons salt, to taste*
1½ teaspoons active dry yeast	*2 teaspoons active dry yeast*

Measure the milk and oil into the baking pan of your bread machine and break the egg into it. Add the mashed banana, almond extract, almonds, flour, brown sugar, salt, and, last — unless the instructions for your particular machine direct you to reverse the order in which you add the dry and the liquid ingredients — the yeast. If your machine has a separate dispenser for leavening, spoon the yeast in there.

Select the machine's rapid-bake cycle for this loaf.

A commercial frosting can be used to ice a Banana Almond Loaf, but if you'd like to make petits fours, here's a basic, simple, uncooked icing that will make delectable ones.

BASIC PETIT FOUR ICING

2 cups confectioners' sugar
1 tablespoon unsalted butter, softened
¼ cup water, lemon or orange juice,
    strong coffee, or other liquid of your
    choice
1 teaspoon vanilla or other extract
a few drops food coloring (optional)
assorted nuts, fresh fruit, and mint
    leaves for garnish

In a small bowl, blend the confectioners' sugar, butter, and, starting with a small amount and adding it gradually, the water, juice, coffee, or other liquid. Add the vanilla or other extract and the food coloring if desired. Beat the mixture until it is very smooth, adding more liquid if necessary. The icing should be thin enough to be poured, even though you're not actually going to pour it, but not so diluted that it will simply run off the cake squares. If the icing becomes too thin, simply add more confectioners' sugar until the right consistency for spreading is reached. If it becomes too stiff, just add more liquid. You can't ruin this icing.

In its most basic form, petit four icing uses for the necessary moisture plain tap water and, if something a little flashier than a plain white frosting is desired, a drop or two of food coloring. But any liquid can be substituted for the water to add both color and flavor. Besides coffee and fruit juices, you can use syrup drained from canned fruit, maple syrup, chocolate syrup — the possible variations on this basic recipe are almost limitless.

To assemble the petits fours, first trim the crusts from your Banana Almond Loaf. If you trim them generously so a little of the moist inner part goes with them, these outer slices can be frozen for later use in a fondue. They complement a butterscotch fondue nicely.

Cut the remaining block into 1- to 2-inch cubes. Spear the cubes with a fork one by one and dip them into the bowl holding the icing. When they are well coated on all sides but the bottom, ease them off onto a rack to dry.

Wait half an hour for the icing to set, then decorate the top of each petit four with a single strawberry, raspberry, or nut resting against a fresh mint leaf. Arranging the squares on individual small doilies will not only add a dainty touch, but make serving the petits fours easier as well.

Sweet Peppermint Poppy Seed Loaf

Peppermint Petit Four Icing

Poppy seeds scattered lightly over rolls or bagels, a decorative touch in miniature black pointillism on a glazed crust, are a familiar sight in this country. Rarely are they seen in more concentrated numbers, however. Yet in some European countries poppy seeds are widely used as a flavoring agent.

Something like poppy seed strudel is at best an acquired taste for most of us. But here's a moist, cakelike loaf distinctively peppered all over with poppy seeds, inside and out, that's bound to please just about everyone. Cube it and ice it with a pepperminty frosting, petit-four style, or serve it sliced for tea with a little jug of orange butter — simply cream ½ cup softened unsalted butter with 1 tablespoon confectioners' sugar and ½ teaspoon orange extract.

SMALL	LARGE
1 cup sour cream or yogurt, regular or low-fat	*1⅓ cups sour cream or yogurt, regular or low-fat*
2 tablespoons unsalted butter or canola oil	*3 tablespoons unsalted butter or canola oil*
1 tablespoon honey	*2 tablespoons honey*
1 teaspoon peppermint extract	*1½ teaspoons peppermint extract*
⅓ cup canned poppy seed filling	*½ cup canned poppy seed filling*
2 cups unbleached all-purpose flour	*3 cups unbleached all-purpose flour*
¼ cup cornmeal	*⅓ cup cornmeal*
¼ to 1 teaspoon salt, to taste	*½ to 1½ teaspoons salt, to taste*
1½ teaspoons active dry yeast	*2½ teaspoons active dry yeast*

Scoop the sour cream or yogurt into your bread machine baking pan and add the butter or canola oil, honey, peppermint extract, poppy seed filling, flour, cornmeal, and salt. Add the yeast as directed for your machine. Remember to reverse the order of ingredients if so instructed by the manufacturer's guidelines.

Use your machine's quick cycle for this loaf.

PEPPERMINT PETIT FOUR ICING

2 cups confectioners' sugar
1 tablespoon unsalted butter, softened
¼ cup water
½ teaspoon peppermint extract

crushed peppermint candies for garnish

Measure the confectioners' sugar into a bowl, add the butter and a little of the water, and cream to a smooth paste. Continue adding water, a little at a time, beating until the icing is of a good dipping consistency. Blend in the peppermint extract.

Petits fours dipped in this icing are attractively garnished with bits of bright peppermint candies scattered over the top.

Coffee Nips Coffee Cake

Mocha Buttercream Icing

Why coffee cakes never tasted of coffee was one of those minor mysteries of my childhood long unresolved. That the name derived from the association of the cakes with the coffee they so often accompanied somehow never entered my juvenile mind, probably because I would consume them at any opportunity granted, *sans* coffee.

Here's a coffee cake that's distinctly coffee-flavored, twice so if spread with the Mocha Buttercream Icing that follows the cake recipe. The loaf is silky, soft, moist, and flavorsome. Served simply with butter, it's not as sweet as one might expect from a perusal of the ingredients. Slices iced with the mocha frosting, on the other hand, make a rich nibble indeed.

SMALL	LARGE
⅞ cup milk, whole or skim	1¼ cups milk, whole or skim
3 tablespoons unsalted butter (or canola oil)	⅓ cup unsalted butter (or canola oil)
1 medium egg	1 medium egg
1 teaspoon coffee extract	1½ teaspoons coffee extract
1 cup unbleached all-purpose flour	1⅔ cups unbleached all-purpose flour
1 cup semolina flour	1½ cups semolina flour
½ cup graham cracker crumbs	¾ cup graham cracker crumbs
½ cup sugar	⅔ cup sugar
⅓ cup instant Viennese chocolate coffee	½ cup instant Viennese chocolate coffee
1 tablespoon instant coffee, regular or decaffeinated	2 tablespoons instant coffee, regular or decaffeinated
2 teaspoons active dry yeast	2½ teaspoons active dry yeast

Remember that if the instructions that came with your bread machine call for the yeast to be placed in the baking pan first, the dry ingredients should be added before the liquids. Otherwise, pour the milk into your pan and add the butter (or canola oil), egg, and coffee extract. Then measure in the all-purpose and semolina flours, graham cracker crumbs, sugar, instant Viennese chocolate coffee, and instant coffee. Last, add the yeast, placing it in its own separate dispenser if your machine has one.

Set the machine to its rapid-bake cycle for this loaf.

While a Coffee Nips loaf really needs no accompaniment as a tea or coffee cake, it also lends itself to more decorative treatment for festive occasions. Slice the bread in fairly thick pieces and cut each slice into four triangles, canapé style. Spread the triangles with Mocha Buttercream Icing and garnish each with chocolate coffee beans.

MOCHA BUTTERCREAM ICING

¼ cup heavy cream, well chilled
¼ cup instant coffee, regular or decaf-
feinated, dissolved in ¼ cup cold
water
¼ cup unsalted butter, softened
3 cups confectioners' sugar
1 teaspoon coffee extract
1 teaspoon chocolate extract
1 teaspoon vanilla extract

chocolate coffee beans for garnish

Pour the cream and the dissolved instant coffee into a small mixing bowl, add the butter and 1 cup of the confectioners' sugar, and beat well. Beat in 1 more cup of the confectioners' sugar and then the coffee, chocolate, and vanilla extracts. Add the remaining 1 cup of confectioners' sugar and beat at high speed for 3 to 4 minutes (don't overbeat or the cream may separate) or until the icing is light and fluffy. Spread immediately and garnish with chocolate coffee beans.

Any extra buttercream can be frozen for another day. Simply defrost it as needed, and while it's still quite cold, whip it again for a couple of minutes to fluff it up once more.

Triple Chocolate Loaf

White Buttercream Icing

Chocolate is a flavor that seems particularly difficult to capture with a bread machine. In my quest for a truly chocolaty loaf, I keep experimenting with more and more of it. What I'm striving for is not the ultimate in devastatingly rich chocolate-frosted devil's food cakes, although I'm as much a sucker for those as any chocolate lover. No, what I have in mind is one of those chocolate cakes that are rich but not so sugary that the chocolate is overpowered.

Here's a dense, fine-grained, cakelike chocolate loaf that combines the subtly different triple flavors of cocoa, hot fudge sauce, and chocolate extract. For those who like it sweet, try the White Buttercream Icing that follows the loaf recipe. Freeze any extra pieces of the loaf for a chocolate or a mocha fondue some other day.

SMALL	LARGE
1/3 cup milk, whole or skim	*1/2 cup milk, whole or skim*
1/4 cup unsalted butter (or canola oil)	*6 tablespoons unsalted butter (or canola oil)*
1 medium egg	*1 medium egg*
1 tablespoon unheated hot fudge sauce	*2 tablespoons unheated hot fudge sauce*
1 tablespoon lemon juice	*2 tablespoons lemon juice*
1 teaspoon vanilla extract	*2 teaspoons vanilla extract*
1 teaspoon chocolate extract	*1 1/2 teaspoons chocolate extract*
2 cups unbleached all-purpose flour	*3 cups unbleached all-purpose flour*
1/4 cup sugar	*1/3 cup sugar*
1/4 cup cocoa	*1/3 cup cocoa*
1 tablespoon instant coffee, regular or decaffeinated	*2 tablespoons instant coffee, regular or decaffeinated*
1/4 to 1 teaspoon salt, to taste	*1/2 to 1 1/2 teaspoons salt, to taste*
1 1/2 teaspoons active dry yeast	*2 teaspoons active dry yeast*

Pour the milk into your baking pan, unless the instructions for your machine direct you to place the yeast in the bottom of the pan first thing, in which case the other dry ingredients should be added next, the liquids last. Add the butter (or canola oil). Since a sizable quantity of butter is involved, if yours is still cold from the refrigerator, cut it into chunks before adding it to the milk, to ensure its blending evenly with the other ingredients. Break the egg into the pan and add the hot fudge sauce, lemon juice, and vanilla and chocolate extracts. Measure in the flour, sugar, cocoa, instant coffee, salt, and yeast, placing the leavening in its own separate dispenser if your machine has that device.

To bake the loaf, set the machine to its rapid cycle.

The Triple Chocolate Loaf is fine just plain or lightly buttered still warm from its pan. It's also lovely iced, however. Crown its low top with thick swirls of White Buttercream Icing (set the butter out to soften when you turn on the bread machine, and the icing will be quickly made), or cut the loaf into slices or cubes and ice the individual pieces, cupcake or petit four style. Of course, when you cover the sides too, the visual contrast between the dark chocolate and the white buttercream is lost — until you bite into a piece.

WHITE BUTTERCREAM ICING

¼ cup heavy cream, well chilled
¼ cup unsalted butter, softened
2 cups confectioners' sugar
1 teaspoon vanilla extract

cocoa for garnish

Pour the cream into a small mixing bowl, add the butter and 1 cup of the confectioners' sugar, and beat well. Add the remaining 1 cup of confectioners' sugar and the vanilla extract and beat at high speed for 3 to 5 minutes (just don't overbeat, lest the cream separate) or until the icing is light and easy to spread.

Individual servings of this treat are prettily decorated with cocoa dusted over the top through a paper doily.

Freeze any unused portion of the buttercream for future use. When needed, it can simply be defrosted and whipped up while still cold for a couple of minutes again.

Rose and Orange Loaf

Rose Water Glaze

Flower waters, quaint by today's Western culinary standards, have been popular flavorings for millennia in the Near East. The Turkish delight so popular in this country at the turn of the century was originally none other than bite-size bits of flower-flavored jellies dusted in confectioners' sugar.

In England, these fruit flavorings gained immense popularity during the Crusades, when those returning from the Holy Land brought home rose and orange flower waters. For a couple of hundred years, right into the reign of Queen Victoria, these flavorings were as popular as vanilla is today.

Considering that vanilla is derived from the dried seedpod of an orchid, why should rose flavoring seem so strange? I asked Revell.

"What, eat perfume?" he retorted.

Logic sometimes does not work with a ten-year-old.

In point of fact, the flavor of rose may not work for you either. But try it, at least. The loaf is soft and white, with a cookielike crust, and the flavor is wonderfully delicate. Remarkably, the rose water is not overpowered by the lemon juice. The cake's elusive taste can be accentuated with Rose Water Glaze, which follows the loaf recipe.

One note: when purchasing rose water for cooking, make sure that what you buy is culinary-grade rose water.

SMALL	LARGE
1/2 cup milk, whole or skim	3/4 cup milk, whole or skim
3 tablespoons unsalted butter	1/4 cup unsalted butter
2 tablespoons solid vegetable shortening	3 tablespoons solid vegetable shortening
1 tablespoon rose water	4 1/2 teaspoons rose water
1 tablespoon orange water	4 1/2 teaspoons orange water
1 tablespoon lemon juice	4 1/2 teaspoons lemon juice
2 cups unbleached all-purpose flour	3 cups unbleached all-purpose flour
1/4 cup sugar	1/3 cup sugar
1/4 to 1/2 teaspoon salt, to taste	1/2 to 1 teaspoon salt, to taste
1 1/2 teaspoons active dry yeast	2 teaspoons active dry yeast

If the directions for your bread machine instruct you to place the yeast in the very bottom of the baking pan, you will need to reverse the order in which you incorporate the liquid and the dry ingredients. Otherwise, pour the milk into your pan and add the butter. If you are making the large loaf and using butter still cold from the refrigerator, cut it into pieces to facilitate its blending with the other ingredients. Measure in the shortening, rose and orange waters, lemon juice, flour, sugar, salt, and yeast. Where a separate dispenser is provided for leavening, spoon the yeast in there.

Bake the loaf on your machine's quick cycle.

In *The Compleat Cook*, a compendium of recipes from the late sixteenth and early seventeenth centuries, there appears the following recipe for a rose water sugar glaze: "Against you draw the cake from the Oven have some Rose Water and Sugar finely beaten, and well mixed together to wash the upper side of it, then set it in the Oven to dry out, when you draw it out, it will shew like Ice."

Here's my adaptation. For best results, spread it while your loaf is still warm—but not hot—from its baking pan.

ROSE WATER GLAZE

> 1 tablespoon rose water
> 1 tablespoon heavy cream
> 1½ cups confectioners' sugar

Combine the rose water and cream in a small bowl and stir in enough of the confectioners' sugar to form a smooth paste. Beat in additional confectioners' sugar a little at a time until the glaze is of a good consistency for spreading. If the glazing mixture becomes too thick, add an extra splash of cream.

It's true that they didn't use cream for this glaze in Shakespeare's time. Then again, they didn't use electric mixers in those days either. The cream acts as a binder and helps to smooth the glaze, which does indeed add sparkle to the top of the loaf.

Luau Loaf

Most of the macadamia nuts we buy in our local supermarkets come from Hawaii, as do, of course, a lot of pineapples. Hence the name for this tasty, soft, light-textured loaf. For extra pineapple flavor, when you drain the pineapple rings called for in the recipe, reserve the syrup in which they were packed to boil down and use as a glaze on the finished loaf.

SMALL	LARGE
½ cup heavy cream	⅔ cup heavy cream
¼ cup canola or other light oil	⅓ cup canola or other light oil
1 teaspoon pineapple extract	1½ teaspoons pineapple extract
½ teaspoon orange extract	¾ teaspoon orange extract
¼ to ½ teaspoon coconut extract, to taste	½ to ¾ teaspoon coconut extract, to taste
5 canned pineapple rings, drained, liquid reserved for glazing loaf if desired	8 canned pineapple rings, drained, liquid reserved for glazing loaf if desired
1 cup dry-roasted macadamia nuts	1½ cups dry-roasted macadamia nuts
2¼ cups unbleached all-purpose flour	3¼ cups unbleached all-purpose flour
¼ to 1 teaspoon salt, to taste	½ to 1½ teaspoons salt, to taste
1½ teaspoons active dry yeast	2 teaspoons active dry yeast

Pour the cream and oil into your baking pan and add the pineapple, orange, and coconut extracts, pineapple rings, macadamia nuts, flour, salt, and yeast, placing the leavening in its own separate dispenser if your machine has such a device. If, on the other hand, the instructions that came with your machine specify that the yeast is to be placed in the very bottom of the pan first thing, remember to reverse the order in which you add the liquid and the dry ingredients.

Set the machine to its rapid-bake cycle for this loaf.

While the Luau Loaf is baking, you can make an attractive glaze with which to crown it when it emerges from the electronic oven. Reduce the pineapple syrup reserved from draining the canned pineapple slices by two thirds, boiling it down in a small saucepan. Using a pastry brush, paint the hot loaf as soon as you've taken it from its baking pan with this thickened syrup. For a pretty contrast that will also enhance the flavor of the loaf, sprinkle shredded coconut over the glaze before it has set.

If you just happen to have a chunk of fresh coconut tucked away in the refrigerator, you can make an even more spectacular garnish by paring delicate strips of coconut from the chunk with a vegetable peeler, much as you would pare chocolate curls from a square of semisweet baking chocolate, and then arranging the strips in careless curls atop the glazed loaf. Handle gently, since the curls will not only look, but be, very delicate.

Double Almond Loaf

Quick No-Fail Creamy Hot Fudge Sauce

Supporting my theory that one really can't have a surfeit of almonds when it comes to baking — the more I experiment with almond loaves, the more of these nuts I keep adding in one form or another — here's a recipe that uses both almond paste or marzipan and the nut in its more crunchy, slivered form.

With all that almond paste in it, along with the milk needed to help soften it, the dough for this bread is very moist, which is why there is no separate recipe for a large version of it. A bread machine with a large oblong pan for its loaf would encounter rather unmanageable difficulties, with the greater mass of dough sticking in the corners. A machine with a tall pan for its large loaf would avoid that pitfall, but such a machine will also accommodate the smaller batch, and as you'll see, the recipe given here will result in an amply sized loaf, high-domed and altogether lovely.

1 cup milk, whole or skim
2 tablespoons unsalted butter (or
    canola oil)
1 medium egg
7 ounces almond paste or marzipan,
    coarsely chopped if firm
1/3 cup slivered blanched almonds,
    toasted for accentuated flavor if
    desired
2 1/2 cups unbleached all-purpose flour
2 tablespoons dark brown sugar
1/4 to 1/2 teaspoon salt, to taste
1 1/2 teaspoons active dry yeast

Unless the instructions that came with your machine call for placing the yeast in the very bottom of your baking pan, followed by the other dry ingredients and then the liquids, pour the milk into the pan and add the butter (or canola oil), egg, almond paste or marzipan, almonds, flour, brown sugar, salt, and yeast, reserving the last for its own separate dispenser if your machine has one.

Select your machine's quick cycle for this loaf and take a peek inside the machine to check on the activity about 5 or 10 minutes into the first kneading cycle, since the dough tends to be quite moist and sticky initially. It may be necessary to scrape down the sides of the pan to make sure that all the bits are incorporated.

Susan, who is not only an almond fancier but a puzzle enthusiast as well, combined the two interests in coming up with a way to convert the rectangular loaf of this bread that our machine turns out into a prism-shaped cake that's become known in our house as the Strawberry Ridge, a confection filled with strawberry preserves, covered with hot fudge sauce, and garnished with ripe strawberries. Its assembly takes only a few minutes, really, particularly if you microwave the hot fudge sauce to warm it.

Lay the loaf on its side and trim off the top and bottom crusts. Freeze these, tightly wrapped, and you'll have the makings of excellent cubes for a chocolate or butterscotch fondue someday.

Next, return the trimmed loaf to an upright position and slice it in half diagonally from top to bottom so that you have 2 right-angled triangles. Now, keeping the loaf together, cut each triangle in half again, starting from the same corner. This will give you 4

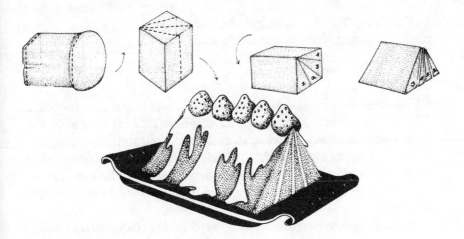

triangles, the 2 center ones of which will be, if you remember your geometry, obtuse ones.

Still holding the loaf together, gently lay it on its side again and flip 2 triangles from one side over to the other side, forming a prism. Separate the wedges enough to spread them with the strawberry preserves, then press them together again.

Pour hot fudge sauce the length of the ridge, letting it flow down the sides, and perch a row of strawberries along the top line.

Another popular version of this cake in our house is a ridge filled with almond paste or marzipan and covered with whipped cream before the strawberries are hoisted into place. Now there's a rich cake!

QUICK NO-FAIL CREAMY HOT FUDGE SAUCE

> 1 fourteen-ounce can sweetened
>   condensed milk
> 2 one-ounce squares unsweetened
>   baking chocolate
> 2 tablespoons unsalted butter
> 2 teaspoons vanilla extract

Scoop the sweetened condensed milk into a heavy saucepan or the top of a double boiler. Add the chocolate and stir over low heat until the chocolate has melted completely and the mixture is thick and smooth. Add the butter, stirring quickly until it is blended into the sauce. Remove the pan from the heat and add the vanilla extract.

"Tastes like melted brownies" is Revell's assessment of this sauce.

Cranberry-Orange Loaf

Quick Orange Glaze

The flavor of cranberries and oranges combined is a uniquely American one. Although wild cranberries are popular in Europe and Russia, in neither area is there a counterpart to the vast cultivated cranberry bogs that dot the sandier areas of coastal New England. As to oranges, well, Floridians may complain about the occasional freeze, but have they ever tried growing citrus fruits in Siberia?

The recipe presented here uses dried cranberries. Their concentrated flavor adds a much more intense accent to the loaf than one could hope to achieve in a bread machine using fresh berries. Also, because the dried cranberries are quite firm, it's possible to simply toss them into the baking pan with all the other ingredients, instead of waiting to add them until after the dough has been mixed and kneaded, and still have whole chunks of delectable berries scattered throughout the finished loaf. Fresh berries subjected to the battering of the kneading blade of a bread machine are mushed into nothingness.

Dubbed by Susan the Constant Comment loaf because of its resemblance to that citrus-accented tea, this one makes lovely petits fours to hide under a lemony or orange-flavored icing or glaze, such as the one following the loaf recipe.

SMALL	LARGE
¾ cup milk, whole or skim	1 cup milk, whole or skim
3 tablespoons unsalted butter	¼ cup unsalted butter
2 tablespoons solid vegetable shortening	3 tablespoons solid vegetable shortening
1 tablespoon orange extract	1½ tablespoons orange extract
1 tablespoon grated orange zest	4½ teaspoons grated orange zest
⅓ cup dried cranberries	½ cup dried cranberries
2½ cups unbleached all-purpose flour	3¼ cups unbleached all-purpose flour
¼ cup sugar	⅓ cup sugar
¼ to 1 teaspoon salt, to taste	½ to 1½ teaspoons salt, to taste
1½ teaspoons active dry yeast	2 teaspoons active dry yeast

Pour the milk into your baking pan and add the butter, cut into chunks if you are making the larger loaf so it will blend more easily with the other ingredients. Measure in the shortening, orange extract, orange zest, cranberries, flour, sugar, salt, and yeast, placing the leavening in its own dispenser if your machine has one. If the instructions that came with your model call for starting with the yeast, however, remember to reverse the order in which you add the liquids and the other dry ingredients.

To bake the loaf, use your machine's quick cycle.

QUICK ORANGE GLAZE
2 tablespoons unsalted butter
juice and grated zest of 1 small
*   orange*
3 cups confectioners' sugar

julienned orange zest and/or
*   cranberries, fresh or dried, for garnish*

Melt the butter in a small saucepan. Stir in the orange juice and zest, then gradually blend in the confectioners' sugar until the glaze is of a good dipping consistency. Let stand for 5 minutes before dipping the petits fours, preferably while the cubes are still slightly warm, and allow them to drain on a cake rack until the glaze is set.

Julienned orange zest adds an attractive finish to petits fours dipped in this glaze. If you don't mind giving away the secret of the little cakes inside, add a dried or fresh cranberry or two to the arrangement.

Chocolate Nut Delight

Dark Chocolate Icing

Chocolate and nuts just go together, and here's a loaf that incorporates generous quantities of both. With the addition of a simple chocolate frosting (see the recipe following the one for the loaf), you can create from it a delicious mock *Rehrücken*, a German torte baked in a long half-round tin, turned out, and iced. This traditional hunting-country dessert is decorated with rows of almonds along its top to resemble the larding strips for the saddle of venison it is meant to imitate.

SMALL	LARGE
1 cup milk, whole or skim	*1½ cups milk, whole or skim*
2 tablespoons canola or other light oil	*3 tablespoons canola or other light oil*
¼ cup unsulphured molasses	*⅓ cup unsulphured molasses*
1 teaspoon chocolate extract	*1½ teaspoons chocolate extract*
¼ cup almonds	*⅓ cup almonds*
¼ cup hazelnuts	*⅓ cup hazelnuts*
¼ cup pecans	*⅓ cup pecans*
2 cups unbleached all-purpose flour	*3¼ cups unbleached all-purpose flour*
¼ cup cocoa	*⅓ cup cocoa*
¼ to 1 teaspoon salt, to taste	*½ to 1½ teaspoons salt, to taste*
2 teaspoons active dry yeast	*2½ teaspoons active dry yeast*

Unless the instructions for your machine specify that the yeast should be placed in the baking pan first thing, followed by the other dry ingredients and then the liquids, pour the milk, oil, and molasses into your baking pan and add the chocolate extract. Toss in the almonds, hazelnuts, and pecans and measure in the flour, cocoa, salt, and, last, the yeast. If your machine has a separate dispenser for leavening, add the yeast there.

Bake the loaf on your machine's quick cycle.

DARK CHOCOLATE ICING

8 one-ounce squares semisweet baking chocolate
½ cup unsalted butter, softened or cut into small chunks
1 teaspoon vanilla extract

whole or sliced blanched almonds for garnish

Place the chocolate in the top of a double boiler or in a heavy saucepan set over very low heat. Do not stir. When the chocolate is soft but not yet altogether liquid, remove from the heat and add the butter, stirring until melted. Blend in the vanilla extract.

To form the mock *Rehrücken,* cut the finished Chocolate Nut Delight in half lengthwise. If yours is a round bread machine pan, the loaf can simply be sliced down the center and the 2 halves laid end to end to make a long Quonset-hut-shaped cake, the traditional shape of this treat. A square cake is best cut on the diagonal. The 2 triangles can be similarly laid end to end to form a long prism.

Ice the cake and, if it's a rounded one, lay 3 rows of blanched almonds, either whole or sliced, along its top to form white stripes against the dark chocolate. Garnish a prism-shaped cake with a roof ridge of the almonds. Either way, the effect is stunning.

21 · Perrie's Delight and Other à la Modes

 DURING MY EARLY TEENAGE YEARS, my family would eat out every couple of weeks at a now-defunct establishment called Perrie's. A neon Eiffel Tower flashed on a sign over the entrance, and the food was very Continental. They even served snails for appetizers, I would tell my startled classmates.

But it wasn't the escargots I reveled in. No, what I looked forward to in eager anticipation was a dessert called Perrie's Delight. It consisted of a slice of toasted pound cake topped by vanilla ice cream, hot fudge sauce, whipped cream, and, of course — this was the fifties, after all — a large maraschino cherry.

There's no way to make a good pound cake in any of the present generation of bread machines, so a true replica of the Perrie's Delight I knew is not possible in the bread machine bakery. However, employing the same principle, similar accessories, and a Butterscotch Brickle, Banana Chocolate, or Peanut Butter–Chocolate Chip Loaf, one can come up with an equally devastating dessert à la mode in next to no time.

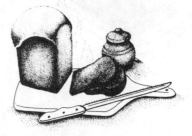

Butterscotch Brickle Loaf

Almond Praline Cream

B utterscotch is one of those flavors that fall into the category of the sublime, and here's a quickly and easily made loaf that gains its blissful flavor from those bits of brickle found almost everywhere on grocery shelves under the name Bits 'O Brickle.

For bits in the finished bread true to their original size, add the brickles at the end of the first kneading cycle or at the beep with which some machines signal the moment to add whole raisins and whatnot. Simply tossing the brickles in with the other ingredients at the outset will give you an equally delectable and delightfully fragrant loaf, but the butterscotch flavor will be dispersed throughout the bread. That's okay too, if you don't mind skipping the textural contrast of biting into those little nuggets of caramelized crunch.

Lightly toasted slices of this bread are heavenly with French vanilla ice cream, topped by — what else? — hot butterscotch. A rich, creamy, homemade almond praline sauce (see the recipe following the one for the loaf), easy to whip up in advance and tuck away in the refrigerator till needed, adds a particularly opulent touch to this dish.

SMALL	LARGE
⅞ cup milk, whole or skim	1¼ cups milk, whole or skim
3 tablespoons unsalted butter (or canola oil)	¼ cup unsalted butter (or canola oil)
2 teaspoons unsulphured molasses	1 tablespoon unsulphured molasses
2 cups unbleached all-purpose flour	3 cups unbleached all-purpose flour
½ cup graham cracker crumbs	½ cup graham cracker crumbs
¼ to 1 teaspoon salt, to taste	½ to 1½ teaspoons salt, to taste
2 teaspoons active dry yeast	2½ teaspoons active dry yeast
¾ cup butterscotch brickles	1 cup butterscotch brickles

Pour the milk into the baking pan of your bread machine and add the butter (or canola oil), molasses, flour, graham cracker crumbs, salt, and yeast, placing the leavening in its own separate dispenser if your machine has one. Remember, however, that if the instructions accompanying your model call for placing the leavening in the bottom of the pan first thing, then the other dry ingredients should be added next, before the milk and butter (or canola oil).

Set your machine to its rapid-bake cycle for this loaf, and toss in the butterscotch brickles at the beep or after the first kneading.

To serve à la mode, toast slices of the loaf lightly to bring out their flavor, heap them with French vanilla ice cream, and ladle a liberal measure of hot butterscotch sauce over each helping. The toppings available commercially are fine, but for a real taste treat, try the Almond Praline Cream below.

ALMOND PRALINE CREAM

½ cup unsalted butter
2 cups firmly packed dark brown sugar
2 teaspoons lemon juice
2 cups heavy cream
3 tablespoons toasted blanched
  almonds

Melt the butter in a heavy saucepan set over very low heat. Remove from the heat and add the brown sugar, creaming the mixture to a smooth paste. Add the lemon juice and mix well. Stir in the cream, return the pan to the stove, bring the sauce to a boil, and allow it to cook without stirring for 3 to 5 minutes or until a knife dipped in the syrup comes out very thickly coated. Just before serving, toss in the toasted almonds. The contrast between the crunchy nuts and the smooth butterscotch cream is wonderful.

Cherry Milk Loaf

The dried cherries that have recently become available at gourmet and bake shops are a real boon for bread machine enthusiasts. In an attempt to impart the piquant flavor of cherries to a yeast-based tea bread, I spent a lot of time experimenting with cherry pie fillings, cherry jams, and fresh cherries. The inevitable result was failure. The high sugar content of the pie fillings and jams simply overwhelmed the yeast required as the leavener in almost all bread machine baking, because the machines can't manage to whip eggs and don't handle quick breads reliably. Fresh cherries, which would seem the most elegant solution to the problem — discounting the messy job of pitting them all — simply don't add the concentrated fruit essence needed to create a loaf that is identifiably a cherry one.

Dried cherries, on the other hand, particularly the Montmorencies from Washington State, provide an incredible burst of flavor for their size. Add them after the machine's first kneading, or at the beep if your model features that signaling device, and you'll have a luscious loaf with a golden crust and bright cherries throughout.

SMALL	LARGE
1/2 cup milk, whole or skim	*3/4 cup milk, whole or skim*
3 tablespoons unsalted butter (or canola oil)	*1/4 cup unsalted butter (or canola oil)*
1 tablespoon dark corn syrup	*2 tablespoons dark corn syrup*
3 medium eggs	*3 medium eggs*
2 cups white whole-wheat flour	*3 1/2 cups white whole-wheat flour*
1/4 to 1 teaspoon salt, to taste	*1/2 to 1 1/2 teaspoons salt, to taste*
1 1/2 teaspoons active dry yeast	*2 teaspoons active dry yeast*
1/3 cup dried cherries	*1/2 cup dried cherries*

Pour the milk into your baking pan and add the butter (or canola oil), unless the directions for your model instruct you to place the leavening in the very bottom of the pan first, the other dry ingredients next, and the liquids last. If you are making a large loaf and using butter straight from the refrigerator, cut the butter into chunks before placing it in the pan, since otherwise, being cold and hard, it will fail to blend evenly with the other ingredients. Spoon in the corn syrup and break the eggs into the pan. Add the flour, salt, and yeast, placing the yeast in its own separate dispenser if your machine has one.

Set the machine to its rapid-bake cycle for this loaf, and after the first kneading cycle or when the machine beeps its last call for ingredients, if yours does that, add the cherries.

This is a great loaf for leisurely brunches. It also makes a marvelous dessert sliced or cubed fresh from the oven and served in individual portions with a scoop of cherry vanilla ice cream, almost hidden beneath a slathering of walnuts in syrup and a dollop of whipped cream. Oh, yes, and, above everything — why not? — a bright big maraschino cherry.

Banana Chocolate Loaf

Real Honest-to-Goodness Hot Fudge Sauce

The flavors of banana and chocolate have a natural affinity for each other that is nowhere more evident than in this loaf, beneath whose unassuming pumpernickel-colored crust lies astonishing flavor. It owes its success to dried bananas, whose concentrated essence seems made for the bread machine bakery.

Dried bananas are now available in small, compressed packages in the exotic or tropical fruit section of many supermarkets. They last well, and you can have a couple of packs at the ready for when the sweet tooth strikes, without having to worry about the fruit turning black, as the fresh variety does all too soon.

SMALL	LARGE
¾ cup milk, whole or skim	1 cup milk
2 tablespoons unsalted butter	3 tablespoons unsalted butter
1 medium egg	1 medium egg
⅓ cup chopped pecans	½ cup chopped pecans
⅓ cup chopped dried bananas	½ cup chopped dried bananas
2¼ cups unbleached all-purpose flour	3 cups unbleached all-purpose flour
⅓ cup sugar	½ cup sugar
⅓ cup cocoa	½ cup cocoa
¼ to 1 teaspoon salt, to taste	½ to 1½ teaspoons salt, to taste
1½ teaspoons active dry yeast	2 teaspoons active dry yeast

Pour the milk into your bread machine baking pan and add the butter, egg, pecans, bananas, flour, sugar, cocoa, and salt. If your machine has a separate dispenser for leavening, spoon the yeast in there. Otherwise, scatter it over the rest of the ingredients in the pan, unless the instructions for the machine you have specify that it is to be placed in the very bottom of the pan first thing, in which case the other dry ingredients should be added next, the liquids last.

Bake the loaf on your machine's quick cycle.

Now here's the ultimate gooey Perrie's Delight. Slice a Banana Chocolate Loaf into individual servings while it's still warm. Mound vanilla ice cream on each slice, cover it with hot fudge sauce — the old-fashioned, preferably homemade, kind that hardens on the cold ice cream, as in the recipe below — and spoon over it some of those wonderful walnuts that come packed in syrup.

Then again, if that sounds too rich, Banana Chocolate Loaf is great simply sliced and served with butter.

REAL HONEST-TO-GOODNESS HOT FUDGE SAUCE

4 one-ounce squares unsweetened baking chocolate
3 tablespoons unsalted butter
⅔ cup water
1¾ cups sugar
¼ cup dark corn syrup
1 teaspoon vanilla extract

Melt the chocolate and butter in a heavy saucepan over very low heat. In a separate small pan, bring the water to a boil, then add it slowly to the chocolate-butter mixture, stirring constantly. Stir in the sugar and corn syrup and bring the sauce to a boil. Let it bubble, but not boil up, in the pan — and don't stir — for exactly 8 minutes. Remove it from the heat and add the vanilla extract, stirring until well blended.

Contrary to its name, hot fudge sauce is best served warm, not piping hot from the stove. It can be refrigerated and reheated, but in our house it's never, ever around long enough for that.

Peanut Butter–Chocolate Chip Loaf

Quick Chocolate-Candy-Bar Sauce

The favored flavors of the United States are epitomized in chocolate chips and peanut butter, here combined in a single loaf. I find the peanut butter a bit overwhelming myself, but Revell and his friends like ice cream and chocolate sauce sandwiches made with slices of the loaf.

Keep some chocolate chips in the freezer for this one. Freezing the chips isn't mandatory; the flavor of the loaf will be fine if you simply add room-temperature morsels in the normal course of events. But they'll be mushed by the bread machine's kneading blade, and then you won't bite into those dark, still-melted beads of chocolate that are such a treat when the loaf is still warm from the oven — which brings to mind grilled peanut butter sandwiches. Remember those? This bread is wonderful for them. The bits of chocolate melt all over again!

As any kid with braces can tell you, peanut butter varies a lot in consistency, from a spread as soft as yogurt to one firm enough to cement pieces of bread together. Should the product of your baking efforts be still uncooked in the center when you cut it open, reduce the liquid in the recipe by a few tablespoonfuls next time if you're still on the same jar of peanut butter.

Another thing to consider, if the peanut butter in your house is of the salted variety — ours isn't, so that's what I used in the recipe — be sparing in the measure of salt you use.

> 1 1/4 cups milk, whole or skim
> 1/3 cup peanut butter, creamy or chunky
> 3 tablespoons dark brown sugar
> 2 cups unbleached all-purpose flour
> 1/4 cup wheat germ
> 1/4 to 1 teaspoon salt, to taste, depend-
> ing especially on the seasoning of the
> peanut butter
> 1 1/2 teaspoons active dry yeast
> 3/4 cup frozen chocolate chips

Pour the milk into your bread machine baking pan and scoop in the peanut butter, unless the instructions that came with your machine call for placing the yeast in the bottom of the pan and reserving the liquids till last. Add the brown sugar, flour, wheat germ, and salt. If your machine features a separate dispenser for leavening, add the yeast there; otherwise, scatter it over the rest of the ingredients in the pan.

Set the machine to its rapid-bake cycle, and if your machine has a separate control for bread color, set it to light, since on the regular color setting the crust will be quite dark, although still acceptably so. Remember to toss in the frozen chocolate chips when the machine beeps its readiness to accept such whole entities. Failing that, add the chips when the first kneading cycle has been completed.

While the bread is still warm and the chocolate chips still gooey and the peanut butter still fragrant, cut the crusts from the loaf, slice it, and spread slightly softened vanilla ice cream and Quick Chocolate-Candy-Bar Sauce (see below) between pairs of slices. Serve to hungry after-schoolers.

QUICK CHOCOLATE-CANDY-BAR SAUCE

> 1 1/4 cups milk, whole or skim
> 1 five-ounce milk chocolate candy bar
> 1 teaspoon sugar
> 4 lightly beaten egg yolks
> 1/2 teaspoon vanilla extract

Place the milk, candy bar, and sugar in a heavy saucepan over low heat or in the top of a double boiler and stir constantly until the chocolate and sugar are melted. Remove from the heat and add the egg yolks in a slow stream, beating briskly. Return the pan to the stove and stir for 2 or 3 minutes longer or until the sauce thickens. Remove from the heat again and add the vanilla extract. Blend until smooth and creamy.

Raspberry Cream Loaf

Raspberry Melba Sauce

Fruit flavors are my favorites, although being asked to decide which one I like best of all would present a tough choice. I know that the rare durian, that queen of fruits prized above all others in the Orient, is not it. Fantasies and tales of the durian's fabulous taste once had Susan and me traipsing all over the hills of Sarawak, in Borneo, in search of this legendary delight. When we finally found some to sample, it tasted overwhelmingly of garlic butter gone rancid. Its pungent smell permeated the entire village, which was apparently celebrating its harvest with gustatory fervor, overcoming the olfactory glands.

No, my favorite fruit flavor would be something more traditional to the Western world. Either raspberry or strawberry would be it. Here's a raspberry winner.

> 3/4 cup sour cream or yogurt, regular or
>   low-fat
> 2 tablespoons unsalted butter (or
>   canola oil)
> 1 1/2 teaspoons raspberry extract
> 1/3 cup canned raspberry filling
> 2 cups unbleached all-purpose flour
> 1/2 cup wheat germ
> 1/4 to 1 teaspoon salt, to taste
> 1 1/2 teaspoons active dry yeast

If the instructions that came with your bread machine call for the yeast to be placed in the baking pan first thing, remember to add the other dry ingredients before the liquids. Otherwise, scoop the sour cream or yogurt into your pan and add the butter (or canola oil), raspberry extract, raspberry filling, flour, wheat germ, and salt. Scatter the yeast over the top of the other ingredients or place it in its own separate dispenser if your machine has such a device.

Set the machine to its rapid-bake cycle for this loaf.

Once the loaf has cooled enough so that it can be sliced without difficulty, remove the top and bottom crusts and cut the remaining square or round into slices 1 to 1½ inches thick.

Serve the slices warm with a scoop of raspberry sorbet, a ladling of raspberry syrup or the Raspberry Melba Sauce below, and a few fresh raspberries scattered on top of it all. Talk about fruit flavor!

RASPBERRY MELBA SAUCE

⅓ cup red currant jelly
1 ten-ounce package frozen raspberries
* in syrup*
1 teaspoon lemon juice
2 teaspoons water
1 tablespoon cornstarch

In a heavy saucepan set over low heat or in the top of a double boiler, melt the currant jelly. Add and stir the raspberries until thawed and bubbly. In a separate small bowl, mix the lemon juice and water and stir in the cornstarch to form a smooth paste. Blend this mixture into the berries. Bring the sauce to a boil, stirring constantly, and boil for 1 minute or until thickened.

This sauce is delectable either poured warm over a sorbet or served chilled, especially if there are a few fresh berries available to stir into the syrup just before serving.

Piña Colada Loaf

Polvo de Amor

The flavor of piña colada can be overwhelming. In this sweet, nutty-textured loaf, however, it is subtle, provoking one of those "Gee, it's great, reminds me of something" experiences we have when a taste is familiar but elusive, so that we can almost, but not quite, identify it.

The bits of coconut that get toasted into the crust as the loaf bakes are real taste treats, and they give you some idea of how good *Polvo de Amor*, or toasted coconut cream (see the recipe following the one for the loaf), is as an accompaniment.

You'll find the piña colada mix called for in the recipe among the beverage mixes at your supermarket.

SMALL
1 cup piña colada mix
¼ cup canola or other light oil
½ cup firmly packed shredded
  coconut
½ cup pecan halves
2½ cups unbleached all-purpose
  flour
½ to 1 teaspoon salt, to taste
1½ teaspoons active dry yeast

LARGE
1½ cups piña colada mix
⅓ cup canola or other light oil
¾ cup firmly packed shredded
  coconut
⅔ cup pecan halves
3½ cups unbleached all-purpose
  flour
1 to 2 teaspoons salt, to taste
2 teaspoons active dry yeast

Pour the piña colada mix and oil into your baking pan and add the coconut, pecans, flour, salt, and yeast. Be sure to follow the directions that came with your particular machine for incorporating the leavening, since the instructions for some models specify reversing the order in which the ingredients are placed in the pan.

To bake the loaf, set the machine to its quick cycle.

A Piña Colada Loaf lends itself to a sweet molasses glaze made by beating together 1 tablespoon unsulphured molasses and 1 tablespoon of hot water. The glaze can be brushed over the crown of the loaf when it emerges from the electronic oven and, for super visual appeal, dusted with toasted shredded coconut, which adheres well to the sticky glaze. To brown this extra coconut, spread the strands out on a cookie sheet and bake them in an oven preheated to 350 degrees F. for about 10 minutes.

Another attractive presentation for the loaf is à la mode, with a simply made but delectable topping called *Polvo de Amor* in Spanish. The coconut cream called for in the recipe is found canned in the Latin American section of many grocery stores.

POLVO DE AMOR
1 cup canned coconut cream
3 tablespoons sugar

Pour the coconut cream into a small saucepan and add the sugar. Stir and cook over low heat until the mixture browns attractively.

To serve, lay generous individual slices of the Piña Colada Loaf on dessert plates, put a scoop of vanilla ice cream on each, and top with the *Polvo de Amor* as you would with a hot fudge sauce. For true coconut enthusiasts.

Peach Praline Loaf

Creamy Caramel Sauce

Here's a simple, quickly made loaf that originated because my daughter Tanya so often left half a canful of peaches in the refrigerator after making a snack of the rest. The canned fruit adds more softness and tenderness than actual taste to the finished product. However, while the flavor is mild, slices of the loaf, particularly when toasted, make a great base on which to float a large scoop of peach ice cream or frozen yogurt covered by Creamy Caramel Sauce (see the recipe following the one for the loaf).

The canned peaches to be found in our refrigerator, and hence in this loaf, are of the no-sugar-added variety.

If your machine has difficulty with this dough, which is very dry until the moisture is extracted from the peaches by the machine's kneading action, liquefy the peaches in a blender before adding them to the baking pan.

SMALL	LARGE
1 cup canned sliced unsweetened peaches, with liquid	1½ cups canned sliced unsweetened peaches, with liquid
1 teaspoon unsalted butter (or canola oil)	2 teaspoons unsalted butter (or canola oil)
1 medium egg	1 medium egg
½ teaspoon vanilla extract	1 teaspoon vanilla extract
¼ teaspoon almond extract	½ teaspoon almond extract
½ cup pecan halves	¾ cup pecan halves
2 cups unbleached all-purpose flour	3 cups unbleached all-purpose flour
½ cup semolina flour	¾ cup semolina flour
¼ to 1 teaspoon salt, to taste	½ to 1½ teaspoons salt, to taste
1½ teaspoons active dry yeast	2 teaspoons active dry yeast

Place the peaches together with their canning liquid in the baking pan of your bread machine, unless the instructions that came with your machine specify that the yeast is to be placed first in the bottom of the pan, followed by the other dry ingredients and, last, the liquids. Add the butter (or canola oil), egg, vanilla and almond extracts, pecans, all-purpose and semolina flours, salt, and yeast. If your machine has a separate dispenser for leavening, spoon the yeast in there; otherwise, scatter it over the rest of the ingredients.

Use the machine's rapid-bake cycle for this loaf.

While a peach praline dessert can certainly be concocted with a ready-made topping, no commercial variety can match the following simple homemade caramel sauce for this dessert.

CREAMY CARAMEL SAUCE

    2 cups sugar
    2 cups heavy cream, heated
    1 teaspoon vanilla extract

Place the sugar in a large heavy saucepan or skillet set over very low heat and stir it with a long-handled wooden spoon just until melted. It will lump as it melts. Not to worry. Remove it from the heat and carefully, keeping your distance (since the next step may result in some sizzle and steam), add the heated cream a little at a time, stirring constantly. Return the pan to the heat and cook the sauce, stirring slowly, until it is smooth and syrupy. Remove from the heat and blend in the vanilla extract. Serve immediately.

Yet Another Chocolate Loaf

Chocolate Buttercream Filling
Satin Chocolate Glaze

Can one have too much chocolate? Not according to Tanya and Revell. Perhaps for that reason, I couldn't resist adding one more recipe for a chocolate loaf as a grand finale to this chapter. Especially when I discovered that this one — which has a rich, dense, fudgy texture, although not the sweetness of true fudge — is wonderfully and wickedly complemented by Chocolate Buttercream Filling, Satin Chocolate Glaze (see the recipes following the one for the loaf), and ice cream over all. The contrast of the satin glaze with the soft ice cream is marvelous.

A greater quantity of dough than that of the recipe below is more than a bread machine can handle. Let that not deter you from making the so-called small loaf.

> ½ cup buttermilk
> ⅓ cup milk, whole or skim
> 1 medium egg
> 1 teaspoon chocolate extract
> ½ teaspoon vanilla extract
> 1 cup unbleached all-purpose flour
> ⅓ cup barley flour
> ¼ cup semolina flour
> ¼ cup millet flour
> ¼ cup graham cracker crumbs
> ¼ cup cocoa
> ⅓ cup sugar
> 1 tablespoon instant coffee, regular or
>   decaffeinated
> ¼ to 1 teaspoon salt, to taste
> 2 teaspoons active dry yeast

Unless the instructions for your particular bread machine specify that the yeast is to be placed in the bottom of the pan first thing, followed by the other dry ingredients and then the liquids, pour the buttermilk and milk into your baking pan. Break the egg into the pan and add the chocolate and vanilla extracts, followed by the all-purpose, barley, semolina, and millet flours. Measure in the graham cracker crumbs, cocoa, sugar, instant coffee, salt, and yeast, placing the leavening in its own separate dispenser if your machine has that feature.

Bake the loaf on the machine's quick cycle.

Because it is rich but not sugary, this cake can be lavishly spread with buttercream without becoming a too cloyingly sweet confection. Buttercream can be used to ice the top of the loaf as well, but it is lovely with the deep, dark Satin Chocolate Glaze, especially if servings are to be topped with ice cream.

CHOCOLATE BUTTERCREAM FILLING

3 tablespoons unsalted butter
1 cup confectioners' sugar
⅓ cup cocoa
1 tablespoon dark corn syrup
2 tablespoons heavy cream
½ teaspoon vanilla extract

Cream the butter in a small bowl. Mix the confectioners' sugar and cocoa together and blend them into the butter a little at a time. Stir in the corn syrup, cream, and vanilla extract, and beat the mixture at high speed for 2 to 3 minutes or until the buttercream is of a good spreading consistency.

Cut the top and bottom crusts from the chocolate loaf, slice it crosswise to make layers, and fill with the buttercream. Content yourself with a buttercream topping as well, or take just a few minutes to create the following handsome glossy glaze for the cake.

SATIN CHOCOLATE GLAZE

2 tablespoons sugar
2 tablespoons water
½ cup semisweet chocolate chips

In a small saucepan, bring the sugar and water to a boil, stirring until the sugar is completely dissolved. Melt the chocolate chips into the mix, remove from the heat, and stir until the icing is fairly stiff but still spreadable. It will harden to a smooth, satiny glaze.

Slices of this treat served à la mode need no further enrichment.

22 · Sauced and Soused Loaves

A DESSERT DRENCHED in a sauce has about it a certain down-home quality associated in many people's minds with the treat looked forward to as children all through the obligatory dinner preceding it. The simple cake or square of some other floury delicacy filled up those corners left hungry by the mandatory forkful of the vegetable of the day, and the sauce, frequently a warm one — and certainly a sweet one — was oh so satisfying. Thus, these desserts often have great comfort appeal.

Despite the homely inspiration for such desserts, the offerings in this chapter are by no means plain and simple. The choice of possible embellishments is nearly endless, and the yield from your bread machine bakery with a sauce or a mousse filling can be quite elegant, as witness the nobly domed *Zuccotto* (see page 277). So let your imagination, and perhaps memories, play with the desserts in this chapter.

Lemon Suzette Loaf

Suzette Sauce

Citrus oils are quite volatile, and their flavor often vanishes during prolonged cooking. This is why breads calling for citrus zest or citrus oil are so often baking-powder loaves, whose cooking time is normally shorter than that of yeast breads. Since the bread machines on the market as yet have no really short cycle to accommodate these quick breads, however, I've had to work around that limitation.

Here's a yeast-based loaf formulated especially for bread machines that's very nearly a cake and certainly lemony. Serve slices of it flooded with warm Suzette Sauce (see the recipe below the one for the loaf) — yes, it's the sauce of crepes, but it can be so much more! — with or without a layer of vanilla ice cream or lemon sherbet in between.

SMALL	LARGE
1 cup milk, whole or skim	1¼ cups milk, whole or skim
3 tablespoons unsalted butter (or canola oil)	¼ cup unsalted butter (or canola oil)
1 tablespoon lemon juice	1 tablespoon + 2 teaspoons lemon juice
grated zest of 1 small lemon	grated zest of 1 large or 2 small lemons
1½ cups semolina flour	2 cups semolina flour
1 cup unbleached all-purpose flour	1⅓ cups unbleached all-purpose flour
½ cup sugar	⅔ cup sugar
¼ to 1 teaspoon salt, to taste	½ to 1½ teaspoons salt, to taste
1½ teaspoons active dry yeast	2 teaspoons active dry yeast

Pour the milk into the baking pan of your bread machine and add the butter (or canola oil), lemon juice, lemon zest, semolina and all-purpose flours, sugar, salt, and yeast, placing the leavening in its own separate dispenser if your machine has one. Remember, however, that if the instructions accompanying your model call for placing the leavening in the bottom of the pan first thing, then the other dry ingredients should be added next, before the liquids.

Bake the loaf on your machine's quick cycle.

SUZETTE SAUCE

½ cup unsalted butter
½ cup sugar
2 tablespoons orange juice
2 to 3 teaspoons grated orange zest, to
  taste

Melt the butter in a small heavy saucepan and stir in the sugar. Add the orange juice and orange zest and bring the mixture to a boil. Lower the heat and simmer for 2 minutes. Pour into a warmed pitcher and let everyone help themselves.

Currant Ginger Loaf

Hard Sauce

Here's a loaf my father would have loved. Ginger was one of his favorite spices, and, as Susan put it, "This one's for people who really like ginger." If the gingerroot you procure happens to be very fresh and the flavor promises to be too strong to suit your taste, reduce the amount of ginger called for in the recipe.

The currants found among the ingredients for this loaf lend it contrast in both taste and texture when they're kept whole. This can be achieved by reserving them to toss into the baking pan when the machine beeps, if it's the type of machine that does that, or after the first kneading cycle, if your machine is the strong, silent type.

For a real treat, serve warm slices of this bread with homemade rum- or brandy-flavored Hard Sauce (see the recipe following the one for the loaf).

SMALL	LARGE
½ cup buttermilk	¾ cup buttermilk
2 tablespoons unsalted butter (or canola oil)	3 tablespoons unsalted butter (or canola oil)
1 medium egg	1 large egg
2 tablespoons thinly sliced peeled fresh ginger	3 tablespoons thinly sliced peeled fresh ginger
2 teaspoons lemon juice	1 tablespoon lemon juice
2 cups unbleached all-purpose flour	3 cups unbleached all-purpose flour
¼ cup uncooked oatmeal (not instant)	⅓ cup uncooked oatmeal (not instant)
2 tablespoons dark brown sugar	3 tablespoons dark brown sugar
¼ to 1 teaspoon salt, to taste	½ to 1½ teaspoons salt, to taste
1½ teaspoons active dry yeast	2 teaspoons active dry yeast
½ cup dried currants	¾ cup dried currants

Unless the instructions for your bread machine specify that the yeast is to be placed in the bottom of the baking pan, followed by the other dry ingredients and then the liquids, measure the buttermilk into your pan and add the butter (or canola oil), egg, ginger, lemon juice, flour, oatmeal, brown sugar, salt, and yeast, placing the leavening in its own separate dispenser if your machine has that feature.

Set the machine to its rapid-bake cycle and let it start churning away. At the beep or, failing that, after the first kneading cycle, add the currants. If you're planning on the homemade Hard Sauce below as an accompaniment to this loaf, you might want to whip it up while you're waiting for the beep, so it can be chilling while the bread bakes.

HARD SAUCE

½ cup unsalted butter, softened
¾ cup confectioners' sugar
1 to 2 tablespoons rum or brandy or
  your own favorite liqueur

In a small bowl, cream the butter until smooth. Slowly add the confectioners' sugar and beat until fluffy. Blend in the rum, brandy, or other liqueur.

While the Hard Sauce can be served simply chilled in a small bowl and perhaps garnished with a few sprigs of mint, for a pretty display it can also be piped into individual rosettes, using a pastry tube or a cookie press fitted with a star tip. Pipe the rosettes onto a foil-lined cookie sheet or tray, freeze them uncovered until hard, transfer them to a regular freezer container, and you'll have decorative rosettes ready anytime you need them.

Pudding Bread

Lemon Sauce

At the conclusion of a dinner we were having at the home of some friends in London, their daughter Lucy, on seeing the ice cream for dessert, exclaimed, "Oh, my favorite pudding!"

Our own daughter Tanya looked rather nonplussed. "But that's not pudding, is it? It's ice cream."

"Well, yes, we're having ice cream for pudding."

The word "pudding" was bandied about with considerable mirth until we colonials finally understood that what we call dessert the English call pudding — whether it is or not.

Well, here's a pudding that's actually bread, or vice versa. Hard sauce is the traditional accompaniment to a pudding; see the recipe immediately preceding, which is presented as a topping for the Currant Ginger Loaf. Served with this sauce or Lemon Sauce (see the recipe below the one for the Pudding Bread), it's a fine winter dessert. Buttered like scones, it belongs in front of a crackling fire with some tea. In either case, it's substantial fare, as you might

surmise from the absence of a recipe for a large loaf. There are big chunks of apricots and nuts in every rich, rough-textured bite.

> *1 cup sour cream or yogurt, regular or*
>   *low-fat*
> *½ cup apple cider*
> *¼ cup unsulphured molasses*
> *1 medium egg*
> *½ cup dried apricots*
> *½ cup dried apples*
> *½ cup hazelnuts*
> *½ cup pecan halves*
> *1½ cups wheat bran*
> *¾ cup unbleached all-purpose flour*
> *½ cup cornmeal*
> *½ to 1 teaspoon salt, to taste*
> *2 teaspoons active dry yeast*

Scoop the sour cream or yogurt into the baking pan of your bread machine and add the cider and molasses, unless the instructions for your particular machine specify that the leavening is to be placed in the pan first and the liquids last. Break the egg into the pan, then measure in the apricots, apples, hazelnuts, pecans, wheat bran, flour, cornmeal, and salt. Distribute the yeast according to the instructions for your machine.

Bake on the machine's quick cycle.

For a lovely piquant accent to this pudding, try the following sunny Lemon Sauce.

LEMON SAUCE

> *1 tablespoon cornstarch*
> *1 cup water*
> *6 tablespoons lemon juice*
> *½ cup sugar*
> *grated zest of 1 medium lemon*

Place the cornstarch in a small bowl and gradually stir in ¼ cup of the water, pouring the rest into a small saucepan or the top of a double boiler. Blend the cornstarch solution until smooth. To the water in the saucepan add the lemon juice and sugar. Heat these ingredients, stirring until the sugar is completely dissolved. Then blend the cornstarch solution into the lemon mixture and simmer, stirring constantly, until the sauce is thick and clear. Add the lemon zest and transfer the hot sauce to an attractive small pitcher from which it can be poured over individual helpings of the Pudding Bread as desired.

Pear Loaf

Cherry Sauce

Pears are one of the few fruits that ripen well off the tree. Stone fruits, such as peaches and plums, harvested early never seem to attain the sweet, redolent flavor of those picked by hand in the dappled shade of the orchard at the very moment they are about to drop. In fact, it's not unusual for a store-bought plum to go from rock to rot without much flavor in between.

Pears are different. They actually ripen better off a tree than on it. They also dry exceedingly well, and in their dried form they add a very pleasant tangy flavor to a loaf. Try serving slices of this one fresh from the electronic oven with a simple, warm, sweet Cherry Sauce (see the recipe following the one for the loaf).

3/4 cup yogurt, regular or low-fat
3 tablespoons unsalted butter (or
canola oil)
2 tablespoons honey
3/4 cup dried pears
2 1/4 cups unbleached all-purpose flour
1/2 to 1 teaspoon salt, to taste
1 1/2 teaspoons active dry yeast

Spoon the yogurt into your bread machine baking pan and add the butter (or canola oil), honey, pears, flour, salt, and yeast, placing the leavening in its own separate dispenser if your machine has one. Where the instructions for your particular machine call for placing the yeast in the bottom of the pan first thing, remember to reverse the order in which you add the liquids and the other dry ingredients.

Set the machine to its rapid-bake cycle for this loaf.

To serve with a cherry sauce, first remove the crusts of your Pear Loaf. If you make the cut for the crusts about 1 inch in from the sides and freeze these edges, they will enhance your next chocolate fondue wonderfully. The flavors of pear and chocolate are glorious together.

Slice the remaining loaf into 1-inch-thick pieces. Pour some cherry sauce onto individual dessert dishes and place a slice of Pear Loaf in the sauce on each plate. Grace the top with a liberal dollop of whipped cream and decorate with grated chocolate or, for a really pretty effect, a generous sprinkling of chocolate curls.

The sauce for this dessert can be a commercial one or simply the contents of a can of tart red cherry pie filling heated in a saucepan over medium heat. But for a memorable treat, try the homemade sauce with dried cherries given below. Since you don't have to pit them, stirring up this sauce takes next to no time, and it's truly luscious.

CHERRY SAUCE

1 cup dried cherries
1½ cups water
¼ cup sugar
¼ cup dark corn syrup
1 tablespoon cornstarch

Place the cherries in a heavy saucepan, cover them with 1¼ cups of the water, and bring the mixture to a simmer over very low heat. Continue to simmer for 5 minutes or until the cherries are plump and tender.

Remove the pan from the heat, add the remaining ¼ cup of water to cool the contents just a bit, and transfer the cherries to your food processor or blender. Puree them until they are very smooth.

Return the puree to the saucepan, add the sugar, and cook for another minute. Pour the corn syrup into a measuring cup, add the cornstarch, and blend this mixture to a smooth paste. Stir the paste into the sauce and simmer very slowly, stirring constantly, until the sauce is dark and thick. Serve hot and fragrant.

Crunchy Caramel Apple–Granola Loaf

Butterscotch Sauce Pure and Simple

One of the toughest choices facing our kids every August and September was whether to have the caramel-covered apples or the red sugar-coated ones at the Woodstock and Brooklyn fairs. The cotton candy was easily chosen — always red, never blue, always on a paper cone, never in a bag. Ah, life's choices should always remain so clear-cut.

For me the choice in apples was simple. The caramel-covered ones didn't stick to the teeth. The same holds true for this easy-to-make treat.

SMALL	LARGE
1 cup sour cream or yogurt, regular or low-fat	1 1/3 cups sour cream or yogurt, regular or low-fat
1 tablespoon unsalted butter or canola oil	2 tablespoons unsalted butter or canola oil
1/2 cup honey	2/3 cup honey
1 medium egg	1 medium egg
1 small unpeeled but cored apple, diced	1 large unpeeled but cored apple, diced
1 3/4 cups unbleached all-purpose flour	3 cups unbleached all-purpose flour
1 cup granola	1 1/2 cups granola
1 teaspoon ground nutmeg	1 1/2 teaspoons ground nutmeg
1/4 to 1 teaspoon salt, to taste	1/2 to 1 1/2 teaspoons salt, to taste
1 1/2 teaspoons active dry yeast	2 teaspoons active dry yeast

Unless the instructions that came with your bread machine call for starting with the leavening, scoop the sour cream or yogurt into your baking pan and add the butter or canola oil, honey, egg, apple, flour, granola, nutmeg, and salt. If your machine has a separate dispenser for the yeast, measure it in there. If not, scatter it over the other dry ingredients.

Set your machine to its rapid-bake cycle for this loaf.

The dough will be quite stiff. So if you're not dashing out the door, check the bread pan 5 or 10 minutes into the kneading cycle, especially if you are making the big loaf in an oblong pan, to be sure the machine is collecting all the ingredients from the corners of the pan. If it's not, scrape the sides down once, using a rubber spatula, to make sure everything is incorporated into the dough.

For a lovely dessert, once the loaf is baked and cooled, cut off the top and bottom crusts along with about 1 inch of the inner crumb. Freeze these slices for later use with a fondue or in a bread pudding.

Cut the remaining loaf into 1-inch-thick slices, place them on individual serving plates, and cover them with a good butterscotch sauce, store-bought or homemade (see below). Top that with whipped cream for extra opulence and sprinkle a little extra crunchy granola over all.

BUTTERSCOTCH SAUCE PURE AND SIMPLE

½ cup unsalted butter
1 cup dark corn syrup
2 cups dark brown sugar
½ cup heavy cream
1 teaspoon vanilla extract

Melt the butter in a heavy saucepan over low heat. Add the corn syrup and then, gradually, the brown sugar, stirring until blended. Bring the mixture to a boil, reduce the heat, and simmer, stirring constantly, for 3 to 5 minutes or until the sauce is the consistency of heavy syrup. Remove from the heat and blend in the cream and vanilla extract. The aroma of this sauce is heavenly.

Figs and Cream Loaf

Prune Sauce

H ere's a dark, rich, substantial confection in the tradition of English holiday desserts that will have you thinking of Dickens. A compact cake with a muffin-y crust, it's wonderful sliced thin and spread with sweet butter for tea. For a company dinner, serve ample squares of it with the thick, syrupy Prune Sauce that follows the cake recipe.

SMALL	LARGE
1 cup heavy cream	1 1/2 cups heavy cream
2 tablespoons unsalted butter (or canola oil)	3 tablespoons unsalted butter (or canola oil)
2 tablespoons honey	3 tablespoons honey
1/2 cup dried figs, stems removed, quartered	3/4 cup dried figs, stems removed, quartered
1 cup unbleached all-purpose flour	1 1/2 cups unbleached all-purpose flour
1 cup whole-wheat flour	1 1/2 cups whole-wheat flour
1/4 teaspoon ground cloves	1/2 teaspoon ground cloves
1/4 teaspoon ground allspice	1/2 teaspoon ground allspice
1/2 to 1 teaspoon salt, to taste	1 to 2 teaspoons salt, to taste
1 1/2 teaspoons active dry yeast	2 teaspoons active dry yeast

Remember that if the instructions accompanying your bread machine call for the yeast to be placed in the baking pan first, the dry ingredients should be added before the liquids. Otherwise, pour the cream into your pan and add the butter (or canola oil), honey, figs, all-purpose and whole-wheat flours, cloves, allspice, salt, and yeast. If your machine has a separate dispenser for leavening, spoon the yeast in there after all the other ingredients have been measured into the baking pan.

Set your machine to its quick setting for this loaf.

The following dark, velvety Prune Sauce complements a Figs and Cream cake superbly. Neither the cake nor the sauce is cloyingly sweet, although the latter is rich and full-bodied, and together they provide a surprisingly healthy dose of fiber, vitamins, and minerals — in all honesty, not an unhealthful dessert.

PRUNE SAUCE

1 cup pitted prunes, firmly packed
water to cover
2 tablespoons lemon juice
1 tablespoon grated orange zest
½ teaspoon ground cloves
¼ teaspoon ground nutmeg
¼ teaspoon ground cinnamon
½ cup sugar
½ cup red wine or port

Place the prunes in a heavy saucepan, barely cover with water, and stir in the lemon juice, orange zest, cloves, nutmeg, and cinnamon. Bring the mixture to the boiling point, then lower the heat and gently simmer for 15 minutes or until the prunes are soft, stirring occasionally.

Transfer the mixture to the bowl of a food processor or a blender and puree until smooth.

Return the puree to the saucepan, add the sugar and wine or port, and continue to cook the sauce over low heat until it is velvety and hot.

Squares of the Figs and Cream cake are attractively served simply topped by a dollop of whipped cream, with the Prune Sauce as an accompaniment to be ladled over individual helpings as modestly or generously as desired.

Zuccotto

Zuccotto Filling
Zuccotto Frosting

The quintessentially Florentine *Zuccotto* is a showy centerpiece confection that's quickly assembled. It will want 4 to 6 hours of chilling in the refrigerator once it's put together, so that much advance planning is required. But this very fact is what makes it such a wonderful company dessert, for it's finished long before the guests arrive or you need to turn your attention to other dinner preparations.

A spectacular half-sphere of a cake completely enveloped in snowy whipped cream, the *Zuccotto* discloses its true nature only upon being sliced, for it is a filled cake whose creamy center comes in many different flavors. The recipe adapted here for the bread machine bakery uses a filling quickly and easily made, to go with the bread so effortlessly conjured up by your bread machine. One time-saver deserves another, after all.

The unique contour of *zuccotti* is traditionally achieved with the help of a special half-round mold suggesting a gourd or a pumpkin cut in two: hence the name *zuccotto*, or "little pumpkin." Doubtless the specialty bakers' catalogs in this country will soon carry such molds, but an ordinary 2½-quart glass or stainless steel mixing bowl works just fine for this dish.

Traditionally, the base for *zuccotti* is a sponge cake. Here a certain adjustment had to be made for the bread machine bakery, since bread machines can't make true sponge cakes. But loaves such as the Light Citrus, Banana Almond, and Lemon Suzette, whose recipes are found earlier in this volume, make very respectable shells for a *zuccotto*, even though not completely authentic renderings of the original.

If you haven't much of any of the loaves mentioned left among the slices tucked away in your freezer, you can use lots of tops and bottoms saved from other loaves, provided they aren't too strongly flavored in any one direction. And, of course, you can always toss the ingredients for, say, a fresh citrus loaf into your bread machine if you know a little in advance that you'll be wanting to serve this elegant dessert.

ZUCCOTTO FILLING

8 one-ounce squares semisweet baking
  chocolate
1¼ cups heavy cream, well chilled
1 tablespoon instant espresso
1 package (3⅜ ounces) vanilla
  pudding mix
1½ cups milk, whole or skim
1 teaspoon almond extract

almond liqueur (approximately ¼
  cup)

Coarsely grate 4 squares of the semisweet chocolate. (To save fingers, I grate just half of each square, working my way across it parallel to that convenient groove provided for cutting the block in half, and grating right up to the notch. To get the 4 ounces called for, I thus grate the first half, so to speak, of 8 squares of chocolate.) Set the grated chocolate aside for the moment.

In a small heavy saucepan over very low heat or in a glass bowl in the microwave, melt the other 4 ounces of the chocolate. Set this aside as well.

Pour the cream into a chilled mixing bowl and whip lightly. Add the instant espresso and continue beating until the cream forms stiff peaks.

In a separate bowl, combine the vanilla pudding mix with the milk and stir in the almond extract. Fold the grated chocolate and whipped cream into the pudding.

To assemble the *Zuccotto*, cut the loaf you plan to use into slices about ½ inch thick. If you're using leftover slices, it doesn't matter

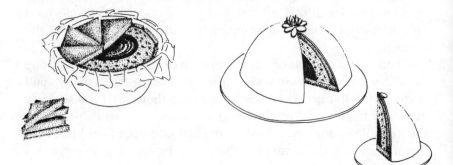

if they happen to be a little fatter or a little thinner than that. They should all be about the same thickness, though.

Stack the slices together and cut the stack in half diagonally so that you end up with 2 piles of triangles or, in the case of a round loaf, half-rounds. Separate the triangles or half-circles and sprinkle them with the almond liqueur.

Line your ersatz *Zuccotto* mold with plastic wrap. Reserving enough of the bread to cover the top of the bowl, wedge the remaining triangles or half-rounds snugly into the bowl, facing them all the same way so that their bottom points meet at the center and they radiate out in a star pattern. What you're striving for is a compact concave shell. This concentrated endeavor leads to fairly fragrant hands. The first time I made a *Zuccotto* the kids commented on my new after-shave.

Line the inside of the shell you've created with about half the pudding mixture, keeping to the outside of the bowl in order to leave room at the center for the remainder of the pudding. Then fold the melted chocolate into the remaining half of the pudding and fill in the center of the shell with this darker mixture.

Now cover the top of the pudding with the reserved triangles or half-rounds. This top will be the bottom once you invert the bowl, which you will do to serve the dessert, so don't worry about the pieces fitting together perfectly. But trim their edges so they don't extend beyond the bowl.

Cover the bowl tightly with plastic wrap and refrigerate the *Zuccotto* for 4 to 6 hours. An overnight's resting doesn't hurt it at all. The serving plate you intend to use can be inverted over it to stay cold as well.

ZUCCOTTO FROSTING

¾ cup heavy cream, well chilled
3 tablespoons confectioners' sugar
1 tablespoon instant espresso

blanched almonds for garnish

In a small chilled bowl, beat the cream lightly, add the confectioners' sugar and instant espresso, and continue to beat until the frosting is thick and fluffy.

Take the *Zuccotto* from the refrigerator, uncover and invert the bowl over the chilled serving plate, and unmold the cake. Carefully remove the plastic wrap around it and frost it with the whipped cream. Garnish the dome with golden toasted almonds.

23 · Dessert Fondues

 In these retro-fifties days when Buddy Holly is alive and well and touring the country on countless car radios via classic rock stations and the King is taking his lickings courtesy of the U.S. Postal Service, my receipt of a fondue set as a Christmas present from our with-it teenager Tanya should have come as no surprise. But I had forgotten all about this culinary device, long since relegated to the musty corners of my memory, along with chafing dishes fashioned for tiny hot dogs and ring molds designed to imprint bold designs on green Jell-O suffused with canned fruit cocktail.

As it turned out, the fondue set was a great inducement to relaxed and rather cozy family dinners. Fondues are by nature a sociable yet informal event. Everyone seems to talk more around a fondue pot, particularly if its contents are sweet.

The original fondue was, of course, melted cheese. The long forks dipped into the communal pot held bite-size cubes of a homely bread, and a mellow wine cleared the palate between leisurely nibbles. Later, fondue bourguignonne made its appearance. The cheese gave way to oil and the bread was replaced by meat. Then finally, or so the story goes, sometime in the late fifties, a Swiss chef forgot a Toblerone bar beside the stove, and the chocolate melted.

He dipped his finger in some, licked it off, and, voilà, the Toblerone fondue was born.

Chocolate and other dessert fondues provide an ideal use for leftover coffee breads, and particularly their crusts, if generous enough in their proportions. A fondue calls for a crusty bread anyway, to help give the fork something to hold on to when a cube of it is lifted from the dip. So when you trim a Banana Almond Loaf for petits fours or a Raspberry Cream one to be served à la mode, trim a little extravagantly so that what you are paring off isn't crust alone. Freeze these outer slices, and when you plan a fondue you'll have your bread on hand, needing only a brief defrosting period before it's ready to be cubed for serving. The bread will not be at its piping-hot-from-the-oven freshest, obviously. But that's all to the good. Truly fresh bread always has to be aged a little for a fondue.

One of the nice things about the home bread machine bakery is that, making your own loaves effortlessly and often, you can mix and match breads with fondues. Fruit breads go particularly well with chocolate fondues, for example, spice and nut loaves with butterscotch ones. Try cubes of Raspberry Cream and Pear loaves — pears and chocolate are made for each other — with a Toblerone Fondue, and serve squares of a Triple Chocolate Loaf with a mocha or mint dip. Dice the crusts of a Crunchy Caramel Apple-Granola Loaf or a Figs and Cream cake to accompany an Apple or a Hot Buttered Rum Fondue, and add some cubes made from the round slices left over in making a *Panettone Farcito*.

The palate can have too much of a good thing, of course. So when you serve a fondue, for a respite from these rich combinations do add to your bread board some squares from simpler loaves — Light Citrus, perhaps, or Sweet Peppermint Poppy Seed, Rose and Orange, or Peach Praline.

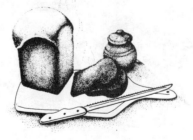

Toblerone Fondue

A chocolate fondue can be made from many kinds of chocolate — unsweetened, semisweet, sweet, chocolate chips — but there's something about those creamy Toblerone bars with their bits of nuts that makes a chocolate fondue special. So that's the chocolate I suggest here.

> *½ cup heavy cream*
> *12 ounces Toblerone chocolate*
> *½ teaspoon vanilla extract*
> *¼ teaspoon lemon extract or 1*
> *tablespoon good brandy*

Warm the cream in a small saucepan, break the chocolate into pieces, and drop them into the cream, stirring over low heat until the chocolate is completely melted. Remove the pan from the heat and slowly, stirring gently, add the vanilla and lemon extracts, or the vanilla extract and brandy. Pour the sauce into a small fondue pot that you've warmed with hot tap water and place it over its burner.

Your bread selection for a Toblerone Fondue might include some Light Citrus, Sour Cream Blueberry, Banana Almond, Kumquat Delight, Raspberry Cream, and Pear. For intense chocolate on chocolate, add cubes from a Triple Chocolate Loaf. On the side, set out a fruit platter with an attractive arrangement of fresh strawberries, grapes, and sliced kiwifruit garnished with sprigs of mint. In the wintertime, substitute a bowl of sun-dried apricots and pears. They'll all get dipped.

Mocha Fondue

Coffee and chocolate are a great combination. Blended into a fondue, they turn any homely dunking bread into an opulent dessert.

> *½ cup strong black coffee or espresso*
> *8 one-ounce squares semisweet baking*
> *chocolate*
> *⅓ cup heavy cream*
> *1 teaspoon coffee extract*
> *pinch of ground or freshly grated*
> *nutmeg*

Heat the coffee or espresso in a small saucepan over low heat and add the chocolate, stirring until the chocolate is melted. Blend in the cream, coffee extract, and nutmeg. Transfer the sauce to a fondue pot, warmed with hot tap water, and keep it quite hot over your fondue burner.

Probably by simple association, I think of squares of Coffee Nips Coffee Cake in connection with this fondue. But cubes from Rose and Orange, Double Almond, Chocolate Nut Delight, Cranberry-Orange, and Cherry Milk loaves are also excellent complements to a Mocha Fondue.

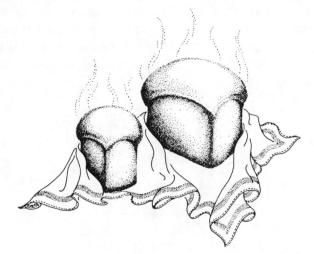

Super-Quick Chocolate-Mint Fondue

For an impromptu two-minute fondue that kids love after a cold day outside and adults aren't exactly impartial to either, take some of your frozen bread trimmings from the freezer and pop them into the microwave to defrost. Then turn your attention to this quick fondue sauce. Junior Mints are a fine choice for it. So are Peppermint Patties, After Eights, and other after-dinner mints.

> *12 ounces chocolate-covered mints*
> *2 tablespoons unsalted butter*
> *¼ cup heavy cream*

For microwave preparation, place the mints in a microwave-safe bowl, add the butter and cream, and microwave for 2 to 3 minutes, until the mints are melted and the fondue is hot. Meanwhile, fill your fondue pot with hot tap water to preheat it. While the mints are melting, you can be cubing the bread. When you're ready to serve the fondue, empty the water from the fondue pot, shake off the excess moisture, and pour in the sauce.

For stovetop preparation, melt the butter in a small saucepan over very low heat, add the mints and stir until melted, then blend in the cream and stir until well warmed. Transfer to your preheated fondue pot.

Dish up cubes from a Banana Chocolate or a Peanut Butter–Chocolate Chip Loaf with this one if it's for the kids, and add some marshmallows to the bowl.

Mint-Chocolate Fondue

In our family, there can't be too much mint chocolate or too many chocolate mints. That goes for family fondue gatherings as well as other occasions. There's something special about the match between the cool mint flavor and the smooth sweetness of the chocolate that is quite compelling.

This fondue is even richer and mintier than the preceding one.

½ cup heavy cream
8 one-ounce squares semisweet baking
  chocolate
2 tablespoons peppermint liqueur or 1
  tablespoon peppermint extract

peppermint candy canes for garnish

Pour the cream into a small saucepan, add the chocolate, and stir over low heat until the chocolate is melted and the mixture is hot. Remove from the heat to blend in the peppermint liqueur or extract. It might be a good idea to sample the mixture as you go. The dip may want a little less, or a little more, of the mint flavor than the recipe lists. Peppermint is a matter of taste.

Serve the fondue garnished at the last minute with bright bits of peppermint candy cane, and provide plenty of bite-size morsels from your last Cherries and Cheese and Yet Another Chocolate loaves. Toss a few fresh mint sprigs, if you have them, into the basket with the bread.

Super-Quick Butterscotch Fondue

There's something about a crisp fall or cold winter evening that seems to bring on the urge for something sweet and warm to nibble on. This fondue is for whipping up in next to no time when the craving for a rich caramel treat hits.

> *½ cup heavy cream*
> *2 cups commercial butterscotch sauce*
> *or ½ pound cream caramels*

Heat the cream in a small saucepan, blend in the butterscotch sauce or cream caramels, stir until smooth and hot, and serve in a fondue pot that has been preheated with hot tap water. Add some marshmallows, for the kids, and dates, for the grown-ups, to the bread basket. That's all there is to it, and the dipping is a delight.

Real Down-Home Butterscotch Fondue

A butterscotch fondue, like a chocolate one, goes particularly well with nut and spice loaves, and one made from this easy recipe leaves any store-bought butterscotch out in the cold.

> *1 cup dark brown sugar*
> *2 tablespoons unbleached all-purpose*
> *   flour*
> *⅛ teaspoon salt*
> *1 cup evaporated milk*
> *2 egg yolks, lightly beaten*
> *2 tablespoons unsalted butter*
> *¼ teaspoon vanilla extract*

Stir the brown sugar, flour, and salt together in a heavy saucepan or in the top of a double boiler, then slowly blend in the evaporated milk. Place the pan or double boiler over low heat and, stirring constantly, add the beaten egg yolks and the butter. Cook the sauce, stirring often, until it is thick and creamy. Remove the pan from the heat and blend in the vanilla extract.

To serve, transfer the dip to a fondue pot that has been warmed with hot tap water and set it on its burner. Supply an assortment of Apple Wheat, Butterscotch Brickle, Peach Praline, and Crunchy Caramel Apple-Granola cubes. Small figs and apple wedges, fresh or dried, are marvelous dipped in this fondue as well.

Apple Fondue

Not all sweet fondues are based on chocolate or other confectionery sweets. Some fit right into the health-food, fruit-and-veggies, body-conscious mind-set of the nineties. A little wine (red, of course) is also healthful, according to research initiated where else but in France.

2 teaspoons unsalted butter
2 teaspoons unbleached all-purpose
 flour
1 cup good red table wine
2 tablespoons sugar
1/2 cup smooth applesauce
1/2 teaspoon ground cinnamon
zest of 1/2 medium lemon
1 cup apple juice
1/2 teaspoon cornstarch

cinnamon sticks for garnish

Melt the butter in a saucepan over low heat and stir in the flour to form a smooth paste. Let the roux brown slightly, then slowly add a little of the wine, stirring quickly to avoid lumping. As the mixture thins and becomes smooth, pour in the rest of the wine, add the sugar, and heat until the sugar is dissolved. Blend in the applesauce, cinnamon, and lemon zest. Blend a little of the apple juice with the cornstarch in a small bowl and stir to a paste. Add the rest of the juice to the sauce and heat well, but do not allow the mixture to boil. Stir in the dissolved cornstarch a little at a time until the fondue is thick enough to cling to a cube of bread dipped in it. You may not need to use all of the cornstarch solution. Pour the dip into a fondue pot that has been warmed with hot tap water and set the pot over its burner.

Toss in a cinnamon stick or two to keep the aroma lingering above the fondue, and serve with cubes from *Pepparkaka*, *Panettone*, Pumpkin-Pie-Spice, Currant Ginger, and Figs and Cream loaves. Set out a small bowl of orange sections or quartered kumquats for both visual and gustatory sparkle.

Raspberry Fondue

A berry fondue is a wondrous thing. Need I say more? Our family favorite is probably a raspberry one. Another kind of berries can be substituted for the raspberries listed in this recipe.

> *1 ten-ounce package frozen raspberries*
> *½ cup heavy cream*
> *1 teaspoon lemon juice*

Let the berries defrost, then empty the package into a blender or a food processor and puree until smooth and fine. Pour the puree into a small heavy saucepan, add the cream, and stir constantly over low heat until the mixture is well heated and smooth.

Add the lemon juice at the last minute and serve the dip from your fondue pot, preheated with hot tap water, with any and all the chocolate bread cubes you can find, along with some from a Kumquat Delight, Sweet Peppermint Poppy Seed, Cranberry-Orange, Raspberry Cream, or Lemon Suzette Loaf.

Hot Buttered Rum Fondue

Sweet fondues are often flavored with brandy, wine, or a liqueur, as in the Mint-Chocolate and Apple Fondue recipes above. Here's one to serve on winter evenings when the snow is swirling silently around the house.

> ½ cup unsalted butter
> 1 cup firmly packed dark brown sugar
> 4 egg yolks
> ½ cup dark rum
> a few cloves

In a small heavy saucepan set over low heat, melt the butter and stir in the brown sugar, blending until the mixture is smooth. Once the sugar is dissolved, remove the pan from the heat and beat in the egg yolks one at a time. Return the pan to the heat and allow the mixture to thicken, stirring constantly. Just before serving, blend in the rum, toss in the cloves, and reheat the sauce briefly before transferring it to a fondue pot, prewarmed with hot tap water, set over its burner.

Checker a bread tray with cubes of a chocolate bread and a substantial white loaf, such as Light Citrus, to go with this fondue. *Panettone*, Currant Ginger, Peach Praline, Figs and Cream, and even Pudding Bread are also good choices here.

24 · Brown Betty, Crumb Crusts, and Bread Puddings

OUR PIONEER FOREFATHERS OR, for that matter, many of our parents would have found it strange that we actually buy ordinary leftovers for cooking these days. Croutons and bread crumbs found their niche in the culinary corner of the home as ways to use stale bread — not that there was that much of it. In those days every crust counted.

Well, the good news is that with a bread machine you won't have to buy commercial baked-goods leftovers anymore. You'll have plenty of your own. The even better news is that they make possible a variety of outstanding desserts.

Consider the simple bread crumb, for instance. Take some stale crusts trimmed from a loaf destined for petits fours, a layer cake, or some other sweet. Feed them through your blender or food processor until you have reasonably fine, evenly textured crumbs. These are crumbs the likes of which you can't buy. Chocolate, coconut, citrus — whatever the flavor of the bread used, it will accent the crumbs.

Slices of leftover bread for crumbs can simply be left to air-dry in an undisturbed corner of the kitchen. If needed in a hurry, they can also be toasted lightly in your toaster or, if they're too thick to fit in the slots, on an ungreased cookie sheet placed in a 350-degree F. oven for 10 to 15 minutes. Also, while a blender or food processor makes the quickest work of turning crusts into crumbs, the dry slices can be crushed between sheets of waxed paper or in a closed bag, graham cracker style.

Store your crumbs in an airtight container or freeze them for long-term safekeeping, and you'll be ready at a moment's notice to make, say, a homey brown Betty or a distinctive crumb-crust pie.

Take the matter of cardamom bread, for instance. It makes such a superlative bread pudding that even when we use regular bread for the pudding, we now add a little cardamom for flavoring.

For French toast, it's well worth baking a whole extra loaf of bread just for that favorite of the kids, so I really shouldn't include it here as an answer to the leftovers quandary. Let me confine myself to suggesting that if you do make French toast from your homemade bread, and if you slice the loaf into inch-thick slabs and let them stale for half a day or so before sinking them into their coating batter, you'll have on your breakfast or supper plates a delicacy fit for a king — or at least a *fattiga riddare,* or poor knight, as the dish is known in Sweden.

Besides providing excellent crumbs, bread crusts make wonderful dog bones, of all things. My children have developed that all-American habit of slicing off the heel, or "corner house," as it's referred to in Germany, of a loaf and helping themselves to the second slice in. How on earth this custom evolved in our family I don't know, since the heel, well slathered with butter, is my favorite part of the bread. Nevertheless, there it is, and one time when we were accumulating heels, which aren't all that great for bread pudding, and had more than enough bread crumbs on hand, I gave a couple to our dogs, Crisscross and Zechy. They loved the rye.

Ever since, whenever there's a surfeit of leftover bread, I cut slices of the dark, heavy loaves into oblong thirds and let them air-dry on a rack for a couple of days, by this simple feat transforming them into dog bones. I'll bet when the Japanese invented the bread machine, they had no idea how happy our dogs were going to be.

Apple Brown Betty

Vanilla Cream

W hen I was a child, I always wondered who this Betty was who could come up with such a yummy dessert. I was never quite sure which I liked more, the homemade vanilla sauce with which I would attempt to levitate and float the brown Betty in its dish or the brown Betty itself. In all probability it was the combination of the two, which is unbeatable.

Crumbs from a citrus or a spice bread are particularly suited to this quickly assembled dessert, the perfect warm and fragrant addition to an evening meal on a wintry day.

> 2 cups crumbs, crushed between sheets
> of waxed paper with a rolling pin or
> pulsed in a blender or food processor
> ¾ cup unsalted butter
> 3 cups diced peeled apples
> ¾ cup firmly packed dark brown sugar
> 1 teaspoon grated lemon zest
> 1 teaspoon ground cinnamon
> ¼ teaspoon ground nutmeg
> ¼ teaspoon ground cloves
> ¼ teaspoon salt
> 3 tablespoons lemon juice
> 3 tablespoons water

Melt ½ cup of the butter and mix it into the crumbs. Use a third of this crumb mixture to line the bottom of a generously buttered or oiled deep baking dish, preferably one that has its own lid.

Cover the layer of crumbs with 1½ cups of the apples.

Mix together the brown sugar, lemon zest, cinnamon, nutmeg, cloves, and salt. Sprinkle half of this mixture over the apples in the dish and dot them lightly with 1 tablespoon of the remaining butter. Then sprinkle them with 1 tablespoon of the lemon juice and 1 tablespoon of the water.

Lay down another third of the crumb mixture, followed by the other 1½ cups of apples. Scatter the remaining spiced sugar mixture over the apples, dot them with 1 more tablespoon of butter, and sprinkle over them the remaining 2 tablespoons of lemon juice and 2 tablespoons of water.

Cover the top apple layer with the last third of the crumbs and dot them with the remaining 2 tablespoons of butter. Put the lid on the baking dish and bake in a 350-degree F. oven for 40 minutes or until the apples are nearly soft when pricked with a toothpick or a fork.

Remove the lid from the dish and increase the oven heat to 400 degrees F. for 15 minutes or until the top of the brown Betty has colored nicely.

Serve the brown Betty hot with a ready-made vanilla sauce or, better yet, a pitcher of chilled homemade Vanilla Cream.

A vanilla sauce for a substantial pudding need not be terribly substantial itself. One doesn't want to overwhelm. The recipe given here is for a delicate, smooth, rich sauce. Those who like it sweet can add a couple more tablespoonfuls of sugar.

VANILLA CREAM

1¾ *cups heavy cream*
3 *egg yolks*
2 *tablespoons sugar*
2 *teaspoons vanilla extract*

Heat 1 cup of the cream in the top of a double boiler. Whisk the egg yolks and sugar together, then add them slowly to the hot cream and stir constantly over low heat until the mixture thickens.

Remove the pan from the heat, add the vanilla extract, and allow the sauce to cool, stirring occasionally.

When ready to serve the sauce, whip the remaining ¾ cup of cream and fold it into the custard mixture. Serve the Vanilla Cream in a pitcher from which it can be poured over individual helpings of the brown Betty. After all, someone may not be able to resist asking for seconds.

Basic Crumb Piecrust

The crumbs from the various loaves whose recipes appear in this volume make great quick piecrusts, needing only to be patted into place in a pie pan with a little melted butter before being filled. Certain pies such as custard and fruit mixtures benefit from having their shells chilled before filling, to keep them firm when the filling is scooped into them, and some benefit from a brief partial baking serving the same purpose. But in either of these cases, the piecrusts can easily be made in advance. Crumb crusts will keep in your freezer, in fact, for up to 3 months, and if you use the lightweight aluminum pie pans, they can be stacked inside each other, taking up reasonably little freezer space. With a premade shell and a quickly prepared filling, you can have a marvelous pie on the table in 15 minutes or less.

A chocolate crumb crust goes well with a creamy pie filling such as key lime or banana. A crust made with crumbs from a Lemon Suzette Loaf or from *Mandelbrot* is a lovely foil for sweetened fresh fruit like strawberries or sliced peaches. Covered with an only slightly extravagant layer of whipped cream and studded with chocolate curls or shaved chocolate, such a confection makes a sparkling and wondrously refreshing summer dessert.

The recipe given here is for a basic crust that derives its flavor primarily from the crumbs used to create it. If you are using crumbs from a strongly flavored loaf — such as chocolate, coconut, or peanut — or from one of the more highly spiced *biscotti*, omit the cinnamon and nutmeg listed in this recipe. The crumbs will give the crust enough flavor themselves.

> 6 tablespoons unsalted butter
> 1 1/2 cups crumbs, crushed between
>   sheets of waxed paper with a rolling
>   pin or pulsed in a blender or food
>   processor
> 1/3 cup confectioners' sugar
> 1/2 teaspoon ground cinnamon
>   (optional)
> 1/2 teaspoon ground nutmeg (optional)

Melt the butter in a small saucepan over low heat. Place the crumbs in a bowl and sprinkle over them the confectioners' sugar as well as the cinnamon and nutmeg if you are using those spices. Stir these ingredients together with a fork until you no longer see swirls of the white sugar. Pour in the melted butter and blend to a uniform pebbled consistency.

Reserve about ⅓ cup of the crumb mixture for a top sprinkling if desired and pat the rest evenly and firmly against the bottom and sides of the pie pan. For a perfectly even crust, take a second pie pan of the same size and press it into the first to firm the crumbs. Leave the pans together if you are freezing the crust, slipping the entire "sandwich" into a large freezer bag. If you reserved some crumbs for topping, slip them into a smaller bag and tuck them into the top pan for safekeeping.

To bake the crust, remove the top pan and place the crust in an oven set to 300 degrees F. for about 15 minutes. Let the piecrust cool before filling.

Deluxe Crumb Piecrust

Delicately flavored custard and cream pies, particularly, are enhanced by a rich piecrust. This one is enriched with nuts and a dash of cream. Save the trimmings from your more lightly flavored loaves such as Cherries and Cheese, Pear, and Rose and Orange, for this shell, so the nut taste comes through.

Almonds, walnuts, hazelnuts, and pecans are all fine nuts for a Deluxe Crumb Piecrust.

> ½ cup unsalted butter
> 1¼ cups light-flavored crumbs, crushed
>   between sheets of waxed paper with a
>   rolling pin or pulsed in a blender or
>   food processor
> ⅓ cup grated nuts
> ⅓ cup firmly packed dark brown sugar
> ⅓ cup heavy cream

Melt the butter in a small saucepan over low heat. Place the crumbs in a small bowl and, with a fork, mix in the nuts and brown sugar. Drizzle the melted butter over the crumbs and blend it in, then do the same with the cream.

Press the crumb mixture evenly and firmly into a pie pan and flatten it with another pan of the same size.

Custard pies definitely want their shells prechilled or prebaked so as not to become soggy. Refrigerate the sandwiched crust to chill well or bake the shell in its bottom pan at 300 degrees F. for about 15 minutes. Allow a baked crust to cool before using it for a custard or cream filling. A shell intended for later use can be frozen still sandwiched between the 2 pans in a freezer bag.

Susan's Bread Pudding

B read puddings are an endless source of dining delight, particularly during the winter months, when their hearty warmth lulls one into a pleasant postprandial drowsiness. There are myriad recipes for bread puddings, most of which fall into one of two categories: those calling for diced bread, and those in which the bread slices are left whole. Susan's Bread Pudding is of the first variety. It's scrumptious made with leftover crusts from a Sour Cream Blueberry, Rose and Orange, Luau, Butterscotch Brickle, Raspberry Cream, Crunchy Caramel Apple–Granola, Scandinavian Cardamom, or any chocolate loaf.

4 cups diced somewhat stale bread
3 cups milk, whole or skim
3 medium eggs
1/2 cup sugar
1 tablespoon lemon juice
1 teaspoon vanilla extract
1 teaspoon grated lemon zest
1/4 teaspoon freshly ground cardamom

Place the bread cubes in a large mixing bowl. Scald the milk in a saucepan and remove it from the heat. Separate the eggs, placing the whites in a small mixing bowl and the yolks in the milk, beating after each addition. Stir the sugar into the milk-and-egg mixture and add the lemon juice, vanilla extract, lemon zest, and salt. Continue stirring until the mixture is smooth and creamy. Pour it slowly over the bread and blend lightly with a fork.

Set the bread aside to soak in this mixture for about 5 minutes. Meanwhile, beat the egg whites until they stand in soft peaks. Fold them gently into the soaked bread.

Pour the pudding mixture into a well-buttered or oiled baking dish. Set the dish in a deep pan of hot water — the water should come at least halfway up the sides of the dish — in an oven pre-heated to 350 degrees F. Bake for about 40 minutes or until the pudding is bubbly and nicely browned.

Serve with a pitcher of cream and, if available, a scattering of fresh berries. They're heavenly with a bread pudding.

French Bread Pudding with Meringue

B read puddings in which the bread slices are left whole, as opposed to being diced, are often called French bread puddings. Why I don't know. Perhaps it's because the whole slices are soaked like French toast. Or perhaps it's that French bread used crust and all makes a particularly attractive presentation of this variety. Of course, if you cover it all with a meringue, you don't see the pleasing array beneath.

Panettone, Sweet Peppermint Poppy Seed, Cranberry-Orange, Cherry Milk, Piña Colada, and, naturally, Yet Another Chocolate are all good loaves for this treat. From the subtle to the dominant, the flavor of the bread used will give its own distinctive signature to the pudding. The variations are almost endless.

> *½ pound bread slices about ½ inch*
>   *thick*
> *¼ cup unsalted butter*
> *4 medium eggs*
> *3 cups heavy cream*

⅓ cup sugar
¼ cup maple syrup
dash salt
½ teaspoon cream of tartar
½ cup confectioners' sugar
½ teaspoon vanilla extract

Spread the bread slices with the butter and lay them buttered side up in a lightly oiled 10-inch deep-dish pie pan or a round baking dish with sides at least 1½ inches high. Depending on how the slices have been cut, they may not all fit evenly into the dish. Just overlap them a bit if need be.

Separate the eggs, placing the whites in a small bowl to be set aside for the moment and breaking the yolks into a larger bowl. To the yolks add the cream, sugar, maple syrup, and salt. Beat well. Pour this mixture slowly over the bread slices and, with a fork, press the slices gently down into the mixture to make sure they all become soaked.

Bake the pudding in a 350-degree F. oven for about 40 minutes or until a toothpick inserted into its center comes out clean.

Beat the egg whites until frothy. Add the cream of tartar and continue beating until the whites form soft peaks. Beat in the confectioners' sugar and vanilla extract. Cover the bread pudding with the egg whites and bake for another 10 to 15 minutes or until the meringue is set and golden.

Serve with the satisfaction of having created a super homemade treat with your bread machine bakery.

Sources for Baking Ingredients

MORE AND MORE GROCERY STORES, even large super-markets, now carry specialty flours and other exotic baking ingredients not found on their shelves a mere few years ago, and what isn't located there can often be procured from one or another of the health-food and alternative-lifestyle shops proliferating in many areas of the country. Still, a few of the rarer flours may not be found even there, and some of us live far from such emporiums. Here mail order often comes to the rescue, and the catalogs and other literature available from the mail-order houses frequently make inspirational reading. The following are sources I have found helpful in my bread-baking ventures.

Birkett Mills

P.O. Box 440
Penn Yan, NY 14527
Tel. (315) 536-3311

FREE PRICE LIST
ACCEPTS MASTERCARD AND VISA CREDIT CARDS
This mill specializes in buckwheat products, carrying flour, stone-ground groats, even seeds for sprouting.

Brewster River Mills

R.D. 1, Box 285
Jeffersonville, VT 05464
Tel. (802) 644-2987

FREE BROCHURE
NO CREDIT CARDS ACCEPTED
Organic flours and meals are available from this supplier.

Ener-G Foods, Inc.
P.O. Box 84487
Seattle, WA 98124
Tel. (800) 331-5222
FREE CATALOG
ACCEPTS AMERICAN EXPRESS, MASTERCARD, AND VISA
CREDIT CARDS
This company carries xanthum gum and gluten-free flours.

Jaffe Bros., Inc.
P.O. Box 636
Valley Center, CA 92082
Tel. (619) 749-1133
FREE CATALOG
ACCEPTS MASTERCARD AND VISA CREDIT CARDS
This firm features a large selection of organic grains, flours, and meals.

Kenyon Corn Meal Co.
Usquepaugh
West Kingston, RI 02892
Tel. (401) 783-4054
      (800) 753-6966
FREE CATALOG
ACCEPTS MASTERCARD AND VISA CREDIT CARDS
Various stone-ground flours and mixes are available through this supplier.

King Arthur Flour Baker's Catalog
P.O. Box 876
Norwich, VT 05055
Tel. (800) 827–6836
FREE CATALOG
ACCEPTS AMERICAN EXPRESS, DISCOVER, MASTERCARD,
AND VISA CREDIT CARDS

This firm carries just about anything a baker could ask for, including white whole-wheat flour.

Sweet Celebrations
7009 Washington Avenue South
Edina, MN 55439
Tel. (800) 328–6722

FREE CATALOG
ACCEPTS MASTERCARD AND VISA CREDIT CARDS

Specializing in cake decorating and hardware, this supplier also carries flavors, extracts, and other baking ingredients.

Tadco/Niblack
900 Jefferson Road, Building 5
Rochester, NY 14623
Tel. (716) 292–0790
    (800) 724–8883

FREE PRICE LIST
ACCEPTS AMERICAN EXPRESS, DISCOVER, MASTERCARD, AND VISA CREDIT CARDS

This firm is a good source for flours, including gluten, gluten-free, and teff, as well as fillings, extracts, spices, barley malt syrup, and caramel color.

The Vermont Country Store
P.O. Box 3000
Manchester Center, VT 05255
Tel. (802) 362–2400

FREE CATALOG
ACCEPTS DISCOVER, MASTERCARD AND VISA CREDIT CARDS

Stone-ground flours and cereals as well as other baking ingredients and supplies are available from this firm.

Walnut Acres
Penns Creek, PA 17862
Tel. (800) 433-3998

FREE CATALOG
ACCEPTS DISCOVER, MASTERCARD, AND VISA
CREDIT CARDS

This company carries flours from millet to teff as well as sourdough starter.

Index

Kumquat Delight (loaf), 229–231

lactose. *See* Low-Lactose
leavening agents
 for bread making, 12–13
 when to add, 16–17
lecithin, for bread making, 15
leftovers, uses for, 32–33, 282, 292–293
Lemon Sauce, 270–271
Lemon Suzette Loaf, 266–267
Light Citrus Loaf, 206–208
Light Onion Bread, 115–116
Light Whole-Wheat Bread, 47
Limpa, Scandinavian, 103–104
liquids
 for bread making, 14
 for sweet loaves, 28
loaves, size of, 19, 21–22. *See also*
 sauced loaves; sweet loaves; tea
 loaves
Low-Lactose Milk Bread, 169
Low-Lactose Whole-Wheat Bread, 170
Luau Loaf, 242–243

Mandelbrot, 200–201
Maple Oat Bread, 205
Melba Sauce, Raspberry, 259
melba toast, how to make, 190
milk, for bread making, 14
Milk Bread, 37–38
 Golden, 38–39
 Low-Lactose, 169
Milk Loaf, Cherry, 253–254
millet, for bread making, 9
Millet Bread, 73
Millet Cornmeal Bread, 72–73
Mini Caraway Salt Loaves, 181–183
Mint-Chocolate Fondue, 286
 Super-Quick, 285
Minty Oat Groats Bread, 100
"mix" breads, using packaged ingredients, 152–163
Mocha Buttercream Icing, 237
Mocha Fondue, 284
Mock Boston Brown Bread, 144–145
Mock Brioche, 204
mock *Rehrücken* (torte), 248–249
Molasses Glaze, 174–175
molasses glaze (with coconut), 260–261
Molasses Rye Bread, 64–65
Moroccan Anise Bread, 102

multigrain breads, 53–78
 Anadama Bread, 70–71
 Brown Rice Amaranth Bread, 69–70
 Brown Rice Bread, 68–69
 Cornell Bread, 54–55
 Ezekiel Bread, 77–78
 Flaxseed Bread, 76–77
 Four-Grains Breakfast Bread, 74–75
 Garlic Pumpernickel Bread, 62–63
 Graham Cracker Bread, 59–60
 Millet Bread, 73
 Millet Cornmeal Bread, 72–73
 Molasses Rye Bread, 64–65
 One Rye Bread, 60–61
 Portuguese Corn Bread, 71–72
 Raisin Pumpernickel Bread, 63–64
 Russian Black Bread, 65–67
 Sesame Semolina Bread, 58–59
 Seven-Grains Bread, 56–57
 Sprouted Wheat Bread, 57–58
 Steel-Cut Oat Bread, 67–68
 Sunflower Bread, 75

No-Fat Bread, 167–168
No-Gluten Bread, 166–167
nut breads. *See* fruit and nut breads
Nut Chocolate Delight (loaf), 248–249
nuts, for topping sweet loaves, 32
Nut Teff Bread, 147–148

Oat Bread
 Maple, 205
 Steel-Cut, 67–68
Oat Groats Bread, Minty, 100
Oatmeal Bread
 Basic, 50–51
 Sesame, 51–52
oats and oatmeal, for bread making,
 10–11
oils, for bread making, 15
Oil Wash, 175
Olive Bread, 117–118
One Rye Bread, 60–61
Onion Bread, Light, 115–116
onions, substituting fresh for dry, 15
Onion Soup Bread, 155–156
Orange and Rose Loaf, 240–241
Orange Barley Malt Bread, 132–133
Orange-Cranberry Loaf, 246–247
Orange Glaze, Quick, 247
orchard breads. *See* fruit and nut
 breads